Super Terrorism

Biological, Chemical, and Nuclear

Yonah Alexander

and

Milton Hoenig

Editors

∥∥ Transnational Publishers, Inc.

0236198

Published and distributed by Transnational Publishers, Inc.
410 Saw Mill River Road
Ardsley, NY 10502, USA

Phone: 914-693-5100
Fax: 914-693-4430
E-mail: info@transnationalpubs.com
Web: www.transnationalpubs.com

Library of Congress Cataloging-in-Publication Data

Super terrorism: biological, chemical, and nuclear / edited by Yonah Alexander
and Milton Hoenig
    p.cm.
    ISBN 1-57105-218-6
    1. Bioterrorism. 2. Chemical terrorism. 3. Nuclear terrorism. I. Alexander,
Yonah. II. Hoenig, Milton M.

HV6431 .S86 2001
358'.3—dc21   2001042680

Manufactured in the United States of America

Contents

II. Dire Threat?

III. Ready to Respond

IV. Is the Homeland Safe?

V. Loose Nukes and Bought Brains

VI. Intelligence and Technology

VII. Laws and Directives

Preface

Terrorism may be defined as the calculated employment or threat of violence by individuals, sub-national, and state actors to attain political, social, and economic objectives in violation of law, intended to create an overwhelming fear in a target area larger than the victims attacked or threatened. It constitutes a permanent fixture of contemporary life.

The bombing of the World Trade Center in New York City in 1993 and the Alfred P. Murrah Federal Building in Oklahoma City in 1995 underscores this reality. These incidents took the lives of many people. We foresee the possibility of even worse times ahead because we may be moving into a new "age of super-terrorism" with very real prospects for the use of weapons of mass destruction. Such a prospect has frightening consequences for the survival of civilization, as we know it.

It is likely that terrorism will continue to plague the world in the future as it did in the era of superpower rivalry. What raises the stakes of terrorism in the "new world order" is the threat that the coming years may witness more actors (nations, organizations, and individuals) with the intent and capability to use weapons of mass destruction (biological, chemical, and nuclear), and greater availability of the knowledge and technology needed to manufacture and deliver such weapons.

Improved weapons technology gives terrorists advantages that they lacked in earlier times. For example, a person could, in principle, carry in his pocket enough chemical agents to kill many people in the World Trade Center in New York City. The packet of deadly material would be so small that even a security official inspecting visitors to the building would not be able to spot a bulge in the terrorist's pocket.

This terrorist could introduce the chemical agents into the air circulation system of the building. By the time people inside the building developed symptoms indicating illness, it would be too late to do anything to save them. Such an attack could easily take a toll of hundreds of lives.

This is but one example of the danger of technology in the hands of terrorists, and there are many examples involving biological, chemical, and nuclear materials or weapons. The events in Oklahoma City and the World Trade Center suggest that the same mind-set that allowed men to use a bomb against innocent civilians could be directed to even more spectacular and large-scale violence. Governments would be unwise to ignore the possibility that a terrorist organization will raise the stakes of violence to unprecedented new heights of awareness.

The bombings in Oklahoma City and the World Trade Center suggest that the United States is much more vulnerable to terrorism than ever before. Domestic groups with an anti-government agenda and foreign agents that see the United States as a supreme enemy can take advantage of the many targets symbolizing the United States to cause cataclysmic damage in the United States on a scale that the country has never before experienced.

Biological And Chemical Issues

When the chemical agent Sarin was released in a Tokyo subway in March 1995, world attention turned to the dangers of chemical terrorism. The casualty rate was high enough, but some observers claimed that if the chemical concentration had been higher, the number of deaths could have been in the hundreds.

What is particularly significant about the Tokyo incident is that it demonstrated that chemical terrorism is a danger to states from non-state organizations. This incident was undertaken by Aum Shinrikyo, a private religious organization. If the practice of using chemical agents to kill people becomes a pattern for non-state actors, the danger of biological and chemical attack can come from a variety of sources, including scientists with advanced doctoral degrees in chemistry, who are experts in narrow aspects of biology and chemistry relevant to the goals of groups intent on killing people.

Ever since the 1995 attack scholars have discussed some basic questions: To what extent is Tokyo a singular event or a harbinger of things to come? Has this incident broken whatever taboo existed with respect to terrorist use of these kinds of materials, or is this group an anomaly?

Some experts have argued that the kinds of self-imposed restraints in terrorist use of these materials that existed in the past will continue for the same reasons that have been traditionally important. In the international community, which in the past has successfully imposed constraints upon the use of such weapons.

From the perspective of the United States, this view seems to be dominant. Most Americans seems not to have become alarmed about a Tokyo-type attack in the United States. They have not endorsed big programs to defend the American public against such attacks.

Other observers maintain that we have crossed the threshold into a new era in which we will see more super-terrorism in a sustained systematic manner, in the same way we saw skyjackings in the late 1960's and 1970's. Only time will tell which view is correct.

Biological and chemical terrorism may pose greater dangers to civilized society than nuclear terrorism. With nuclear materials, governments have more security and safeguards arrangements for materials and weapons than are possible for biological and chemical items that can be turned into products for creating death and destruction.

In a free society, such as the United States, it is impossible to control those non-nuclear materials or the groups that might be interested in them so rigorously that we make ourselves invulnerable to a terrorist incident. The problem of security against terrorism has increased as a result of a changing world economic structure.

A consequence of developing a global economy is the placement of non-military facilities in many different countries. For example, pharmaceutical plants, which can produce ingredients used to create explosions in the manner of Oklahoma City, are emerging in developed and developing nations.

As more companies build facilities in places where international control regimes are weak, there is an increased risk of biological and chemical terrorism. In many developing countries, government officials do not have the same attitude toward public safety as exists in advanced industrial societies. Totalitarian countries clearly do not even regard the rule of law in the same way that industrial nations do. Therefore, as the world moves forward economically, the normal processes of development are going to expand to such an extent that industrial facilities will produce enticing items for use by terrorists.

The potential for an enormous disaster is significant. Antiterrorist efforts must be strengthened to the degree that all nations adopt the kind of attitude that the military shows in the handling of certain types of weapons and on its vessels: namely, zero tolerance for safety violations. If super-terrorism is to be thwarted, a safety culture must be the responsibility of everyone involved, from the person in the boardroom to the person who drives the pickup truck. Safety is a cultural issue that must be imposed on these companies.

Creating a safety culture is easier said than done. In the United States, we used to have fire drills in peacetime and air raid drills in wartime. We had all sorts of things to sensitize people to safety matters. We need to sensitize people from a very early age that safety is everybody's business if we are to begin to control the elements of biological and chemical terrorism that terrorists find inviting. We also need to enforce the Chemical Weapons Convention and complete a protocol that includes inspections under the Biological Weapons Convention.

Even with the best of safety precautions, however, the availability of biological and chemical weapons is widespread. It does not take much skill to use biological and chemical weapons for terrorist purposes. Simple kinds of bacteriological and chemical materials can be made in sufficient quantities to kill large numbers of people.

The types of materials that can be dangerous include items used in the manufacture of products ranging from paint to ball-point pens. Some materials are components in flame-retardant products. All of these have chemicals that could be used in a chemical attack. In addition, chemicals and biological cultures that are shared on a daily basis by the medical community around the world are exactly the types of materials that are attractive for use in biological weapons.

Nuclear Issues

While biological and chemical weapons in the short term are technologically feasible, in the long term, nuclear terrorism—the explosion of a nuclear bomb, the use of fissionable material as a radioactive poison, or the seizure and sabotage of nuclear facilities—is plausible and perhaps inevitable. Nuclear materials for commercial purposes will increasingly be shipped by land, sea, and air. The possibility of hijacking shipments of such material and using it to build nuclear weapons or radiological devices is no longer just the subject of movie thrillers but remains a real prospect for terrorists.

Fears of such dangers were expressed in connection with Japan's shipment of plutonium on the high seas in 1992. But more realistic fears were felt after the break-up of the Soviet Union and the weakening security of existing nuclear storage facilities in the newly independent republics.

It may be possible for a group of terrorists to build a crude nuclear weapon if they possess the essential expertise as well as the materials and components. A terrorist group could also steal a weapon from the thousands stored in nuclear weapon states. However, such a group would find it difficult to construct a sophisticated nuclear weapon without state sponsorship because of requirements for testing and securing safe havens. Terrorists could also seize medical isotopes from hospitals or radioactive wastes from commercial nuclear fuel reprocessing plants.

In sum, all of these factors indicate that terrorists might find these tactics particularly desirable for future operations. Such a prospect highlights the need for both thorough analysis and strong preventive measures to avert the threat of such seizure and attacks.

Policy Issues

Clearly, there are a number of public policy issues that need to be studied. One concern involved: To what extent does the government want to intensify awareness of the danger of super-terrorism? There are arguments for and against sensitizing the public. To some degree, people do not want to think about the subject of super-terrorism. Further, highlighting the danger of super-terrorism can breed a lack of confidence in government if the public senses that there is a danger that government may not be able to deal with the threat.

Failure to respond adequately to crises poses dangers to government. For example, Chernobyl, which placed a very heavy responsibility on the officials responding to the nuclear incident, produced a direct erosion of authority of the Soviet government. In the United States, Hurricane Andrew and the failure of the federal government to respond adequately had direct negative political consequences for President George Bush. Considering the biological and chemical issue, the government would have to respond even if ill prepared to deal with a cataclysmic event. An inadequate response would damage its authority.

Some experts contend that there should be no reticence in discussing these types of issues. An expert group should be able to explain the tradeoffs. Government must tell the people of the world what they are facing and identify the threat.

Then there is the issue of the amount of publicity that government should give to this subject. Will increased warnings about super-terrorism produce a self-fulfilling prophecy as terrorists direct their attention to even greater devastating acts?

There are also concerns about the international implications of biological and chemical terrorism. How should be United States work with foreign nations in meeting the challenge of super-terrorism?

Clearly, there is a tremendous need to educate the government agencies that will serve as front-line operators and first-line responders to an act of super-terrorism. Preparation for a disaster is complicated, however. Better equipment is needed to deal with such a cataclysmic event of super-terrorism. To take the necessary precautions, such as stockpiling vaccines, costs money. The FBI and the Federal Emergency Management Agency (FEMA) has been tasked to play a key role in such an emergency. Many other agencies must be involved.

More funding is needed for research and development. It was only about 30 years ago that the development of technological capabilities to deal with natural disasters began to receive support. We need much more research and development in this area than we are currently supporting. Specifically, there should be more of a focus on the decontamination of urban areas.

Another major issue of public policy involves the conflict between national security and civil liberties—a persistent issue in the United States during the Cold War. Will increased wiretaps and increased surveillance produce greater security? How much and what kind of tradeoffs must be made?

One issue of public policy involves the political resolve to take steps against foreign enemies who are exporting terrorism. It was noted that the desire and effort to carry through on a consistent policy from the top has been lacking for decades. A good example is the attempt to enact sanctions on those countries that deal with Iran and do business with the United States. There has been no real desire to impose tough and consistent restrictions in the so-called sanctions that the United States employs against Iran.

Another concern centered on the best way to publicize the prospect of super-terrorism. Some observers argue that the discussion should be conducted mostly within the government and one should not debate contingency plans, for indeed, they may generate a self-fulfilling prophecy. What is lacking in the use of intelligence that does exist, classified and unclassified, resulting in decisive action. On the basis of information supplied by government agencies in cases of clear and present danger, the President and no one else should go before the nation and explain the situation. When that happens, public opinion coalesces around the President and national action results.

The aforementioned issues are some of the considerations addressed in this volume. There are many other aspects related both to the threat and responses to super-terrorism that are discussed by politicians, members of Congress, and leading experts. By presenting these deliberations we attempted to lay out a roadmap for understanding American views on this growing challenge to national and international security.

Acknowledgements

To be sure, this volume represents another research effort in this important field of public concern that was formally initiated over a dozen years ago at the Terrorism Studies Program of The George Washington University. Numerous seminars and conferences dealing with different aspects of the challenges were organized.

We wish to acknowledge in particular the support of the Smith Richardson Foundation for a related research project on "Counter Terrorism Strategies for the 21st Century: National, Regional, and Global Agenda," which resulted in the publication of Volumes 15-23, *Terrorism: Documents of International and Local Control* (Dobbs Ferry, N.Y.: Oceana Publications, 1999-2001), edited by Yonah Alexander and Donald J. Musch as well as the four-volume set on *Cyber Terrorism and Information Warfare: Threats and Reponses* (Dobbs Ferry, N.Y.: Oceana Publications, 2000), edited by Yonah Alexander and Michael S. Swetnam. Thanks are also due to the Stella and Charles Guttman Foundation, Inc., for their assistance in the publication of a four-volume set on *Legal Aspects of Terrorism in the United States* (Dobbs Ferry, N.Y.: Oceana Publications, 2000), edited by Yonah Alexander and Edgar H. Brenner.

Special gratitude goes to Professor Yuval Ne'eman of Tel Aviv University for his wise guidance, and to Timothy F. Wuliger for his continuing support of the multidisciplinary project on "Preventing Super-Terrorism: Biological, Chemical, and Nuclear Terrorism."

Finally, we wish to thank Michael S. Swetnam, president and chairman of the board, Potomac Institute for Policy Studies, for his continuing encouragement and support. We also wish to thank Herbert M. Levine, James T. Kirkhope, Allyson Kozal, Alon Lanir, Peter H. Leddy, Brian M. Miller, and Vivek Narayanan at the International Center for Terrorism Studies, Potomac Institute for Policy Studies and the Inter-University Center for Legal Studies, International Law Institute for their research role.

Yonah Alexander
and
Milton M. Hoenig
Washington, D.C.
May 15, 2001

I.
Setting the Scene

Letter of Albert Einstein to President Roosevelt on the Possibility of Developing and Delivering an Atomic Bomb*

Albert Einstein
Old Grove Rd.
Nassau Point
Peconic, Long Island
August 2d, 1939

F.D. Roosevelt
President of the United States
White House
Washington, D.C.

Sir:

Some recent work by E. Fermi and L. Szilard, which has been communicated to me in manuscript, leads me to expect that the element uranium may be turned into a new and important source of energy in the immediate future. Certain aspects of the situation which has arisen seem to call for watchfulness and, if necessary, quick action on the part of the Administration. I believe therefore that it is my duty to bring to your attention the following facts and recommendations.

In the course of the last four months it has been made probable—through the work of Joliot in France as well as Fermi and Szilard in America—that it may become possible to set up a nuclear chain reaction in a large mass of uranium, by which vast amounts of power and large quantities of new radium-like elements would be generated. Now it appears almost certain that this could be achieved in the immediate future.

---

* This is the text of the letter signed by Albert Einstein which was delivered to President Franklin D. Roosevelt by Alexander Sachs on October 11, 1939. The chief author is believed to be Leo Szilard.

This new phenomenon would also lead to the construction of bombs, and it is conceivable—though much less certain—that extremely powerful bombs of a new type may thus be constructed. A single bomb of this type, carried by boat and exploded in a port, might very well destroy the whole port together with some of the surrounding territory. However, such bombs might very well prove to be too heavy for transportation by air.

The United States has only very poor ores of uranium in moderate quantities. There is good ore in Canada and the former Czechoslovakia, while the most important source of uranium is the Belgian Congo.

In view of this situation you may think it desirable to have some permanent contact maintained between the Administration and the group of physicists working on chain reactions in America. One possible way of achieving this might be for you to entrust with this task a person who has your confidence who could perhaps serve in an unofficial capacity. His task might comprise the following:

a) to approach Government Departments, keep them informed of the further development, and put forward recommendations for Government action, giving particular attention to the problems of securing a supply of uranium ore for the United States.

b) to speed up the experimental work, which is at present being carried on within the limits of the budgets of University laboratories, by providing funds, if such funds be required, through his contacts with private persons who are willing to make contributions for this cause, and perhaps also by obtaining the co-operation of industrial laboratories which have the necessary equipment.

I understand that Germany has actually stopped the sale of uranium from the Czechoslovakian mines which she has taken over. That she should have taken such early action might perhaps be understood on the ground that the son of the German Under-Secretary of State, von Weizaecker, is attached to the Kaiser-Wilhelm-Institut in Berlin where some of the American work on uranium is now being repeated.

Yours very truly
(signed) A. Einstein

Ways for Non-Missile WMD Delivery into the United States*

National Intelligence Council
September 1999

Although non-missile means of delivering weapons of mass destruction (WMD) do not provide the same prestige or degree of deterrence and coercive diplomacy associated with an intercontinental ballistic missile (ICBM), such options are of significant concern. Countries or non-state actors could pursue non-missile delivery options, most of which:

- Are less expensive than developing and producing ICBMs.
- Can be covertly developed and employed; the source of the weapon could be masked in an attempt to evade retaliation.
- Probably would be more reliable than ICBMs that have not completed rigorous testing and validation programs.
- Probably would be more accurate than emerging ICBMs over the next 15 years.
- Probably would be more effective for disseminating biological warfare agent than a ballistic missile.
- Would avoid missile defenses.

The requirements for missile delivery of WMD impose additional, stringent design requirements on the already difficult technical problem of designing such weapons. For example, initial indigenous nuclear weapon designs are likely to be too large and heavy for a modest-sized ballistic missile but still suitable for delivery by ship, truck, or even airplane. Furthermore, a country (or non-state actor) is likely to have only a few nuclear weapons, at least

---

*Excerpt from " Foreign Missile Developments and the Ballistic Missile Threat to the United States Through 2015," National Intelligence Council. Prepared under the auspices of the National Intelligence Officer for Strategic and Nuclear Programs, Bob Walpole. The National Intelligence Council, comprised of experts drawn from the intelligence community and outside the government, serves the Director of Central Intelligence as a center for strategic thinking to assist policymakers as they pursue shifting interests and foreign policy priorities.

during the next 15 years. Reliability of delivery would be a critical factor; covert delivery methods could offer reliability advantages over a missile. Not only would a country want the warhead to reach its target, it would want to avoid an accident with a WMD warhead at the missile-launch area.

On the other hand, a ship sailing into a port could provide secure delivery to limited locations, and a nuclear detonation, either in the ship or on the dock, could achieve the intended purpose. An airplane, either manned or unmanned, could also deliver a nuclear weapon before any local inspection, and perhaps before landing. Finally, a nuclear weapon might also be smuggled across a border or brought ashore covertly.

Foreign non-state actors, including some terrorist or extremist groups, have used, possessed, or are interested in weapons of mass destruction or the materials to build them. Most of these groups have threatened the United States or its interests. We cannot count on obtaining warning of all planned terrorist attacks, despite the high priority we assign to this goal.

Recent trends suggest the likelihood is increasing that a foreign group or individual will conduct a terrorist attack against US interests using chemical agents or toxic industrial chemicals in an attempt to produce a significant number of casualties, damage infrastructure, or create fear among a population. Past terrorist events, such as the World Trade Center bombing and the Aum Shinrikyo chemical attack on the Tokyo subway system, demonstrated the feasibility and willingness to undertake an attack capable of producing massive casualties.

The 1988 Chemical Weapons Attack on Halabja, Iraq

Christine M. Gosden*

Introduction

I have recently witnessed the long-term effects of the chemical weapons attack on the large civilian population in Northern Iraq, in the town of Halabja. My experiences of the devastating power of these weapons have emphasized the importance of protecting individuals and nations against chemical and biological weapons attacks. This journey and the horrifying findings have shocked and devastated me to an extent that I had not believed possible.

At first glance, it might not appear that Saddam Hussein's use of poison gas against his own people in 1988 has much relevance to today's issue of domestic preparedness in the United States. However, I believe there are at least three "lessons learned" from Halabja.

— First, national plans for responding to chemical or biological weapons incidents in the United States (or the United Kingdom for that matter) must take into account the possibility that multiple types of chemical and biological agents may be used in the attack, greatly complicating an effective response;

— Second, that treating immediately the victims of chemical attack is absolutely critical not only for saving lives, but for preventing long-term radiation-like medical and genetic problems; and

— Third, and most important, given that technological and other barriers against chemical weapons use have fallen away, it is vitally important that each of our nations maintain adequately funded national medical preparedness programs to treat potential chemical weapons casualties, both civilian and military.

*Dr. Goden is Professor of Medical Genetics, University of Liverpool, United Kingdom. Excerpt from testimony before the Senate Judiciary Subcommittee on Technology, Terrorism and Government and the Senate Select Committee on Intelligence on "Chemical and Biological Weapons Threats to America: Are We Prepared?," April 22, 1998.

The Attack on Halabja

The poison gas attack on the Iraqi town of Halabja was the largest-scale chemical weapons (CW) attack against a civilian population in modern times. Halabja was a bustling city in Northern Iraq with a population that was predominantly Kurdish and had sympathized with Iran during the Iran-Iraq war in the 1980s. The population at the time of the attack was about 80,000 people. Troops from the Kurdish Patriotic Union of Kurdistan (PUK) entered Halabja on 15th March 1988 amidst heavy resistance from Iraqi security and military forces.

Halabja fell to the PUK troops (accompanied by Iranian revolutionary guards) four hours later. The Iraqis responded with heavy artillery fire and an early wave of six aircraft bombarded an area near Halabja with ordinary high explosives. The civilians had been prevented from leaving the town by the PUK, hoping that the Iraqis would not attack a town with civilians in it—thus providing a human shield.

The CW attack began early in the evening of March 16th, when a group of eight aircraft began dropping chemical bombs, and the chemical bombardment continued all night. According to Kurdish commanders on the scene, there were 14 aircraft sorties during the night, with seven to eight planes in each group, and they concentrated their attack on the city and all the roads leading out of Halabja. The chemical attacks continued until the 19th. Iraqi planes would attack for about 45 minutes and then, after they had gone, another group would appear 15 minutes later.

This was not the first chemical attack by Saddam Hussein. Previous attacks had been launched by Iraqi aircraft against 20 small villages in 1987. However, the scale and intensity of the chemical campaign against Halabja was entirely different—this was the first time that chemical weapons had been used on a major civilian population of this size. The victims of the attack included women, children and the elderly.

Saddam Hussein's Chemical "Cocktail"

There is something else that sets Halabja apart from other known chemical weapons attacks—including the Aum Shinrikyo attack on the Tokyo subway in 1995. The Halabja attack involved multiple chemical agents—including mustard gas, and the nerve agents SARIN, TABUN and VX. Some sources report that cyanide was also used. It may be that an impure form of TABUN, which has a cyanide residue, released the cyanide compound. Most attempts directed to developing strategies against chemical or biological weapons have been directed towards a single threat. The attack on Halabja illustrates the importance of careful tactical planning directed towards more than one agent, and specific knowledge about the effects of each of the agents. The demands of developing effective treatment regimes for children, the elderly and infirmed are daunting. And the task is ever more daunting when having to treat a chemical weapons "cocktail."

Saddam Hussein clearly intended to complicate the task of treating the Halabja victims. At a minimum, he was using Halabja as part of the Iraqi CW test program. Handbooks for doctors in Iraqi military show sophisticated medical knowledge of the effects of CW. The Iraqi military used mustard gas in the "cocktail" for which there is no defense or antidote. And it is also worth noting that Saddam did *not* use the nerve agent SOMAN. This is noteworthy because it shows that Hussein's experts were also well aware that pyridostigmine bromide—one of the chief treatments against nerve agent—is relatively ineffective against TABUN, SARIN and VX, but highly effective against SOMAN when given as a preventive.

Other medical chemical countermeasures designed to increase protection may be unavailable or ineffective. The drug atropine, the most commonly used for treatment of nerve agent exposure, ameliorates muscarinic effects (shortness of breath, troubled breathing, wheezing or tightness in chest, slow heartbeat; unusual tiredness or weakness), but has little effect on nicotinic effects, such as muscle twitching. And oximes, which also are used to treat nerve gas exposure, are useful in counteracting nicotinic effects but will not function without atropine.

Long Term Effects on the People of Halabja

There had been no systematic and detailed research study carried out in Halabja in the 10 years since the attack. The novel effects such as those on reproductive function, congenital malformations, long term neurological and neuropsychiatric effects, (especially on those who were very young at the time) and cancers in women and children are of special importance. There is no knowledge about the ways in which the serious and long term damage caused by these weapons can be treated.

What we found is sobering, if not frightening. It must serve as a wake-up call about the need for improving our medical preparedness and national and international response plans to chemical weapons attack. For example, eye, respiratory and neuropsychiatric problems do not appear to respond to conventional therapy. It may be necessary to develop new methods of research and treatment.

Severe respiratory problems

These require assessments of lung function, trials of drugs that may be of help and consideration of the possibility of lung transplants for the most severely affected.

Cancers

The cancer risks in this population are high and the people are dying very young of large, aggressive, rapidly metastasizing tumors. There is a need for improved diagnosis, surgery, pathology and better imaging (CT, MR, and bone scans). Methods of chemotherapy and radiotherapy for these chemical weapons induced cancers may be different from those of other cancers and require knowledge of the types of mutations which lead to these cancers.

Congenital malformations

The types and range of congenital malformation are extremely extensive, although certain major effects can be seen. These include congenital heart conditions, mental handicap, neural tube defects and cleft lip and palate. The is a need for pediatric surgeons to repair heart defects, cleft palate etc, improved diagnosis and imaging and many other forms of professional help (e.g., speech therapy, occupational therapy and specialist teaching for the handicapped).

Neurological and psychiatric problems

These are among the most alarming of the effects of these weapons and are also the most difficult to quantify scientifically and diagnose. They are the problems that make the people feel extremely desperate. Many try to commit suicide and there are many examples of failed suicides, the surgeons frequently have to remove bullets from people who have unsuccessfully tried to shoot themselves. Conventional antidepressant drugs may have severe side effects on those with nerve gas or organophosphage poisoning.

Skin and eye problems

The effects of mustard gas burns may persist for life and cause much pain and suffering. Radical forms of therapy, such as corneal grafting for eye problems and skin grafting for severe skin burns, may be the only real forms of effective treatment.

Infertility

Miscarriages, stillbirths, neonatal and infant deaths.

Many of the people in Halabja have two or more major problems. The occurrences of genetic mutations and carcinogenesis in this population appear comparable with those who were one to two kilometers from ground zero in Hiroshima and Nagasaki, and show that the chemicals used in the attack have a general effect on the body similar to that of ionizing radiation.

All the people who were bombarded with this awful cocktail of weapons do not have identical problems. They received different doses; some were drenched in liquid mustard gas and nerve agents, others breathed in vapor; some people were outside, others were inside; and some were wrapped in clothing or wet sheets or washed off the chemicals quickly. It is important to note that people vary in their ability to detoxify and this is genetically determined. Finally, the DNA target for the mutagenesis is the whole of the human genome. Many different genes may be affected; in the body, conferring risks of cancer or disease; and, in eggs or sperm, causing congenital abnormalities or lethality in offspring.

A great deal remains unknown. The long term effects such as those on fertility and congenital malformations are not well characterized. The most effective ways of treating the long term problems are not known.

The Need for Enhanced Medical Preparedness to Treat CW Casualties

In order to provide effective defense against chemical and biological weapons attacks, there is a need for a good comprehensive working knowledge of the chemical and biological weapons. This has to be coupled with an understanding of the principal ways of deploying each of the different types of weapons and the likely civilian and military targets against which they might be deployed. The principal methods of defense against each of these weapons, such as decontamination methods, antidotes and methods of treating casualties to prevent long term effects are extremely important.

Reasons and Rationales Behind Potential CBRN Terrorism

Gilmore Commission First Annual Report *

If, in fact, we are approaching a new era of "super" chemical, biological, radiological or nuclear (CBRN) terrorism, why would groups seek to escalate to this level? One can identify five possible motivating rationales.

First , and at the most basic level, may be simply the desire to kill as many people as possible. CBRN weapons could give a terrorist group the potential ability (especially if a nuclear weapon were used) to wipe out thousands, possibly even hundreds of thousands, in a single strike.

A second reason for groups to seek to escalate to the CBRN level could be to exploit the classic weapon of the terrorist—fear.

A third possible rationale for resorting to CBRN weapons could be the desire to negotiate from a position of unsurpassed strength. A credible threat to use a chemical, biological, or nuclear weapon would be unlikely to go unanswered by a government and could, therefore, provide an organization with a tool of political blackmail of the highest order.

A fourth reason, with specific reference to biological agents, could derive from certain logistical and psychological advantages that such weapons might offer terrorists. A biological attack, unlike a conventional bombing, would not likely attract immediate attention.

Fifth, a group may wish to use CBRN weapons, and more specifically biological agents, to cause economic and social damage by targeting a state's or region's agricultural sector. For example, Tamil separatists in Sri Lanka threatened to infect Sri Lankan rubber and tea plantations with nonindigenous diseases as part of a total biological war strategy designed to cripple the Sinhalese-dominated government.

---

*Excerpt from First Annual Report to The President and The Congress of the Advisory Panel To Assess Domestic Response Capabilities For Terrorism Involving Weapons Of Mass Destruction: *Assessing The Threat*, Gov. James S. Gilmore, chair, December 15, 1999.

Based on this analysis, the most likely terrorist groups that would seek to cause mass civilian casualties with CBRN weapons are fundamentalist religious organizations or cults that embrace adversarial, Manichean worldviews, or other extremist single-issue groups. However, there are two scenarios that are conceivable exceptions to this hypothesis: use by terrorists of biological agents as a way of destroying, or at least undermining, an adversary's agricultural base and state-sponsorship, which has the advantage of enabling terrorists to leapfrog the technical hurdles associated with CBRN weaponization. It is significant that, to date, there is no evidence that any formal link exists between terrorist groups and state-assisted CBRN programs.

The Panel believes that the historically more frequent, lesser-consequence terrorist attack, is more likely in the near term—one involving a weapon on a relatively small-scale incident, using either a chemical, biological or radiological device (and not a nuclear weapon), or conventional explosives. Rather than having the intention of inflicting mass casualties, such an attack could be designed to cause a limited number of casualties, but at the same time cause mass panic. Nevertheless, even limited casualties could precipitate a disproportionate psychological response among the public.

A plausible scenario is a series of simultaneous (or near-simultaneous) terrorist attacks using or threatening to use chemical, biological or radiological materials, mounted across a city, a wider metropolitan area or geographical region, or even a number of locations throughout the United States. The intent would not be to kill large numbers of people or wreak mass destruction but to exhaust the capabilities of local authorities rapidly, thus creating panic, instilling widespread fear, and likely undermining confidence in government

In November 1995, Chechen separatists threatened to detonate radiological devices in and around Moscow. The rebels attempted to back up their threat by directing a Russian television news crew to a site in a popular Moscow park where the Chechens had buried a large radioactive parcel containing cesium-137.

Biological Terrorism

There are at least four primary acquisition routes that terrorists could conceivably pursue in acquiring a biological warfare capability:

- purchasing a biological agent from one of the world's 1,500 germ banks;

- theft from a research laboratory, hospital, or public health service laboratory,
  where agents are cultivated for diagnostic purposes;
- isolation and culturing of a desired agent from natural sources; or
- obtaining biological agents from a rogue state, a disgruntled government scientist, or a state sponsor.

The principal obstacle is the development of a genuinely lethal strain of the biological agent in sufficient quantities to cause mass casualties. The most obvious route would be by attempting to acquire the strain from nature, e.g., obtaining potentially lethal anthrax spores from soil and then culturing sufficient quantities to produce mass casualties. While theoretically conceivable, this is nonetheless difficult in practice and doubtless well beyond the capabilities of most terrorist groups.

In the specific case of botulinum toxins, there are difficulties in purifying these agents, which then will likely become unstable once they are purified. The same problem of maintaining toxicity during the purification process hampered U.S. government researchers during the Cold War.

Although there remains a widespread public perception that it is easy to acquire and use highly lethal biological agents, there is no clear consensus among analysts about how much scientific and technological expertise and prior training are needed.

Terrorists intent on inflicting hundreds of thousands of casualties with biological agents would have to create an aerosol cloud to disseminate the toxin from either a mud-like liquid ("slurry") form or in a dried, talcum powder-like form. In the case of B. anthracis, turning the spores into a powder requires the use of large and expensive centrifuges and drying apparatus. The dissemination itself could conceivably be accomplished in any number of different ways—from low-flying airplanes, crop dusters, trucks equipped with sprayers, or with an aerosol canister situated in one place and activated by a remote timing device.

Chemical Terrorism

Chemical agents fall into four broad categories:

- Choking agents, such as phosgene and chlorine.
- Blood agents, including hydrogen cyanide and cyanogen chloride.
- Blister agents, e.g., mustard gas.

- G-series nerve agents, such as tabun (GA), sarin (GB), and soman (GD); and
- V-series nerve agents, e.g., VX.

It appears likely that terrorists would reject most of them. Sarin, on the other hand, is highly toxic, volatile, and relatively easy to manufacture. Indeed, it was these same qualities that attracted Aum Shinrikyo's scientists to sarin.

Although often referred to as a nerve "gas," sarin is, in fact, a liquid at ambient temperature. When in vapor form, it is heavier than air and, as a result, will cling to floors, sink into basements, and gravitate toward low terrain. While sarin may be less complicated to synthesize than other nerve agents, the expertise required to produce it should not, however, be underestimated.

Moreover, although sarin's high volatility greatly simplifies weaponization, terrorists who may seek to cause mass casualties will need a fairly sophisticated means of spreading the agent in sufficiently large quantities over their intended target area. An airplane equipped with a suitable industrial or crop sprayer could be a satisfactory mechanism for dissemination. Alternatively, terrorists could equip a truck and drive through the target area. Temperature, wind speed, inversion conditions, and other meteorological factors, however, would likely determine the effectiveness of any attack.

Releasing ten kilograms (22 pounds) of sarin into the open air under favorable weather conditions covers about one-hundredth of a square kilometer with lethal effects. Since population densities in U.S. urban areas are typically around 5,000 people per square kilometer, such an attack would kill about 50 people. Releasing 1,000 kilograms would cover several square kilometers, killing about 10,000 people. Thus, only in an open-air attack using amounts approaching 1,000 kilograms of sarin would the effects become distinctly greater than that attainable by such traditional terrorist means as conventional explosives.

Given these impediments, a terrorist interested in harming large numbers of persons might prefer to attempt to engineer a chemical disaster using conventional means to attack an industrial plant or storage facility, rather than develop and use an actual chemical weapon, as the 1984 Bhopal, India, catastrophe demonstrated.

Nuclear Terrorism

Terrorists who were either unable or unwilling to steal a nuclear device or were unsuccessful in obtaining one on the putative black market that has surfaced in the countries of the former Soviet Union and Warsaw Pact, might attempt to build one themselves. Their first hurdle, however, would be in acquiring either highly enriched uranium (HEU) or plutonium (Pu) suitable for fashioning a nuclear device. Mining and processing uranium or building a reactor to create plutonium would of course be impractical (although, it should be noted, Aum's most grandiose aims embraced this possibility); terrorists would, therefore, have to steal it or conceivably purchase it on the black market.

There is disagreement, however, about what level of expertise and other resources are required to construct such a weapon. Although much of the information about nuclear weapons design and production has become public knowledge during the past 50 years, it is still extraordinary for nonstate entities to attempt to embark on a nuclear weapons R&D program. The technical challenges remain immense. In the case of South Africa, for example, it took scientists and engineers—who were endowed with a large and sophisticated infrastructure—four years to build their first gun-type system.

Radiological Terrorism

In the view of some authorities, theft of a nuclear device or building a weapon "in house" are the least-probable courses of action for a prospective nuclear terrorist. Far more likely is the dispersal of radiological material in an effort to contaminate a target population or distinct geographical area. The material could be spread by radiological dispersal devices (or RDDs)—i.e. "dirty bombs" designed to spread radioactive material through passive (aerosol) or active (explosive) means.

Radiological weapons kill or injure by exposing people to radioactive materials, such as cesium-137, iridium-192, or cobalt-60. With high enough levels of exposure, the radiation can sicken and kill. Radiation (particularly gamma rays) damages cells in living tissue through ionization, destroying or altering some of the cell constituents essential to normal cell functions. The effects of a given device will depend on whether the exposure is "acute" (i.e., brief, one time) or "chronic" (i.e., extended).

There are a number of possible sources of material that could be used to fashion such a device, including nuclear waste from fuel reprocessing, or radiological medical isotopes found in many hospitals or research laboratories. Radioactive materials are often sintered in ceramic or metallic pellets. Terrorists could crush the pellets into a powder and put the powder into an RDD. The RDD could then be detonated, spreading the radiological material.

The CBRN Terrorist Threat in Perspective

Because of the extreme consequences that could result from a successful attack involving a CBRN agent, even the remotest likelihood of one cannot be dismissed as insignificant. The challenge, therefore, is to avoid reaction too strongly to only one aspect of the problem, while still preparing adequately for a threat that remains uncertain but could nonetheless have profound repercussions. A critical step in this process is to reconsider the "worst-case scenario" threat assessment approach that has dominated domestic planning and preparedness for potential acts of CBRN terrorism. The narrow focus lower-probability/higher-consequence threats, which in turn posit virtually limitless vulnerabilities, do not reflect the realities of contemporary terrorist behavior and operations. Indeed, of the more than 9,000 incidents since 1968, fewer than 100 evidence any indication of terrorists plotting or attempting to use chemical, biological or radiological weapons, or to steal or otherwise fabricate nuclear devices on their own.

The Diversity of Bio Weapons

Joshua Lederberg*

I will pursue how we might be dealing with present and future technologies for bio attack and defense. Very innovative approaches are being developed (a good part in the national laboratories) for the rapid sensing and diagnosis of infectious agents in the environment and from tissue and blood samples from exposed individuals. That's absolutely critical to recognizing that an attack has happened, that it might be going on, and as well as for the care and treatment of those at risk.

Even so, for the next few years, we would be very lucky to be able to detect a clandestine anthrax or smallpox attack before a substantial number of people have started showing symptoms. That would be squandering two or three days of very precious time that is absolutely crucial to the management of the consequences.

We perhaps put too much stress on an acute incident, an explosion, a compelling notice that something really awful has happened. That would entail the involvement of emergency responders. But no shrewd user of a BW weapon is going to give you that opportunity. The "incident" will be people accumulating illness, disease, death. Finally, then the evidence may become overwhelming that this is out of the ordinary, and the public health system will begin to take hold.

So a very important aspect for defense against BW is to adopt the correct level of paranoia, when possibly random fluctuations of the incidence of disease, an epidemic of a mild, or not so mild, influenza starts bringing people to the hospitals. Or even speculating that a new disease like West Nile now

* Rockefeller University. Dr. Lederberg is President-emeritus of Rockefeller University and recipient of the 1958 Nobel Prize in Physiology and Medicine. Excerpt from talk to RAND Symposium, "Bioterrorism: Homeland Defense: The Next Steps," February 8-10 2000, Santa Monica, CA, co-sponsored by the American Society for Industrial Security, Battelle Memorial Institute, Lawrence Livermore National Laboratory, Los Alamos National Laboratory, Los Angeles County Health Services, Los Angeles Sheriff's Department, Pepperdine University, School of Public Policy, RAND and Sandia National Laboratory.

transmitted by mosquitoes in New York and the crows falling at our feet might that be a BW attack or not.

Advances in diagnosis will march on, depending on specific diseases. I think we will beat the bacterial infections, and we'll recover our overwhelming defense capability even in the face of the waves of antibiotic resistance that bacteria have generated out of careless use of antibiotics. Diagnosis will be important in order to know which agents to use.

I wish I could be quite that optimistic about viral infections for which therapeutic measures are few and far between. Our frustration in dealing with AIDS is an example of that, which has had the most concentrated effort in history at the development of therapeutics. Perhaps there will be some improvement if there is renewed investment in dealing with other virus diseases. That is the only approach that I can see as being feasible on a strategic level in dealing with smallpox. Are we going to persuade ourselves or others that we ought to revaccinate the entire world's population? Once you stop and think about the implications on doing this on a merely regional or national level without the world being involved, you'll see why it is an "all or none" global decision. But if we could have therapeutics that could deal with a smallpox attack once it had started, so that it is not so inevitably lethal as it offers to be at the present time, that would greatly alter the picture.

The same might apply for preparedness for a broad range of other viral attacks. So it's a little bit chancy but one could be moderately optimistic about the pace of development of therapeutic management measures coming from the technologies of the next five to 10 years. Nevertheless, the offense will be preponderant as we understand infectious disease in greater and greater depth: our ability to conduct DNA analysis sequencing, moving bits of DNA from one organism to another, and genetic engineering as it is applied to very beneficent purposes. It's just built in that the knowledge that is being accumulated in the basic biochemistry of infection is going to make it a lot easier to perfect biological weapons than to build defenses against them.

One way of expressing my level of concern is that the technologies are so accessible. Growing anthrax is as easy as baking a pie, finding anthrax seed is not that tough. Outbreaks of it occur in cattle from time to time. Any large farm community will know some field where some cow has died of it and where you could recover anthrax from the soil with a little digging around. High school students are going to have to be added to our roster of potential sources of threat. Thousands of high school kids are doing biotechnology as part of their high school research projects, at a level that is quite sophisticated enough for devising brand new agents. They have laboratory facilities to do it and you buy kits over the counter. When you're a young high school student nothing looks as tough as it may appear to a 30 or 50 year old. It's mostly a metaphor, but something to be taken somewhat seriously about where the technology is heading us.

Now, why is high tech microbiology even more dangerous than natural disease? I used to teach that it would not be. I taught that the evolution of disease agent was very complicated. That putting together all the things needed for a bug to adapt itself to the environment of a host, defeat its defense systems and so forth would make it unlikely that you could synthesize a brand new pathogen, even with quite deep bio-technical knowledge. And that is still true. But I've had further reflection.

Consider the business of our natural infecting agents, the influenza that you'll get, the common cold, your boils, your gut infections, your staph on your skin and so on and so forth. Their economy is not to kill their host. But things happen. They happen as a byproduct of the skirmishing between them and host defenses. If you look around the world of infectious disease, in fact you find that with rare exceptions, our most lethal diseases are almost accidental byproducts of a bug moving away from its natural host. That's outstandingly true of HIV-AIDS which is in equilibrium with its primate hosts and does not cause an enormous amount of mischief there. It has jumped into humans just as plague has jumped into humans, just as Avian flu has jumped into humans, and there can have devastating results . In their natural historical environment, most bugs are selected for moderated virulence, because they will survive better in that natural world if they do not kill the host.

That is where technology would override that natural restraint. If we were to see the importation of, say, botulinum toxin, to a wide variety of other existing pathogens, we might find they would be far more lethal in a way that would be self-destructive to them (and to us) in their natural environment. But these would make even more horrendous kinds of weapons in the artificial circumstance of technical use. There have been two or three published experiments down that line in which anthrax has been used as a vehicle for importing still other toxins. Anthrax is a well-adapted pathogen. Usually there's a local lesion; in cattle it's rarely that fatal. Even in humans you typically have a skin lesion from contact with an infected animal. In its natural mode of transmission, it has a moderately low lethality. Only when it is artificially disseminated by aerosols and by an inhalation portal of entry does it have the features we now recognize for BW. But by putting other toxins into anthrax, this stands a very good chance of defeating the vaccine that we have developed, and we are going to need a very different approach in vaccine design when it is not the natural anthrax toxin but the imported one.

On the other hand, in nature, where do we find botulinum toxin? It's the most potent toxin around by a factor of 100 or so compared to even other bacterial toxins. You do not see it in the ordinary pathogens that cause systemic disease. You see it in the bottom feeders: in the anaerobic bacteria that live in the bottom of lakes, or in sealed cans of food. The human body is a very unnatural part of its life cycle. The bottom of a lake is an anaerobic, non-air environment. We do not find the toxin in other pathogens, not because it couldn't migrate from species to species. We know very well that it could, and there are biological mechanisms for it. But it is too hot to handle. It would be selected against very rapidly as a natural entity because of its high lethality—a rule that would be abrogated in intentional use. So there is a lot to worry about in the future.

But let me turn from that to where solutions might come from. Basically, we have to look at intentions as well as capabilities in this sphere. The capability of doing mischief, for a very long time, has greatly exceeded what has actually been done. BW has not in modern times reached the currency in formal warfare that chemical weapons did, as they did in WWI with a vengeance. BW has been subject to restraints at various times. We do not understand them very well. We experience a very deep sense of moral revulsion and outright fear. Some of this comes from our understanding: you let that tiger loose, he's going to come back and eat you up as well. There is no limit as to what the eventual spread of BW will be. You know, let smallpox loose, you've made war against the world.

We have made some very serious mistakes in the past. Above all, during the Cold War we continued our own offensive BW program for decades during a time when nobody in his right mind really believed we would ever use biological weapons. We never needed them. We had weapons perfectly capable of providing whatever level of deterrence or compellence we needed, and in a far more precisely targeted way then with BW. I do not know what our own doctrine was for the conditions under which they would be applied. I half suggest it was a never very serious one.

Overall, as President Nixon eventually recognized, it was very much against the national interest of this country to continue to fund major offensive programs over the years that we had them. They left a cache of secrets that can't be kept silent that long, that deeply. Not 20, 30, 40 years: the promulgation of the core knowledge of what happened in the offensive program is part of what we are worrying about at this very moment with the prospects that they will be used against us. I was greatly in favor of the BW disarmament convention because we have at least de-legitimated biological weapons. BW programs if they continue on the part of others, will have to be done under some cloak of secrecy and evasion, and we then have a lot of leverage about our own enforcement measures, about how we can mobilize world opinion and mobilize our own resolve in terms of responding to them.

Essentially on political grounds, I do not worry that Russia is going to use BW against the United States. I do worry that there may be leakage from their programs to other countries. Either at official levels, or much more likely at unofficial ones of private individuals who otherwise do not know how to feed their families, going to sell themselves to the devil and provide material and some degree of insight and so on. That's a matter that's been widely discussed. We would be in a very poor position to take measures against that roguery if we did not have the treaty framework as a basis for de-legitimization of these kinds of weapons.

There is one program of a very positive kind that would reinforce it all, and would be a very great benefit to us directly as well. That is to be,even more than we are, a major partner in our global attacks against infectious disease. In this world today 700 to 800 million people are considerably damaged by malaria infection, 200 or 300 million with tuberculosis, and several million a year die from avoidable diseases Even deployment of our existing technology could go a long way to alleviating that kind of distress. There is a very direct connection between cooperation with other populations anywhere around the globe and our own survivability as we sit very comfortably behind our borders. These bugs do not recognize those borders. And it would be a very important part of the bargain that we are tacitly making with underdeveloped countries, who can't afford our sophisticated weapons. The nonproliferation regime says "look, if we're in this game together, you forego the biological weapons that might even the playing field from your point of view and we will continue to be part of that global effort to fight infectious disease as an enemy of all humankind."

Now I will also submit that there would be nothing more devastating to our security that a successful demonstration of the power of an attack with weapons of mass destruction. I do not in any way want to minimize the efforts at organization, at preparedness, at coordination, at anticipation, at intelligence, at warning. The first successful attack will not be the last one. And to the extent that the culprits can get away with it and demonstrate its power, they will be setting an example that will be ever more difficult to avert later on. So there's much, much more at stake than the casualties that might be involved in any single incident. We're really at a turning point in what the future history of biological weapons might be.

Bioterrorist Weapons

Ken Alibek*

What do we know about biological weapons, and what do we know about biological terrorism? That is a very serious issue. Many people say, "Why we are so concerned about biological terrorism, because we haven't seen a lot of cases of biological terrorist attacks?" But that is not correct; there are some cases. We know that in 1984, there was, practically, a biological terrorist act here in the United States by contaminating food. In the logical development of any weapon, it is not a matter of "if," but only a matter of "when." If we look through the history of weapon development, we can see that any weapon invented in the 20th century was finally used, including nuclear weapons.

We see the concern about nuclear weapons. Why be concerned about biological weapons? First of all, because they are very easy to develop and very easy to manufacture. Why are biological agents so attractive to people interested in biological terrorist acts? It's very easy to escape undetected, not just from a place *of* application, but even from a country *for* application. And if one or another highly contagious or highly infective agent were used, the number of cases would be enormous. We are not talking about a couple of people. We are not talking about dozens. We are talking about thousands, possibly hundreds of thousands of people.

It is not a political issue. It is a scientific issue. Some very knowledgeable scientists here in this country say biological terrorism is not very important because it is very difficult to develop a sophisticated weapon. Unfortunately, these scientists use quite obsolete knowledge in this area. Let's just look through all the developments made for the last eight or ten years. What do we see? We see that it's possible to manufacture even very complicated weapons using pretty simple techniques.

---

*Dr. Ken Alibek (Kanatjan Alibekov), prior to arriving in the United States in 1992, was the first deputy chief of Biopreparat in the civilian branch of the Soviet Union's offensive biological weapons program. Excerpt from presentation to seminar on "Emerging Threats Of Biological Terrorism: Recent Developments," Potomac Institute for Policy Studies, Arlington, VA, June, 16, 1998.

I will give you an example. It is a hemorrhagic fever. We (the Soviets) tested it in 1990 using explosive chambers—tested its destructive capacity just to infect. Back in 1977, we had about 40 to 50 percent contact rate. For a long time, people thought it would be impossible to develop such a biologic weapon, because it is still pretty complex, using a so-called reactor technique. But recent developments show it is very easy to manipulate this fever. Using high concentration, 800 grams could cover a territory killing a great many people regardless of the density of population.

If this agent were used in the subway system, imagine what kind of consequences we could expect. We do not know how to contain this type of thing. We need to be prepared as a nation and see where we are not prepared. Unfortunately, we are not prepared yet. In the last four or five years, we did a lot. We started developing new data bases just to get a better understanding of what biological weapons are, what biological terrorism is, what the characteristics of one or another biological agents are, what kind of techniques would be used to infect with agents, and so on.

For example, we started to develop some manuals. I spent a day reviewing a military manual. I found about 100 errors and misleading information and misperceptions. For example, a statement that cholera cannot be used in aerosol form (one of its most appropriate forms of application) is wrong. If you have this type of mistake, it would be very difficult in the future just to contain such epidemics. Another example is smallpox. We know about the incubation period. People contacted with smallpox become contagious, even in the incubation period. But what we see in this manual is that military personnel may remain on duty until they show symptoms. This is a mistake because, in a just a couple of days, this particular person becomes contagious and starts infecting other people.

There is one more problem, when we discuss biological terrorism. It is a very sophisticated and difficult problem because of the huge number of agents that could be used in biological terrorist acts—somewhere between 50 to 70 possible agents, according to our estimation, some of them with big effects and others with lesser effects. For example, if anthrax or a hemorrhagic fever were used, we would unfortunately see a lot of deaths. But with most incapacitating agents, you would see a lot of diseased people, and these people would need a lot of treatment, a lot of involvement of physicians and nurses just to treat people. Now, we do not have a well-developed understanding of how to contain that situation.

So as to reduce the possible severe consequences of biological terrorism, our understanding has to be improved just to know what we need to do, what kind of consequences to expect, and what kind of measures to take just to contain one type of epidemic.

The most serious problem, in my opinion, is in the area of treatment. There is a difference between biological weapons, when we are talking about military applications of biological weapons, and biological terrorist devices. Just to pick an example, we have heard a lot about anthrax vaccination in the United States Army troops. We are talking just about a single agent, anthrax. We knew that anthrax was one of the agents developed by Iraq. Maybe they have developed something else too. But if our intelligence works perfectly and is able to get the information, we will be able to protect our forces.

But when we are talking about preparing the civilian population, we do not know which agent could be used in biological terrorism. We do not know how to contain the situation. If an agent is used in massive amounts, how would we organize measures just to contain the situation? It is a serious problem, and we need to start a discussion. In my opinion, we need to start spending more funding to develop better medical protection. Because you know, our final goal, our ultimate objective is to protect people's lives. With current vaccination technology it is not possible.

It is just not possible to vaccinate everybody in the United States. It is not possible because of many reasons. What agents? Who to vaccinate? With 260 million people, it is not possible. We need to focus our attention toward developing so-called nonspecific immune protection. A human body has two immune systems: the so-called nonspecific immune system and specific immune system. When we develop vaccines, we are working with a specific immune system. What we need is to increase the competence of the nonspecific system.

If we start researching this area, it would be possible to defend against any agent possible. We know it's a long way off. We know it will take years and years just to solve the problem. We can develop all the political and technical measures and physical protection. But you know, finally, we need to develop medical approaches to solve this problem.

Bacterial and Viral Terrorist Weapons

John Huggins*

A person who works to develop antiviral drugs needs to establish conditions to grow the virus well in high concentrations for experiments. We need to select strains for maximum pathogenesis, so we can make a model of particular types of human disease. We also need to develop animal models for drug vaccine evaluation, and that means we need to learn to enhance the virulence of a particular virus, and, in my case, to make a hundred percent lethal model.

The fact is that we know how to enhance virulent organisms. All people that do research on viruses and vaccines learn how to do these things. So what does this mean? There are an a lot of people who have acquired the skills to infect by the aerosol route because their similar research approach to developing a treatment for influenza or tuberculosis also means that they have to master these skills.

I am going to use a couple of examples from my own research to show what those of us on the other side of the fence know how to do. Facilities—university or research labs—contain the biocontainment and the necessary equipment. I think a person working in those could do it.

Potentially of even more concern might be biotechnology companies, because of the products that they're working on. They have biocontainment. They also have production facilities, and they're bought and sold on a very frequent basis. You may track something going into one biotech company and find that that has been sold several times.

---

*Dr. Huggins is chief of the Department of Viral Therapeutics, Biology Division, U.S. Army Medical Research Institute of Infectious Diseases.(USAMRID). Excerpt from presentation to seminar on "Emerging Threats Of Biological Terrorism: Recent Developments," Potomac Institute for Policy Studies, Arlington, VA, June, 16, 1998.

For a number of things I am going to describe, you do not really need a laboratory. If you are some distance away from most populations, you are probably all right.

We all think of biocontainment as a potential production hurdle. At US Army Medical Research Institute of Infectious Diseases (USAMRIID), we can think of large, very complicated engineering suites with multiple redundant systems designed to provide absolute protection not only for the workers but for the community, because we're unwilling for the communities to accept any risk. That's probably not true for bioterrorists. They are primarily concerned about keeping themselves protected and not being detected for a short period of time while they produce the munition. So they might, in fact, need much less of a biocontainment facility. For many of these agents, vaccination of the terrorists against that biocontainment, is quite good enough. It will protect the worker who is working with the agent. In that case a remote facility far away from a population center might be able to work for some reasonable period of time without the virus getting into the environment and letting people know that there's something going on.

The other thing we have learned is flexible isolation technology—plastic sheeting glued together with a negative pressure source—that has been used to construct large biocontainment facilities using off-the-shelf pieces of equipment. Clearly I think I could put together a flexible field system in which I could comfortably work with even Ebola virus.

As far as the production goes, we all have talked about virus growth. Cell culture in small quantity is something that most research facilities can easily do. Large-scale production is very specialized, but there are university facilities. There are certainly biotech facilities, but I think we all forget that embryonated eggs is the way the bio programs used to grow these agents. They are very good. They grow bacteria and viruses. They give high concentrations, and they are exceedingly low tech. The local farm store will sell you—along with 500 farmers in your area—everything that you need to grow embryonated eggs. And we can grow almost all of these. There are multiple examples of animal models like that where clearly, you can produce what you need to using a fairly low-tech environment.

At least in the laboratory, we have solved delivery problems by multiple methods. Animal experimentation for infection models is well known. Dry powder delivery of pharmaceutical products is another way of delivering small amounts of liquids or powders. I think most pharmaceutical companies know that technology quite well. As far as testing, there is equipment to make sure you got the particle in the right size, or you can use animal models. And I think we have to recognize that limited human testing is probably a possibility. People that are going to use weapons of mass destruction may not have the same ethical concerns that we do on that. And for some of these organizations for which there are no good animal models, that may be the way around it. Some of these viruses can be stable for only a few hours. Some can be stable for weeks and months.

Let's go on to an example of what we're really talking about here. Some of you have probably seen it before; it's a classic example of a smallpox spread. In January 1970, a single person coming back from Pakistan was admitted to a hospital and was immediately taken to an isolation ward with a diagnosis of typhoid fever, and, what at that time would have been normal nursing procedure to isolate that patient, was put in place.

The patient did not have a rash but developed it on the third hospitalization day, and bells and whistles went off. They confirmed it by the fifth day, and the case was transferred to a specific smallpox hospital. Immediately after that, all the staff within the hospital were either vaccinated or given an MIG, an immunoglobulal preparation. There were 19 cases of smallpox generated from this single person.

You see that every place that air flowed, you got infected patients. Probably the scariest one was patient no. 8. This visitor entered an administrative area in the hospital, spent 15 minutes and left. That person was still infected with smallpox.

So clearly, these are incredibly infectious aerosol agents, and they can flow with the air very nicely even when naturally generated. So what is the pathology of these diseases? We've all seen the typical smallpox lesions, and I think we think about that as being the disease when we think about smallpox. It's not the skin lesion that causes the pathogenesis. What is it? It is a bronchopneumonia. This is a lung infection. It grows to high concentrations, and that's what you're actually dealing with. Because you have lots of virus in the lung, you have a built in secondary spreader for these infections.

A lot of people have skills that I think, perhaps, have dual use applications. I don't know that necessarily means it's possible to perpetrate biological terrorism, but I think, perhaps, the fact that it hasn't worked so far is that maybe they have gotten the wrong mix of skills involved. I think there clearly are people who have legitimately acquired dual-use skills that could probably do a much better job than what people have done so far.

Transnational Threats to Agriculture and Livestock

DoD Threat & Response 2001*

Transnational proliferation includes those nuclear, chemical or biological (NBC) threats that cross national or regional boundaries. The potential threats to U.S. agriculture and livestock can come from a variety of pathogens and causative agents. With one in eight jobs and 13 percent of the gross national product dependent on U.S. agricultural productivity, economic stability of the country depends on a bountiful and safe food supply system. Similar to the human population, the high health status of crop and livestock assets in the United States creates a great vulnerability to attack with biological agents. Attacks against U.S. agricultural assets, might be tempting, due to the perceived relative ease of attack, the plausible deniability toward accusations, and the limited number of plant seed varieties in use. Indeed, the Soviet Union apparently planned to target U.S. agriculture and livestock as one element of a larger disruptive process and developed a range of biological agents that would be effective in this capacity.

Consequences of compromising the productivity and safety of the U.S. food supply are primarily economic in nature. Disrupting the supply lines for food stocks or threatening the safety of those items supplied also may erode military readiness.

Highly infectious naturally occurring plant and animal pathogens exist outside the U.S. borders and some agents are readily transported, inadvertently or intentionally, with little risk of detection. The Animal and Plant Health Inspection Service (APHIS) of the U.S. Department of Agriculture (USDA) is the regulatory, first-response agency responsible for the diagnosis and management of all suspicious agricultural disease outbreaks. As a result of binding international agreements, select plant and animal disease outbreak confirmation, regardless of magnitude, can immediately have an impact on export trade. Depending on the agent, APHIS authority includes property seizure and total eradication of all plant or animal hosts within concentric zones of quarantine.

---

* From "Proliferation: Threat and Response," U.S. Department of Defense, January 2001.

Public trust in government and political stability can be threatened depending on the extent of disease transmission, the success of regulatory response procedures, and the duration of time to restore normalcy. Additional impacts include: U.S. livestock markets would be vulnerable to the causative agents of diseases including anthrax, Q fever, brucellosis, FMD, Venezuelan equine encephalitis, hog cholera, African swine fever, avian influenza, Newcastle disease, Rift Valley fever, and rinderpest.

Soybean rust, which can easily be introduced and spreads quickly, could cause U.S. soybean producers, processors, livestock producers, and consumers to lose up to $8 billion annually, according to USDA estimates. An outbreak of FMD, which is also easily introduced, highly contagious, and persistent-in the U.S. livestock industry could cost as much as $20 billion over 15 years in increased consumer costs, reduced livestock productivity, and restricted trade, according to the USDA.

Foot and Mouth Disease

The foot and mouth disease (FMD) virus is a member of the *Picornovirus* family, and the disease is endemic in many areas of the world. However, the United States has not dealt with the FMD virus since the 1920s. Therefore, few veterinary practitioners currently have the ability to recognize early stages of FMD infection. This agent is somewhat unique, as the animal becomes infective shortly after exposure and prior to the onset of clinical symptoms. To disseminate the agent, the mere transport of sloughed nasal vesicular tissue and modest preservation in transport could easily start an epidemic. For example, a single infected cow, or particularly a pig, can generate enough viral particles to infect vast geographical areas in a short period of time. FMD is characterized by a sudden rise in temperature, followed by an eruption of blisters in the mouth, nostrils, other areas of tender skin, and on the feet. The blisters grow larger and then break, exposing raw, eroded surfaces. Eating becomes difficult and painful, and because the soft tis-sues under the hoof are inflamed, the animal invariable becomes lame. Livestock raised for meat lose much weight, and dairy cattle and goats give far less milk. FMD usually kills very young animals and causes pregnant females to abort. The Animal and Plant Health Inspection Service (APHIS) of the U.S. Department of Agriculture (USDA) does not permit imports of FMD sero-positive animals. Considerable progress has been made toward developing an effective vaccine against FMD, but the cost (approximately $1 billion annually) of vaccinating all susceptible animals would be prohibitive. Moreover, the vaccine would not eradicate the disease. Consequently, the slaughter and incineration of all exposed animals is the only presently effective countermeasure to FMD. During an outbreak in the United Kingdom in 1967 and 1968, ore example, more than 430,000 animals were destroyed.

Foreign Livestock and Plant Pathogens which Threaten U.S. Agricultural Productivity

Animal Disease
Foot and Mouth Disease
Vesicular Stomatitis
Rinderpest Gibberella
African Swine Fever
Highly Pathogenic Avian Influenza
Rift Valley Fever
Lumpy Skin Disease
Bluetongue
Sheep and Goat Pox
Swine Vesicular Disease
Contagious Bovine Pleuropneumonia
Newcastle Disease
African Horse Sickness
Classical Swine Fever

Plant Disease
Soybean Rust (Soybean Plant)
Ear Rot (Corn)
Karnal Bunt (Wheat)
Ergot (Sorghum)
Bacterial Blight (Rice)
Ring Rot (Potatoes)
Wirrega Blotch (Barley)

Terrorists Going Nuclear

Milton Hoenig*

Introduction

The knowledge of how to make a first-generation nuclear explosive device is no longer a secret held by just a few states. A veteran Los Alamos weapons designer recently noted that "the scientific knowledge and computational expertise required for nuclear weapons design is now widely dispersed."[1] This hardly should be news 56 years after the dropping of the first atomic bombs over Hiroshima and Nagasaki. Data and computer codes on extreme states of matter are now spread over many scientific disciplines and are no longer unique to nuclear weapons design. A small cadre of able scientists, working possibly even without previous nuclear weapons experience, could build a crude nuclear bomb.

No wonder the January 2001 Cutler-Baker "report card" on the U.S. Department of Energy's programs to secure Russia's nuclear weapons materials makes the finding.[2]

In a worst-case scenario, a nuclear engineer graduate with a grapefruit-sized lump of HEU or an orange-sized lump of plutonium, together with material otherwise readily available in commercial markets, could fashion a nuclear device that would fit in a van like the one the terrorist Yosif parked in the World Trade Center in 1993. The explosive effects of such a device would destroy every building in the Wall Street financial area and would level lower Manhattan.

Design

The terrorist team design effort might be already completed in anticipation of other operatives in terrorist network stealing or buying the needed

---

* Dr. Hoenig is a nuclear physicist.
[1] Declaration of Walter Goad in U.S. v. Wen Ho Lee, executed May 17, 2000.
[2] A Report Card on the Department of Energy's Nonproliferation Programs with Russia (Draft). Howard Baker, Lloyd Cutler, Co-Chairs, Russia Task Force, Secretary of Energy Advisory Board, United States Department of Energy, Jan 10, 2001.

fissile materials, plutonium and highly enriched uranium (HEU) ,[3] preferably already in metal form, for the nuclear components. Crude designs of the "implosion" type, made either with plutonium or HEU as the fissile nuclear fuel, or the simpler "gun" type using HEU could be developed with a nominal explosive yield equivalent to ten kilotons (10,000 tons) or more of TNT, and the complete device would require no testing. Terrorists would find it much less difficult to make a gun-type device than an implosion design. The gun-type bomb that exploded over Japan, which did not require testing, fired a "subcritical" HEU projectile into a subcritical HEU target to make a "supercritical" mass.[4] The neutron chain reaction was set to initiate a rapid release of explosive energy only when the HEU projectile was fully seated in its target.

Plutonium cannot be used in a gun-type weapon because the assembly speed (about 1,000 feet per second) is a thousand times too slow, a situation that occurs because the isotope Pu-240 is always present in a small fraction.[5] Pu-240 undergoes "spontaneous fission" to release a steady spurt of neutrons (about 1,000 per gram of Pu-240 per second) that could initiate a chain reaction any time after the projectile-target system becomes supercritical. This so-called "pre-initiation" would blow apart the weapon before assembly is complete, with far less than the nominal yield. A crude gun-type device made with plutonium would probably be no more destructive than the weight of the device in TNT or other high explosive.

The pre-initiation problem in plutonium is greatly reduced by the much faster assembly of the implosion-type design, where a near-critical solid sphere of plutonium is rapidly compressed by a converging symmetric shock wave. The shock wave is generated by the precision-timed detonation of a surrounding "lens" of chemical high explosive, and the assembly time is measured in microseconds. As the shock converges, the density of the plutonium core increases, and it changes from a subcritical mass to a supercritical one, since the size of the critical mass varies inversely as the square of the density. Of course, HEU could also be used in the fissile core. The fabrication and detonation of the chemical explosive lens would need to be thoroughly tested to assure that the converging shock wave generated is symmetrical. For a group with little design experience, that could be a formidable task.[6]

---

[3] Bomb-grade HEU is uranium enriched nominally to greater than 90 percent in the isotope U-235; the balance is the isotope U-238.

[4] The critical mass is the smallest amount of fissile material that sustains a neutron chain reaction.

[5] Weapon-grade plutonium is typically 6% Pu-240, 93.5% Pu-239 and the rest other isotopes.

[6] Richard L. Garwin, "The Future of Nuclear Weapons Without Nuclear Testing," *Arms Control Today*, November/December 1997.

Materials

How much fissile material would be needed for a crude device? That will depend on the design and on the type and thickness of the reflector material that encases the assembled fissile core. It also will depend on the uranium enrichment, and for an implosion design, on the power of the assembly mechanism. The "bare" critical masses, with no neutron reflector, are 52 kilograms of 93 percent enriched uranium and 10 kilograms of weapon-grade plutonium. A heavy metal reflector, such as natural uranium, iron or tungsten, reduces these by a factor of two or more and a beryllium reflector by a factor of about three. For reasonable efficiency, two or three reflected critical masses are needed in the fully assembled device before initiation of the chain reaction. In the implosion design, this is achieved by the maximum shock wave compression of the core prior to initiation.

An estimate of the quantity of material a terrorist group would need comes from the first bombs. The implosion-type Nagasaki bomb ("Fat Man"), which was first tested at Trinity, used 6 kilograms of high purity, alpha-phase plutonium.[7] The gun-type Hiroshima bomb ("Little Boy") used about 60 kilograms of 80 percent enriched uranium.[8] A considerably smaller amount of uranium, about 20 to 25 kilograms of HEU, would suffice to make an implosion device. The "orange" and "grapefruit-sized" lumps of material quoted from the Baker-Cutler report refer to plutonium and HEU cores in a crude implosion design.

Russia's present inventory of over 1000 tons of HEU and over 100 tons of weapon-grade plutonium, plus another 30 tons of reactor-grade plutonium, is a vulnerable target for the diversion of a few weapon's worth of material that would be transported across the country's leaky borders to waiting terrorist groups. Stored worldwide is over 100 tons of reactor-grade plutonium already separated from commercial spent fuel.

Recruitment

A terrorist group determined to design and fabricate a crude nuclear bomb would have to recruit knowledgeable individuals with some degree of expertise in metallurgy, neutronics, radiation effects, high explosives, hydrodynamics and electronics. More than one person may be required, perhaps even a team of three or four specialists. In today's environment, the presence

---

[7] Plutonium in the Nagasaki bomb was produced with only 1 percent Pu-240 to keep the chance of pre-initiation low.

[8] The six withdrawn and disassembled South African bombs each contained 50 kilograms of uranium enriched to 80 to 93 percent in U-235.

of thousands of underemployed weapons scientists in Russia, Ukraine and other former Soviet states offers a workforce market for terrorist groups with sufficient resources.[9] Trained nuclear scientists who are motivated to support terrorist causes or want the money may also be available for recruitment from some states, such as Iran, Iraq and North Korea.

Reactor-Grade Plutonium and Fizzle Yield

Reactor-grade plutonium separated from commercial light water reactor fuel can be used to make nuclear weapons.[10] This is well understood, but often not appreciated.[11] As of 1999 over 200 tons of this grade of plutonium had been recovered from commercial fuel of Japan and Western European countries and Russia. A current Department of Energy assessment states,[12]

At the lowest level of sophistication, a potential proliferating state or subnational group using designs and technologies no more sophisticated than those used in first-generation nuclear weapons could build a nuclear weapon from reactor-grade plutonium that would have an assured, reliable yield of one or a few kilotons (and a probable yield significantly higher than that). At the other end of the spectrum, advanced nuclear-weapon states such as the United States and Russia, using modern designs, could produce weapons from reactor-grade plutonium having reliable explosive yields, weight, and other characteristics generally comparable to those of weapons made from weapons-grade plutonium.

The downside of using reactor-grade plutonium is that per gram it generates about six times as many spontaneous neutrons as weapon-grade plutonium. Using reactor-grade instead of weapon-grade plutonium in a crude implosion device would increase the probability of pre-initiation from the spontaneous fission of Pu-240 and other plutonium isotopes that are present in

[9] J. Carson Mark et al., "Can Terrorists Build Nuclear Weapons" in Paul Leventhal and Yonah Alexander, eds., *Preventing Nuclear Terrorism* (Lexington Mass: Lexington Books, 1987).

[10] Reactor-grade plutonium (separated from fuel burned to 42 megawatt-days per kg) is typically 55% Pu-239 and 23% Pu-240, plus 2% Pu-238, 12% Pu-241, 8% Pu-242. The bare critical of reactor-grade plutonium is about 30 percent greater than for weapon-grade.

[11] For definitive treatment of this topic, see J. Carson Mark, "Explosive Properties of Reactor-Grade Plutonium," *Science & Global Security* 4 (1993): 111-128. For other views and a critique, see Richard L. Garwin, "Reactor-Grade Plutonium Can Be Used to Make Powerful Nuclear Weapons," Garwin Archive, http://www.fas.com.

[12] U.S. Department of Energy, Draft Nonproliferation and Arms Control Assessment of Weapons-usable Fissile Material Storage and Disposition Alternatives (October 1, 1996).

larger fractions than in weapon-grade plutonium, and it also would decrease the certainty of the yield.[13]

The smallest possible yield resulting from pre-initiation is called the "fizzle" yield. When a fizzle occurs, the assembly system functions properly, but the neutron chain reaction is initiated just when the fissile material becomes critical. For a Nagasaki-type assembly system, the fizzle yield would be about 3 percent of the nominal yield—amounting to several hundred tons of TNT.[14] The Nagasaki bomb, which used highly pure plutonium, had an 88 percent probability of reaching the point of maximum compression and achieving its nominal yield. A similar assembly design using reactor-grade plutonium would have an expected yield of a few times the fizzle yield, amounting to 1 kiloton or more and having catastrophic consequences. A mere fizzle yield would be a very damaging explosion, with the effects of blast, heat and prompt radiation extending out to a radius of at least one-third of a mile.

Conclusion

Aside from stealing an intact nuclear weapon, a terrorist group with sufficient resources could proceed to go nuclear by fabricating a crude nuclear device on its own. The group would need to recruit the services of scientists with the required know how and buy or steal the HEU or plutonium for the fissile core. Even the "fizzle" of a crude implosion-type bomb would be equivalent to several hundred tons of TNT in yield—a thousand times the reported yield of the conventional explosive in the fatal terrorist bombing of the destroyer USS Cole in the port of Aden on October 12, 2000. Such a crude nuclear device would have decimated the ship and severely impacted the port and its personnel, inflicting mass casualties and destruction.

---

[13] Reactor-grade plutonium also generates about five times as much decay heat, a problem that can be dealt with by conducting heat out of the core to the outside by an aluminum bridge. In addition, it has a six times greater output of penetrating radiation, which would require more caution in handling and shielding.

[14] J. Carson Mark, "Explosive Properties of Reactor-Grade Plutonium," Science & Global Security 4 (1993), pp. 111-128.

The Potential Terrorist Use of Nuclear and Non-Nuclear Electromagnetic Pulse (EMP)

Bronius Cikotas*

Today with the development of new technology, the tools of warfare and terrorism are merging and their effectiveness is improving dramatically. In the past, the primary targets of terrorism were direct attacks on people, and while that is still true today, the new technologies of nuclear, biological and chemical weapons, which in some cases are available to terrorists today, allow a few individuals to achieve levels of destruction that even armies could not inflict in the past.

To succeed at their goal terrorists want to stay in familiar territory, use tools they understand, e.g., explosives that they know will work. This premise sets up a line which has to be crossed when attempting to use new techniques, tools or to cross into the area of weapons of mass destruction. The potential of massive damage and large psychological impact may tempt them to move across the threshold into the weapons of mass destruction. Because it may be difficult to obtain a nuclear weapon or to build their own and to deal with the complexity of use, these first attempts to cross the threshold are likely to be made by well financed and well organized state-sponsored terrorist groups that have the resources to acquire and use nuclear devices. Although biological and chemical agents are easier to obtain, the same issues apply in dealing with the complexity of effective use and avoidance of self-contamination.

Because of the high threshold and associated risks to move into the WMD area, I believe many individual terrorists, terrorist groups and even state-sponsored terrorists are looking for easier and less direct ways to attack the U.S.

---

* Former EMP Division Chief, U.S. Defense Nuclear Agency. Excerpt from statement presented to the Special Oversight Panel on Terrorism, House of Representatives Committee on Armed Services, May 23, 2000

and its interests. Recently Chinese military writers proposed the use of strategic indirect warfare against powers like the U.S. rather than direct confrontation. This can take the form of political and economic manipulation, disruption of infrastructures, intimidation, various forms of economic warfare, etc. This is an area, where knowledge and tools are expanding rapidly through the internet and where the internet has become the main means for launching the attacks. It is also an area where it is possible to have unwitting surrogates do your work by proliferating powerful tools that on the surface may appear as innocent pranks or play things. In addition, Indian Brigadier Nair wrote a book (1992) on lessons learned from the Gulf War in which he details U.S. military vulnerabilities, with much emphasis on electronic warfare. His audience is third world nations that may confront the U.S.

Because of our growing dependency on computers, there is a new target set for terrorists that includes our infrastructures which are vulnerable to cyber, radio frequency and other forms of attack. If that can be done these types of cyber attacks would have to be classified as weapons of mass destruction attacks. It could be argued that we have deep and extensive infrastructures that could not be attacked in any significant way. The problem is that if you take the power grid down, the rest of them crumble because of interdependencies. Our almost total dependence on our infrastructures for power, food, water, fuel, telecommunications, transportation, etc. and a general lack of reserves brought about by just in time manufacturing, makes us particularly vulnerable to infrastructure disruption. The cities typically have a three-day supply of food on supermarket shelves, the rest is on trains and trucks from the processing plants.

Nuclear EMP, which is generated by high altitude nuclear detonations (typically 30 to 300 kilometers) produces a fast-rising, high-amplitude, short-duration electromagnetic pulse amplitude, (few to tens of thousands of volts per meter) followed by a much lower amplitude, gradually decreasing long duration pulse that lasts for minutes. EMP couples to all conductors including power lines, telephone lines, pipelines and conductors within buildings down to direct interaction with electronic circuits and chips. It can couple enough electrical energy to cause upset and burn out in electronic circuits on a wide scale.

EMP was considered a serious cold war threat that potentially could disable our weapons systems, communications, power grid and other electronically dependent infra structures. The Department of Defense conducted major programs to harden military systems against EMP effects and, in some cases, built their own EMP hardened infrastructures to insure that their capability to respond to a nuclear attack would be affected minimally by the potential failure of the power grid or other critical infrastructures. The vulnerability of our infrastructure and our society has increased with the increased use and dependence on electronics. During the Cold War the EMP attack was considered a precursor to a nuclear attack. Today it could be considered as an intimidating threat, show of intent, coercion or a form of economic warfare.

The question is—what about a terrorist group using a SCUD or a similar missile from a ship off the East coast of the U.S. to launch an EMP attack? EMP is a sophisticated form of attack.. The adversary needs to determine the EMP output of a bomb to match it to a delivery vehicle, in order to figure out how best to use it. If a terrorist group built its own nuclear weapon, or got hold of a Former Soviet Union (FSU) tactical nuclear weapon, put it on a SCUD or a similar missile, launched it and detonated it at altitude, it is unlikely that they would be able to know whether the EMP output would be comparable in terms of damage as compared with explosive power of a small bomb, a grenade or a firecracker.

That is a lot of effort for an outcome that is uncertain, particularly since understanding the effects of EMP on the infrastructure is a complex task. The possibilities of inflicting damage improve when you consider rogue states or a well financed organized state sponsored terrorist organization, particularly if it acquires the support of FSU scientists who have worked in this area. Today the real capability and threat of EMP is posed by the established nuclear powers and it diminishes quickly both in capability and EMP output as you move down the scale to terrorist groups, rogue states, narco cartel, crime syndicate and transnational organizations. It is a job for our intelligence community and the terrorist watchers to continuously assess not only the capability, but also the intent of use of nuclear EMP as a threat against the U.S.

What are our options to deal with this threat? There are no fast or easy solutions, but the following approaches should help. Continue with the National Missile Defense Program and include the EMP attacks from close in SCUD like launches as a threat to the U.S. The other area that needs to be addressed is the vulnerability and the interdependencies of our infrastructures. There are certain key infrastructures which we either need to harden or back up to some extent. The hardening would have to include EMP, cyber, and radio frequency weapons. If the power grid fails other key infrastructures likely would crumble.

Considering its size and complexity of the power grid, hardening it is not a simple option. Building even a limited backup to the power grid is also a very costly option. However, commercialization of fuel cell generating plants, not as back up, but as primary power sources, is going to happen. There are predictions that in the near future new homes, and businesses will be powered by fuel cells that produce electricity and heat, and they will not be connected to the power grid. The government should consider using this trend might as a means to build a limited backup to the power grid to meet critical national needs in case of power grid failure.

The main difference when considering the effects of nuclear and non-nuclear EMP is that effects from a nuclear EMP can be induced hundreds to a few thousand kilometers from the detonation. Radio frequency weapons have ranges from tens of meters to tens of kilometers. The advantage of radio frequency weapons is that they can be hidden in an attache case, suitcase, van or aircraft. The attack can result in computer upsets or burnouts, but generally the computer users would attribute the failures to internal problems. Basically radio frequency weapons require a larger investment in hardware than cyber, and attacks are limited to local area effects rather than world wide as in the case of cyber attacks.

While nuclear generated EMP is not something I expect terrorist groups to start using, that is not the case with radio frequency weapons. Both the U.S., FSU as well as other nations have been working in this area for tens of years and with the fall of the FSU, the technology is proliferating and being commercialized. The commercialization is occurring because there are legitimate uses of this technology like stopping cars at ranges up to 3000 feet as the Swedes have demonstrated. These devices can also be useful in direct and indirect warfare, antiterrorism, terrorism, economic competition, etc. Today Russia, China, France, Great Britain, Germany, Sweden, Japan, U.S. and, I am sure, others have radio frequency weapons programs.

II.
Dire Threat?

Worldwide Threat 2001: National Security in a Changing World

George J. Tenet*

Never in my experience has American intelligence had to deal with such a dynamic set of concerns affecting such a broad range of US interests. Never have we had to deal with such a high quotient of uncertainty. With so many things on our plate, it is important always to establish priorities. For me, the highest priority must invariably be on those things that threaten the lives of Americans or the physical security of the United States. Let me turn first to the challenges posed by international terrorism.

Transnational Issues

The threat from terrorism is real, it is immediate, and it is evolving. State sponsored terrorism appears to have declined over the past five years, but transnational groups—with decentralized leadership that makes them harder to identify and disrupt—are emerging. We are seeing fewer centrally controlled operations, and more acts initiated and executed at lower levels.

Terrorists are also becoming more operationally adept and more technically sophisticated in order to defeat counterterrorism measures. For example, as we have increased security around government and military facilities, terrorists are seeking out "softer" targets that provide opportunities for mass casualties. Employing increasingly advanced devices and using strategies such as simultaneous attacks, the number of people killed or injured in international terrorist attacks rose dramatically in the 1990s, despite a general decline in the number of incidents. Approximately one-third of these incidents involved US interests.

Usama bin Ladin and his global network of lieutenants and associates remain the most immediate and serious threat. Since 1998, Bin Ladin has declared all US citizens legitimate targets of attack. As shown by the bomb-

---

* Director of Central Intelligence. Excerpt from statement before the Senate Select Committee on Intelligence, February 7, 2001.

ing of our Embassies in Africa in 1998 and his Millennium plots last year, he is capable of planning multiple attacks with little or no warning.

His organization is continuing to place emphasis on developing surrogates to carry out attacks in an effort to avoid detection, blame, and retaliation. As a result it is often difficult to attribute terrorist incidents to his group, Al Qa'ida.

At the same time, Islamic militancy is expanding, and the worldwide pool of potential recruits for terrorist networks is growing. In central Asia, the Middle East, and South Asia, Islamic terrorist organizations are trying to attract new recruits, including under the banner of anti-Americanism.

Terrorist groups are actively searching the internet to acquire information and capabilities for chemical, biological, radiological, and even nuclear attacks. Many of the 29 officially designated terrorist organizations have an interest in unconventional weapons, and Usama bin Ladin in 1998 even declared their acquisition a "religious duty."

Nevertheless, we and our Allies have scored some important successes against terrorist groups and their plans. Here, in an open session, let me assure you that the Intelligence Community has designed a robust counterterrorism program that has preempted, disrupted, and defeated international terrorists and their activities. In most instances, we have kept terrorists off-balance, forcing them to worry about their own security and degrading their ability to plan and conduct operations.

Fragmentation and Failure

The final point we have observed this past year is the growing in potential for state fragmentation and failure. Afghanistan obviously falls into this category. The Afghan civil war will continue into the foreseeable future, leaving the country fragmented and unstable. The Taliban remains determined to impose its radical form of Islam on all of Afghanistan, even in the face of resistance from other ethnic groups and the Shia minority.

What we have in Afghanistan is a stark example of the potential dangers of allowing states—even those far from the US—to fail. The chaos here is providing an incubator for narcotics traffickers and militant Islamic groups operating in such places as Kashmir, Chechnya, and Central Asia. Meanwhile the Taliban shows no sign of relinquishing terrorist Usama Bin Ladin, despite strengthened UN sanctions and prospects that Bin Ladin's terrorist operations could lead to retaliatory strikes against Afghanistan. The Taliban and Bin Ladin have a symbiotic relationship—Bin Ladin gets safe haven and in return, he gives the Taliban help in fighting its civil war.

Conclusion

It is inevitable given our position as the world's sole superpower that we would attract the opposition of those who do not share our vision or our goals, and those who feel intimidated by our strength. Many of the threats I've outlined are familiar to you. Many of the trends I've described are not new. The complexity, intricacy, and confluence of these threats, however, is necessitating a fundamental change in the way we, in the Intelligence Community, do our business. To keep pace with these challenges:

- We must aggressively challenge our analytic assumptions, avoid old-think, and embrace alternate analysis and viewpoints.

- We must constantly push the envelope on collection beyond the traditional to exploit new systems and operational opportunities to gain the intelligence needed by our senior policymakers.

- And we must continue to stay ahead on the technology and information fronts by seeking new partnerships with private industry as demonstrated by our IN-Q-TEL initiative.

Motives and Methods of Future Political Violence:

Landscapes of the Early 21st Century

Paul Schulte*

The targeting of various types of objects against which force is used is far greater than we realize, and although the measurable casualties are often small, society is affected psychologically. Those carrying out acts of violence often do so in a strange, unpredictable, and perverse interaction with society and government. We must face the possibility that political violence is likely to come from bizarre, emotionally primitive, or marginalized subcultures acting out oppositional lifestyles, or selective technopolitical rage, rather than from traditional political motivations fostered by motivations like economic redistribution or ethnic destiny.

Globalization, or accelerating world wide contacts, transactions, and interpenetrations; the expanding flows of information, people, goods, ideas, images, behaviors, and money will call forth many different local responses and various demands for protection. Failure to provide protection from perceptions of the corrosiveness of globalism and the resulting feelings of powerlessness may result in violent reactions.

There will also be worldwide scientific changes like genetic alteration or cloning, automated police surveillance, closed caption television surveillance, or computer face recognition. The merging of the Internet with audio-visual media will constantly provide highly emotive and politically persuasive material to feed outrage. These technologies may become a source of political dispute and distrust that could illicit violent protest. Additional drivers of political violence will likely be economic inequalities, lack of employment

* UK Ministry of Defense. Excerpt from presentation to The "New Terrorism," a Conference co-sponsored by the Chemical And Biological Arms Control Institute and the Center For Global Security Research, Lawrence Livermore National Laboratories, April 29-30, 1999.

opportunities or job security, protectionist pressures, regional disparities, and intellectual developments such as technophobia.

People and populations placed under demographic pressures, such as uneven development, economic recession, and climate change, will continue to migrate. How effective will governments be in accommodating, and helping migrants assimilate and succeed? And how will migrant communities express their predicament should they not succeed?

As a general prospect, an apocalyptic breakdown in the United States or Europe should not be expected, but there is likely to be some general decline in civility and dependability of social arrangements. Maybe a few more bombings or shootings, delays and mysterious malfunctions, traffic and data blockages, anxious rumors, growing precaution, personal and corporate and a constant reminder of obscure oppositions and discontents.

The methods of political violence in the future will be instrumental and expressive. Instrumental activities include picketing, obstruction, pre-planned mass demonstrations, cyberwar, high-energy radio frequency guns, covert technologies, and physical assaults on physical and infrastructure rather than on people. Expressive methods imply personal assault, physical destruction, arson, desecration, motiveless rioting, and amateurism.

Significant motivations for these activities will likely be anti-ethnic antagonisms, separatist or nationalist tensions, redistributive movements, radical opposition to technocratic growth, radical right and left, animal rights, anti-nuclear sentiment, ecological commitments, religious sects, anti-military attitudes, pervasive criminality, and externally sponsored groups.

A matrix is the result of this attempt to assign a probability to each conjunction of method and motive. The matrix represents a predictive snapshot and a system for sorting and classifying the daily flux of news reports. Overall, the statistical chance of an individual being the target of an attack is very low, but our collective level of media-fed fascination remains high.

This may be where mass casualty terrorism comes in as a potentially presiding cultural anxiety. Imagine a looming cloud of mass destruction that engulfs the landscape in intolerable unfairness, but helps to equalize, correct, and avenge international, inter-ethnic, and societal distributions of goods, opportunities, and power. It is too easy to forget this in the undifferentiated craziness of mass casualty terrorism, and we need to try to deduce the mental topographies of potential terrorist groups. As technical capabilities diffuse within societies and across borders and so diminish as a limiting factor, the understanding of these internal dynamics and world views will grow in importance.

This highlights the general uncertainty of the mass casualty threat. Some allege it is merely a "Rent a Threat" to boost up budgets and enhance careers, while others insist it is inevitable and fear it as the way that our endlessly enhanced military arsenals will be overcome. It should be noted that nothing in history warrants a belief that military hegemony will ever go unresented or unchallenged.

Although it is important to inform publics of the threat so they support efforts to reduce or meet it, it is also important that we avoid creating a mood of fatalism if we want to retain public support for effective engagement in 21st century crises. The United States and some allies are stressing preparedness for the War of the Future, intervention campaigns in an uncertain world using global reach. We must anticipate asymmetrical responses like Information Warfare, weapons of mass destruction, and transnational terrorism.

The War of the Future that may be emerging as an imagined inevitability is not inevitable, but it is not unthinkable either. It is certainly worth consideration, and we should think hard about how it could be averted, or contained, and, if absolutely necessary, won. Above all, we must address how we can prevent it from becoming a self fulfilling prophesy.

Threats to U. S. National Security

Louis J. Freeh*

International terrorism

The threat of international terrorism directed at Americans and U.S. national interests is following the general pattern we have identified in terrorist activity worldwide. Although the number of attacks directed at American interests remains comparatively low, the trend toward more large-scale incidents designed for maximum destruction, terror, and media impact actually places more Americans at risk.

The international terrorist threat can be divided into three general categories. Each poses a serious and distinct threat, and each has a presence in the United States.

The first category, state-sponsored terrorism, violates every convention of international law. State sponsors of terrorism include Iran, Iraq, Syria, Sudan, Libya, Cuba, and North Korea. Put simply, these nations view terrorism as a tool of foreign policy. In recent years, the terrorist activities of Cuba and North Korea have declined as their economies have deteriorated. However, the activities of the other states I mentioned continue and, in some cases, have intensified during the past several years.

The second category of international terrorist threat is made up of formalized terrorist organizations. These autonomous, generally transnational organizations have their own infrastructures, personnel, financial arrangements, and training facilities. They are able to plan and mount terrorist campaigns on an international basis, and actively support terrorist activities in the United States.

Extremist groups such as Lebanese Hizballah, the Egyptian Al-Gamat Al-Islamiya, and the Palestinian Hamas have placed followers inside the United States who could be used to support an act of terrorism here.

---

* Director, Federal Bureau of Investigation. Excerpt from statement before the Senate Select Committee on Intelligence, January 28, 1998.

The third category of international terrorist threat stems from loosely affiliated extremists—characterized by the World Trade Center bombers and rogue terrorists such as Ramzi Ahmed Yousef. These loosely affiliated extremists may pose the most urgent threat to the United States at this time because their membership is relatively unknown to law enforcement, and because they can exploit the mobility that emerging technology and a loose organizational structure offer.

The FBI believes that the threat posed by international terrorists in each of these three categories will continue for the foreseeable future.

To enhance its mission the FBI centralized many specialized operational and analytical functions in the Counterterrorism Center. Established in 1996, the Counterterrorism Center combats terrorism on three fronts: International terrorism operations both within the United States and in support of extraterritorial investigations, domestic terrorism operations, and counterterrorism relating to both international and domestic terrorism.

But the threat of international terrorism demands continued vigilance. Today's terrorists have learned from the successes and mistakes of terrorists who have gone before them. The terrorists of tomorrow will have an even more dangerous arsenal of weapons and technologies available to further their destructive ambitions. Compounding the enhanced capabilities of contemporary terrorists is another disturbing aspect of modern terrorism. As recent events have shown, this "web of terrorism" perpetuates violence upon violence and poses a particular challenge to nations that take a strong stand against terrorism.

In the 15 years since President Reagan designated the FBI as the lead agency for countering terrorism in the United States, Congress and the executive branch have taken important steps to enhance the federal government's counterterrorism capabilities. The FBI's counterterrorism responsibilities were further expanded in 1984 and 1986, when Congress passed laws permitting the Bureau to exercise federal jurisdiction overseas when a U.S. national is murdered, assaulted, or taken hostage by terrorists, or when certain U.S. interests are attacked. Since the mid 1980s, the FBI has investigated more than 350 extraterritorial cases.

More recently, the Antiterrorism and Intelligence Authorization Acts and the Antiterrorism and Effective Death Penalty Act of 1996 (AEDPA) have broadened the FBI's ability to combat international terrorism. Enactment of the AEDPA will enhance the ability of the U.S. Government to respond to terrorist threats.

As the United States develops a stronger investigative and prosecutorial response to international terrorism, we may witness more attempts at reprisal both at home and abroad. Also, reliance on computers and other amazing technologies has inadvertently created vulnerabilities that can be exploited from anywhere in the world. Modern transportation and modern technology give terrorists abilities unheard of only a few years ago.

Weapons of mass destruction

The FBI views the proliferation of weapons of mass destruction (WMD) as a serious and growing threat to our national security. Pursuant to our terrorism mandate and statutory requirements, we are developing within the inter-agency setting broad-based, pro-active programs in support of our mission to detect, deter, or prevent the threat of nuclear, chemical and biological weapons, their delivery systems, and WMD proliferation activities occurring in or directed at the United States.

Our programs cover the broad spectrum of Foreign Counterintelligence (FCI), criminal and counterterrorism investigations, focusing on persons or organizations involved in WMD proliferation

During 1997, the FBI initiated over 100 criminal cases pertaining to nuclear, biological and chemical threats, incidents, or investigations (excluding Proliferation cases). Many of these threats were determined to be noncredible; however, this represents a threefold increase over 1996. Credible cases have resulted in arrests and prosecutions by the FBI, and state and local authorities. In support of this growing problem, legislative changes by Congress over the past three years have strengthened the FBI's powers to investigate and bring to prosecution those individuals involved in WMD proliferation.

The FBI has also investigated and responded to a number of threats which involved biological agents and are attributed to various types of groups or individuals. For example, there have been apocalyptic-type threats which actually advocate destruction of the world through the use of WMD. We have also been made aware of interest in biological agents by individuals espousing white-supremacist beliefs to achieve social change; individuals engaging in criminal activity, frequently arising from jealousy or interpersonal conflict; individuals and small anti-tax groups, and some cult interest. In most cases, threats have been limited in scope and have targeted individuals rather than groups, facilities, or critical infrastructure. Threats have surfaced which advocate dissemination of a chemical agent through air ventilation systems. Most have made little mention of the type of device or delivery system to be employed, and for this reason have been deemed technically not feasible. Some threats have been validated. As an example, during 1997, a group with white supremacist views pled guilty to planning to explode tanks containing the deadly industrial chemical hydrogen sulfide as a diversionary act to their primary activity, an armored car robbery.

The FBI has experienced an increase in the number of cases involving terrorist or criminal use of WMD. These cases frequently have been small in scale and committed primarily by individuals or smaller splinter/extremist elements of right wing groups which are unrelated to larger terrorist organizations.

For example: As most of you will remember, on April 24, 1997, B'nai B'rith headquarters in Washington, D.C. received a package containing a petri dish labeled "Anthracis Yersinia," a non-existent substance and a threat letter. Although testing failed to substantiate the perceived threat, the significant response mobilized to mitigate the situation highlights the disruption, fears, and complexity associated with these types of cases.

On September 17, 1997, an individual was indicted in violation of Title 18, U.S.C. Section 175(A)/Biological Weapons Anti-Terrorism Act for knowingly possessing a toxin (ricin and nicotine sulfate) for use as a weapon and knowingly possessing a delivery system designed to deliver or disseminate a toxin. On October 28, 1997, he pled guilty to manufacturing a toxin (ricin) for use as a weapon. On January 7,1998, he was sentenced to 12 years and 7 months in federal prison to be followed by 5 years of supervised release.

In what the FBI considers a significant prevention, the FBI arrested four members of a white supremacist organization in Dallas, Texas, who planned to bomb a natural gas refinery, which could have caused a release of a deadly cloud of Hydrogen Sulfide. This act was planned to divert law enforcement attention from the groups original objective of committing an armored car robbery. On video, the subjects discussed their complete disregard for the devastating consequences of their intended actions. The four were indicted on several charges to include Use of Weapons of Mass Destruction. The group pled guilty to several criminal charges and are awaiting sentencing.

Notwithstanding that which we have already faced and continually plan for, the potential for WMD to damage our national security does exist and trends are troublesome. The ease of manufacturing or obtaining biological and chemical agents is disturbing. Available public source material makes our law enforcement mission a continuous challenge.

Combating Terrorism:
Assessing Threats,
Risk Management, and Establishing Priorities

John V. Parachini*

The United States government has moved rapidly to address the dangers posed by new trends in terrorism that emerged in the last decade. With local responder training ongoing in many cities around the nations, the establishment of the Joint Task Force, and a number of important R&D program underway, now is an appropriate time to review national efforts and make improvements where necessary.

While I believe the United States has made great strides in recent years to enhance federal, state and local capabilities to combat terrorism, particularly terrorist use of weapons of mass destruction (WMD), I am concerned that many of the efforts launched in the mid-1990s need to be reconsidered. I particularly fear that our national anxiousness to address the so-called "New Terrorism" may be inadvertently adding to the danger. As a result, we are spending big, but not spending smart (See Figure 1).

Terrorism Threat Assessments and Risk Management Strategies

The United States currently lacks a comprehensive and integrated intelligence assessment to inform policymaker thinking on how to prioritize spending decisions to support the government's programs to combat terrorism. The General Accounting Office (GAO) has indicated repeatedly that part of the problem with the current executive branch approach to terrorism is the lack of "threat and risk assessments that would suggest priorities and appropriate

---

* Center for Nonproliferation Studies, Monterey Institute of International Studies. Excerpt from statement before the House Subcommittee on National Security, Veterans Affairs, and International Relations, July 26, 2000.

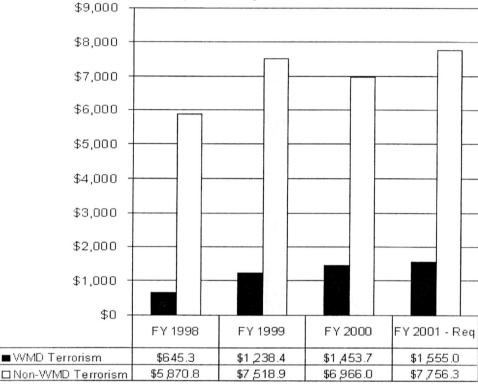

Figure I:
Federal Funding to Combat Terrorism
($ in Millions)

	FY 1998	FY 1999	FY 2000	FY 2001 - Req
■ WMD Terrorism	$645.3	$1,238.4	$1,453.7	$1,555.0
□ Non-WMD Terrorism	$5,870.8	$7,518.9	$6,966.0	$7,756.3

countermeasures."[1] The GAO's observation is extremely important and should be addressed in a serious manner.

The last formal National Intelligence Estimate (NIE) on terrorist threats occurred three years ago. While this estimate was broad in scope, it was not intended to serve as a national assessment to assist policymakers in calibrating government efforts and spending decisions. Currently there is no single person who serves as a National Intelligence Officer (NIO) for terrorism. In a de facto fashion, the Director of Center Intelligence's (DCI) Counterterrorist Center generally serves this role. Given the jurisdictional restraints on the

---

[1] U.S. General Accounting Office. *Combating Terrorism: Observations on Federal Spending to Combat Terrorism.* Statement of Henry L. Hinton, Jr., Assistant Comptroller General, National Security and International Affairs Division, Before the Subcommittee on National Security, Veterans Affairs, and International Relations, Committee on Government Reform, U.S. House of Representatives, March 11, 1999, p. 13.

Central Intelligence Agency, the Counterterrorist Center cannot assemble an assessment that combines information on both domestic and international terrorism.

With a security threat as fluid and elusive as terrorism, the challenge of crafting effective short and long term measures is very difficult. Intelligence on terrorist threats is significantly different than intelligence on military threats from nation-states. While the threat posed by terrorism is much more difficult to gauge, analysis of the threat certainly deserves as thorough a review. What is missing from our national discussion on how to best combat terrorism is a regular, comprehensive threat assessment that integrates assessment of both domestic and international terrorist threats.

The view of the intelligence community should serve as a critical baseline for the decisions of policymakers. Given the transnational and increasingly loose networks of individuals conducting terrorist acts, policymakers must have a picture of both domestic and international terrorist threats. Examining one set of threats in isolation from the other may hinder early identification of key warning signs.

One option, and the best in my opinion, is to have the Interagency Intelligence Committee on Terrorism conduct a comprehensive and integrated assessment every year or two. Another option is to establish a National Intelligence Officer for terrorism. In order to ensure that the assessment integrated information on foreign terrorism with domestic terrorism, it is worth considering an equivalent officer in the Federal Bureau of Investigation. Given the constitutional restrictions, the FBI's Counterterrorism Threat Assessment and Warning Unit may be the proper office to charge with stitching together the assessments of foreign and domestic terrorist threats.

Creating a national strategy to address a threat for which there is not a clear consensus on the magnitude of the threat leaves the task of crafting a strategy without context. In recent years, United States policy to combat the threat of terrorist use of weapons of mass destruction has been driven by perceptions of vulnerability to such attacks rather than the likelihood. A comprehensive threat assessment would presumably factor in capabilities and motivations in addition to vulnerabilities. The inordinate focus of our antiterrorism policy on vulnerabilities and worst-case planning may skew precious federal resources to less critical aspects of the terrorism problem.

The historical record on terrorism and the intelligence community both suggest that conventional explosives continue to be the weapon of choice for terrorists. Low consequence attacks with multiple-use chemicals and non-contagious biological agents trails behind conventional explosives as the likely weapon of choice. There is a low probability of high consequence attacks that may involve the full range of unconventional weapons materials.

By focusing on the low probability, high consequence events we may tend to categorize too many of them involving unconventional weapons materials as federal events when state and/or local resources may be more appropriate. Given the potential for demands on federal assets to meet American interest abroad as well as at home, they should be saved for when they are appropriately required.

Frequent discussion about our vulnerabilities draws attention to them. Most of the WMD cases the FBI investigated in recent years were anthrax hoaxes. Our public communication about the terrorist threat is inadvertently eliciting threats that distract our resources from real attacks by determined terrorists. Inordinate concern about catastrophic domestic terrorism may lead policymakers to call upon the military to perform missions at home that should be the domain of non-military service government organizations.

Both executive and legislative branches of government seek to address the threat posed by catastrophic terrorist attacks. Senior officials say that they will accept criticism for being over-prepared and over-compensating for the threat. Some congressional staff suggest that the political danger of being parsimonious with spending to combat terrorism is too great to do anything but prepare for the worse-case scenario. A balance must be struck between responsible preparedness and mere political hedging.

Far too many policymakers and researchers rendering assessments about terrorist use of unconventional weapons focus on what they *imagine* terrorists could do, not on what they have done in the past, which leads them to substitute their thinking for that of the terrorists.

Comprehensive Terrorism Threat Assessment and a National Strategy for Combating Terrorism

A comprehensive terrorism threat assessment is an essential component for crafting a national strategy for combating terrorism. A national strategy should guide the creation of programs and allocations of resources to implement the strategy. The report submitted by the Director of the Office of Management and Budget (OMB) provides a useful basis for congressional and public review of the executive branch's policies and programs.[2]

The year 2000 OMB Annual Report notes that the Clinton administration's terrorism policy is outlined in Presidential Decision Directives (PDD) 39, 62 and 63 and specific agency guidance such as the Attorney General's "Five-Year Interagency Counter-Terrorism Plan." These documents, issued over the course of the last several years, form a basis for a national strategy. The current budget review process described in the OMB annual

---

[2] Annual Report to Congress on Combating Terrorism, "Including Defense Against Weapons of Mass Destruction/Domestic Preparedness and Critical Infrastructure Protection," May 18, 2000 (hereafter "The 2000 OMB Annual Report").

report is not a substitute for a comprehensive threat assessment. PDD-39 was issued in 1995 shortly after the sarin attack on the Tokyo subway and the bombing of the Murrah Federal Building in Oklahoma City. PDD-62 and PDD-63 were issued in 1998. A collection of policy documents is simply not equivalent to a national strategy like that recommended by the Gilmore commission.

Conclusion

Far too much of the government's policy on terrorism is driven by perceptions of vulnerability and planning for worst-case scenarios. Inordinate attention to vulnerabilities and worst-case scenarios may be skewing resources in ways that do not effectively add to the government's effort to protect our personnel and facilities, private businesses, and citizens at home and abroad. Producing a comprehensive and integrated national threat assessment that takes into account vulnerabilities to attack as well as the capabilities and motivations of terrorists will improve our national understanding of the threat and should inform the President and the Congress as they decide upon investments in short and long term programs to combat terrorism.

Threat Assessments

W. Seth Carus*

Assessing the threat posed by terrorist use of CBRN weapons has proven to be a remarkably difficult process. During the past year, a contentious debate has developed over the likelihood and potential magnitude of the threat from terrorist use of CBRN weapons. Some analysts argue that there is no identifiable CBRN terrorist threat, while others contend that there is an imminent risk of catastrophic use of such weapons.

Misconceptions About the Threat

Understanding of the threat from CBRN weapons continues to be undermined by the persistence of certain misconceptions about the nature of the threat. Specifically, many people appear to believe that the sole source of CBRN threats to the territory of the United States comes from terrorist groups.

Terrorists Are Not The Main Threat

The primary threat from CBRN weapons comes not from terrorists but from hostile states. While there is considerable controversy about the prospects for terrorists use of CBRN weapons, we know for certain that hostile states have acquired these weapons to threaten and/or use against the U.S. military and the territory of the United States. The Soviet Union had a massive biological weapons program targeted at the United States, including pathogens aimed at both our people and our agricultural sector.

Many argue that no adversary would dare target the United States, apparently believing that the leaders of hostile states would fear the potential U.S. response to such use. While it is true that the United States has military capabilities, including its nuclear deterrent, that will give pause to any aggressor, there is legitimate reason to worry that we may not be able to deter use of

* National Defense University. Excerpt rom testimony before the House Subcommittee on National Security, Veterans Affairs and International Relations of the Committee on Government Reform, July 26, 2000.

CBRN weapons. The conditions for deterrence are significantly different today than they were during the Cold War. The states of current concern, such as North Korea or Iraq, differ in significant ways from the Soviet Union. Their leaders may be more prone to risk taking than was the Soviet leadership. Certainly, an adversary who believed that we threatened the very survival of their regime is likely to have few qualms about threatening to attack U.S. territory. A hostile state might also calculate that it possessed escalation options of its own, and thus come to believe that it could deter the United States from retaliation involving a full range of military responses.

Threat assessments focused exclusively on terrorism provide a skewed view of the challenge and are of little value in determining the appropriate level of resources required for resources. A terrorist use of a biological agent may look identical to a covert release engineered by operatives of a state. Hence, steps taken to deal with the terrorist threat will also deal with the state challenge, just as efforts aimed primarily at state threats will have utility in dealing with terrorist actions.

Threat Assessments Are Not Just Intelligence Assessments

Let me now turn my attention to a second misconception about CBRN threat assessments, that the primary focus of threat assessments is intelligence analysis.

Clearly, we want to rely on accurate and detailed intelligence analyses to guide decision making. Unfortunately, the intelligence community cannot always provide that type of information. This problem becomes more evident in specific areas where the intelligence community may find it difficult to collect critical types of data. CIA Director George Tenet made some significant observations on this point in Congressional testimony earlier this year. He told the Senate Foreign Relations Committee, "Biological and chemical weapons pose, arguably, the most daunting challenge for intelligence collectors and analysts." For this reason, he added, "There are, and will remain, significant gaps in our knowledge. As I have said before, there is continued and growing risk of surprise."

Threat assessments consist of several components. Although the process necessarily includes intelligence collection and analysis, it encompasses additional elements, including analyses of response capabilities and an understanding of the potential impact of the adversary's activities. Finally, threat assessments cannot reflect a linear extrapolation from past possibilities. This is especially true in an area as scientifically dynamic as biological warfare. There is little doubt that the challenges we will face in the coming decades will differ radically in important respects from the ones that we have had to deal with to this time.

In terms of addressing the new kinds of threats that we expect to face in the future, we also need to incorporate three other kinds of assessment: scenarios, scientific bench-marking, and red teaming.

Scenarios are often used to help understand the potential impact of CBRN use. They permit exploration of alternative means of using such weapons, and help bound the problem, including by development of "worst plausible cases."

Scientific research can help establish a technical basis for evaluating the potential threat posed by particular capabilities developed by adversaries. This would include microbiological and medical research into the activities of particular organisms, as well as engineering research into the practicality of particular means for disseminating organisms

Finally, red teaming studies make it possible to assess the kinds of capabilities that groups may be able to obtain given certain constraints. Thus, by providing indications of what a terrorist group could credibly accomplish with CBRN weapons under different circumstances, it is possible to provide an indication of what types of response capabilities may be needed.

Assessing CBRN Terrorist Threats

Let me now turn to the problem posed by terrorist use of CBRN weapons. This is an area rife with disagreements. Some analysts totally discount the threat, and argue that as a result the United States is grossly overspending on response efforts. Others contend that the challenge is far greater than often considered, and that insufficient resources are being devoted to the problem. The available evidence does not support either perspective.

The Absence of Evidence is Not the Absence of Threat

There is a real risk that we will expect too much from the intelligence community. Certainly, we hope that they would discover reliable and complete information about terrorist involvement with CBRN. And it is clear that the U.S. government is doing a much better job of addressing this problem today than it did prior to the Aum Shinrikyo attack. Hence, there is a greater probability that activities like Aum's would now be detected. But given the difficulties associated with collection in this arena, we must expect surprises. Hence, the right answer is to develop policies that do not depend on the ability of the intelligence community to accurately assess what is almost certainly a low probability, but very high consequence event.

Lessons From the History of Bioterrorism

My views on this subject are largely molded by my research during the past three years into the illicit use of biological agents by terrorists and criminals.

First, it is clear that in the past there was limited interest by terrorist groups in use of biological weapons.

Second, while most terrorists are not interested in causing mass, indiscriminate casualties, there have been a few terrorists who wanted to kill large numbers of people. In this sense, the mere existence of a group like the Aum Shinrikyo, which was responsible for the Tokyo sarin attack, demonstrates that groups can exist that will want to inflict mass casualties.

Third, technical limitations have been the real barrier to past use of biological agents. Contrary to views often expressed that biological agents are trivially easy to employ, it is still extremely difficult to develop an effective biological weapon. There is no reason to believe that such capabilities are currently available to non-state actors.

This experience appears to suggest that those attempting to generate threat assessments face particularly difficult challenges. Only a small percentage of terrorist groups are likely to develop an interest in CBRN weapons, and the groups that do may have unconventional characteristics that make it difficult to identify them.

There is also the possibility that state sponsors of terrorism could provide capabilities to terrorist organizations. Concerns about potential misuse of such weapons will tend to limit the willingness of most states to provide such types of assistance. On the other hand, it is possible to imagine certain circumstances in which a state might believe it to be in their interest to support terrorist capabilities against the West, especially if they believed it could be done without being traced back to the source.

Responding to the Challenge

How should the United States as a nation respond to a threat of uncertain dimensions? There are two aspects to this problem: calculating the extent of the resources needed, and determining the character of responses that ought to be developed.

Invest in Dual Use Capabilities

As a starting point, we should emphasize investments that will prove beneficial even in the absence of a CBRN terrorist attack. The model for such a program is the Epidemic Intelligence Service (EIS), a component of the Centers for Disease Control and Prevention that investigates disease outbreaks in support of state and local governments

As it happens, much of the investment in CBRN response is being made in areas where it appears similar benefits will accrue. The Domestic Preparedness Program, which was created to enhance the ability of cities to respond to chemical and biological threats, has enhanced the ability of those cities to address any incident that causes mass casualties. Similarly, much of the spending by the Department of Health and Human Services will go to create capabilities that will benefit the country on a regular basis. Hence, CDC's Bioterrorism Preparedness and Response Program is devoting considerable resources to enhancing disease surveillance systems and public health laboratories. Similarly, the National Disaster Medical System has been strengthened by the investments in CBRN response, which means that it is better able to address other kinds of medical emergencies.

In the final analysis, many of the investments being made to respond to CBRN threats are actually addressing fundamental deficiencies in the national infrastructure. Accordingly, many of the investments will provide significant benefits even in the absence of a terrorism threat.

Conclusion

Let me reiterate four points:

First, the threat from CBRN weapons is not limited to terrorists. The United States must worry about the potential state use of CBRN weapons. For that reason, we have a clear need to develop robust CBRN response capabilities independent of the terrorism threat.

Second, it is difficult to precisely define the probability that terrorists may acquire and use CBRN weapons. It appears that technical constraints have been the key factor accounting for the failure of such groups to cause mass casualties. There is reason for concern that this will not remain the case. In addition, it is possible that terrorists might obtain CBRN capabilities from state sponsors of terrorism.

Third, many of the responses to use of CBRN weapons depend on the capabilities of federal, state, and local emergency management agencies and public health organizations. As a result, investments needed to address consequence management requirements usually reflect underlying weaknesses in government response capabilities. Consequence management capabilities to address CBRN terrorist incidents will also be available to tackle attacks mounted by hostile states.

Finally, the Department of Defense plays a critical role in supporting national efforts to respond to CBRN terrorism. It possess unique capabilities for dealing with such threats. It is appropriate that such capabilities be viewed as part of a national system for confronting CBRN threats.

The Bioterrorism Threat:
Technological and Political Considerations

Joseph F. Pilat*

Bioterrorism is high on the US national security agenda. It poses a potential threat to the US population, agriculture, interests, friends and allies, and military forces (asymmetric threats). Yet these possibilities have not been widely pursued or realized by terrorists. The perceived threat is far worse than anything experienced to date and is largely technologically driven.

There is no consensus on the current threat, but threat perceptions appear to be driven by several factors: the chemical attack by Aum Shinrikyo on the Tokyo subway, which is seen to have broken a taboo on weapons of mass destruction (WMD); Aum's failed efforts to disseminate the biological agents, anthrax and botulinum toxin; the interest in biological agents by US militias, white supremacists and others and the scores of recent anthrax hoaxes across the United States; the impact of media; and the prospective impact of the biotechnology revolution in terms of increasing the threat and the potential horror of any attacks.

From a technological perspective, the threat seems grave, and inevitably getting graver. However, the historical experience and growing analytical base on bioterrorism incidents suggests that lower consequence events-hoaxes and conspiracies, along with amateurish, inconsequential and even deadly but low-casualty attacks, including poisonings, have largely defined the real-world threat to date and may do so for the foreseeable future.

Any bioterrorism that may occur is unlikely to be apocalyptic. Even some observers who recognize this still speak of death tolls in the thousands, tens of thousands and hundreds of thousands (if not millions) and devastating

---

* Safeguards Systems Group, Los Alamos National Laboratory. Excerpt from presentation to RAND Symposium, "Bioterrorism: Homeland Defense: The Next Steps," February 8-10 2000, Santa Monica, CA.

impacts on states and societies. This is the sense behind such terms as "superterrorism" or "grand terrorism" or "catastrophic terrorism." In contrast, the bioterrorism experienced to date, with far more limited effects, raises questions about this characterization and future threat projections based upon it. It must be recalled that the Tokyo attack, the only significant act of NBC terrorism to date, killed twelve people. Bioterrorism will not necessarily produce greater effects than the high explosives historically preferred by terrorist groups. Of course, particularly at the high-impact end, it is technically possible to go well beyond these effects.

Crude bioterrorism does not really require advanced technologies or specialized equipment. In any case, the production of biological agents can be undertaken in a small facility, with no readily identifiable distinguishing features or signatures. Few precursor materials are essential, although growth media are needed to produce significant quantities of an agent. Culture can be obtained from commercial houses (although this avenue is coming under better control) or from nature, and relatively small quantities are required.

For high-impact bioterrorism, significant barriers remain, especially those involving effective dissemination. Challenges such as aerosolization thwarted Aum Shinrikyo. And the requirements for significant bioterrorism include extensive human and material resources, infrastructure, testing, etc. The impact of the biotechnology revolution could change this in the future, but there is no reason to believe that technology change will become the driver of the threats all of a sudden.

The barriers are eroding as a result of technology diffusion via the Internet and other means; the proliferation of technologies, equipment, agents and materials, most of which are "dual use;" and the collapse of the Soviet Union, which increased not only the insecurity of nuclear weapons, but also of biological and chemical weapons.

Advances in biotechnology could, in principle, increase the threat by enhancing the potency or survivability of the agent or toxin, or leading to the creation of entirely new and perhaps more virulent organisms. However, developing or otherwise obtaining exotic pathogens and mastering sophisticated dispersal methods would pose serious and perhaps insoluble problems for most terrorist groups and for individuals that may contemplate bioterrorism.

In a realistic assessment of the threat, political considerations are more important than those centered on technological issues. Biological or other unconventional terrorism may be inconsistent with their objectives. The terrorists may also have feared public repulsion and governmental reactions. It is argued that these political barriers are eroding with the use of new, or postmodern, terrorists. This is surely true, but it is important to recall that these barriers have not disappeared. New terrorists or old, in the future as in the past, most terrorists may not wish to kill large numbers of people indiscriminately because they see it as unnecessary, counterproductive or immoral. These practical, political calculations will have force so long as terrorists are not wholly irrational.

Biological threats are also inconsistent with established terrorist operational patterns. Terrorists remain operationally conservative, although some groups have demonstrated a significant tactical adaptability. Despite immense technological possibilities, terrorists today, as they have in the past, favor guns and bombs, with bombings being the most common actions of terrorists. High-technology weaponry and complex operations increase the chances of failure, and have not generally been appealing to terrorists who have desired predictable and easily controllable effects, and successful actions.

The greatest fears of bioterrorism are based on the belief that technology diffusion will increase the technical capabilities of the terrorists. This view assumes technical barriers have been the primary reason terrorists have not engaged in serious bioterrorism to date. This is not the case.

The erosion of political barriers is potentially more significant for the future of the threat. It is difficult to know what, if any, political developments would open the floodgates of significant bioterrorism. Much has been made of emerging new terrorist groups as potential, or even probable, authors of mass destruction. These groups, which already reveal greater lethality, less clear political motivations, and other elements of the extremism believed a requirement for mass-destruction terrorism, demonstrate clearly that old political constraints have eroded without necessarily leading to a wave of bioterrorism or other unconventional terrorism. The greatest threats appear to be posed by religious-based and radical right groups, both domestic and international.

In principle, state sponsorship can and does provide terrorists with more resources than they would have otherwise, particularly funding, intelligence and technical expertise. But most states, including unstable and aggressive regional regimes known to support terrorism, would most likely resist providing biological agents or weapons to terrorist groups, or offering sanctuary to terrorists who were planning or had conducted an act of bioterrorism. States might conclude that bioweapons provided to terrorists constituted an unacceptable danger and also fear that any support would result in intense political pressures and the possibility of isolation or even of large-scale military action against them.

Many elements of the future threat are cloudy and need to be better analyzed. First, the agents that may be utilized by terrorists, especially in the longer term, are unknown. Truly apocalyptic plagues and designer bugs have uncertain futures, less for technological than political reasons. On the other hand, toxins are attractive for terrorists, and production methods are changing that make them more accessible.

Second, the manner in which terrorists may use biological agents or weapons is unknown. For states and terrorists, biological weapons may be seen as an instrument to be used for revenge and punishment; asymmetric warfare to undermine coalitions, disrupt power projection forces, etc.; or perhaps other new objectives. More traditional motivations, from political objectives to extortion to publicity may, in principle, be served by bioterrorism. However, the increased risks, the unpredictability of the effect (which is likely to be less than expected), and the presence of a lag time of from hours to weeks for many classical agents before any significant effects appear raise questions about the utility of bioterrorism in the pursuit of traditional terrorist ends.

If dramatic, destructive results are desired by terrorists, they might in theory find nuclear terrorism more appealing than biological or chemical terrorism. The potential advantages are probably outweighed by the disadvantages for a terrorist, however, particularly the technological difficulties posed by a nuclear act.

Chemical and biological weapons are more accessible and may more likely be used by terrorists than nuclear materials or weapons. Of the two, chemicals may be preferred. Observers have noted the potential advantages of biological terrorism from a terrorist perspective, albeit unconvincingly. Save for toxins, which have characteristics similar to chemicals, biological weapons may be seen as too challenging to terrorists on technological grounds.

Bioterrorism is a real threat for the 21st century, albeit one that is not fully understood and likely to be quite different from current threat perception. The bioterrorism threat is perhaps in the "too difficult" box, but it should not be either hyped or downplayed for this reason. Perceptions of the threat are being shaped, to a large extent, by academics, policy makers and analysts, the media and others, rather than by terrorist behavior. There is a need to find a balance between overreacting and inaction.

The Nuclear Threat

John M. Deutch*

Overview

The threat of a nuclear attack involving hundreds or thousands of weapons from the former Soviet Union has been much diminished. Another threat has arisen, the potential acquisition of nuclear materials or even nuclear weapons by states hostile to the US or by terrorists intent on staging incidents harmful to US interests. We currently have no evidence that any terrorist organization has obtained contraband nuclear materials. However, we are concerned because only a small amount of material is necessary to terrorize populated areas.

The chilling reality is that nuclear materials and technologies are more accessible now than at any other time in history—due primarily to the dissolution of the former Soviet Union and the region's worsening economic conditions. This problem is exacerbated by the increasing diffusion of modern technology through the growth of the world market, making it harder to detect illicit diversions of materials and technologies relevant to a nuclear weapons program.

Russia and the other states of the former Soviet Union are not the only potential sources of nuclear weapons or materials. The reported theft of approximately 130 barrels of enriched uranium waste from a storage facility in South Africa, which was covered in the press in August 1994, demonstrates that this problem can begin in any state where there are nuclear materials, reactors, or fuel cycle facilities.

The Intelligence Community is taking all possible measures to aggressively support US Government efforts to ensure the security of nuclear materials and technologies. Let me first review why we are concerned about the security of nuclear materials.

---

* Director Central Intelligence. Excerpt from testimony before the Permanent Subcommittee on Investigations of the Senate Committee on Government Affairs, March 20 1996.

A few countries whose interests are inimical to the US are attempting to acquire nuclear weapons—Iraq and Iran being two of our greatest concerns. Should one of these countries, or a terrorist group, acquire one or more nuclear weapons, they could enormously complicate US political or military activity, threaten or attack deployed US forces or allies, or possibly conduct an attack against the US.

Years ago there were two impediments to would-be proliferators: the technical know-how for building a bomb and the acquisition of the fissile material. Fissile material is the highly enriched uranium or plutonium atoms that split apart in a chain reaction and create the energy of an atomic bomb.

Today the major impediment to a nation committed to acquiring a nuclear capability is the acquisition of fissile material. While it is by no means easy to make a nuclear weapon, knowledge of weapons design is sufficiently widespread that trying to maintain a shroud of secrecy around this technical knowledge no longer offers adequate protection.

The protection of fissile material in the Former Soviet Union has thus become even more critical at the same time that it has become more difficult. Many of the institutional mechanisms that once curtailed the spread of nuclear materials, technology, and knowledge no longer exist or are present only in a weakened capacity and effective new methods of control have yet to be fully implemented for a large portion of the world's nuclear related materials, technology, and information.

The Former Soviet Nuclear Complex

During the cold war the security of Soviet nuclear weapons and fissile material in the weapons program was based on a highly centralized, regimented military system operating within a strong political authority. Nuclear weapons security ultimately depended on a responsible, competent, well-disciplined military establishment at the command and operating level. There was intrusive human oversight, and procedures and technical controls on what individuals could do. But the breakup of the Soviet Union, the opening of Russian society, and its economic difficulties have subjected the security system to stresses and risks it was not designed to withstand. All these changes have worked together to raise both Russian and US concerns about the security of Russian weapons.

- The military is now facing a crisis situation in housing, pay, food, manning levels, and social services, all of which have resulted in plummeting morale and lapses in discipline. Although nuclear weapon handlers traditionally were among the best treated and loyal in the Russian military, they are now suffering hardships similar to those of the rest of the armed forces.

- The new openness in Russia has reduced the effective distance between personnel who have access to nuclear know-how or weapons, and those who may hope to profit from the theft of a nuclear weapon.

In addition to personnel issues, accountability for nuclear materials is a major concern.

- Tons of weapons-usable material have been distributed over the last 40 years to non-military organizations, institutes, and centers for various nuclear projects, none of these has what we regard as sufficient accountability.
- Hundreds of tons more weapons-usable material will be recovered from the nuclear warhead elimination program as a result of unilateral and multilateral commitments. The accountability system for this material also is uncertain.

The net result from all this is first, a large disaffected population (potentially thousands of people in Russiaís nuclear complex) with knowledge and access to nuclear materials; second, an uncertain nuclear material inventory with a questionable accounting system; and, third, an ongoing demand for such material by proliferating countries and possibly terrorists. Both we and the Russians recognize the potential for loss of weapons-usable material, and its security implications.

The countries of Central Asia and the Caucasus—Kazakhstan, Armenia, Azerbaijan, Kyrgyzstan, and Uzbekistan—form transit links between Asia and the West, and the Middle East and the West. The breakup of the Soviet Union has resulted in the breakdown of the institutions that kept many smugglers and questionable traders out of this region. The pervasive control once exerted by a combination of the Soviet KGB, the Soviet military, and the Soviet border guards no longer exist. Even before the breakup, however, some of the southern borders, especially with Afghanistan, were penetrable. According to anecdotal information from recent travelers to these areas, anything can go across the borders in these countries for a minimal price. Travelers have discussed bribing border guards with as little as a bottle of vodka to allow them passage without papers, to as much as a few hundred dollars to arrange for a carload of goods and travelers to cross without inspection or questions.

There is little hard evidence to support the plethora of unconfirmed reports and anecdotal information that this region has been a source of proliferation concern, but weapons of mass destruction-related materials—to include weapons-grade fissile material and other radioactive materials, nuclear and missile technology, and scientific expertise—are present in the region, and the potential for diversion exists.

There is no evidence that existing narcotics transit routes are being used to smuggle nuclear materials. The fact that they are well established and successful, however, leads us to believe that they easily could be used for nuclear materials diversion.

The Threat from Terrorists and Other Non-State Actors

The list of potential proliferators is not limited to states with nuclear weapons ambitions. There are many non-state actors, such as separatist and terrorist groups, criminal organizations, and individual thieves who could choose to further their cause by using fissile or non-fissile (but radioactive) nuclear materials. Despite the number of press articles claiming numerous instances of nuclear trafficking worldwide, we have no evidence that any fissile materials have actually been acquired by any terrorist organization. We also have no indication of state-sponsored attempts to arm terrorist organizations with the capability to use any type of nuclear materials, fissile or non-fissile, in a terrorist act. Unfortunately, this does not preclude the possibility that a terrorist or other group could acquire, potentially through illicit trading, enough radioactive material to conduct an operation, especially one designed to traumatize a population.

A non-state actor would not necessarily need fissile material for its purposes. Depending upon the group's objectives, any nuclear or radioactive material could suffice. The consequences of a nuclear explosion are well appreciated and feared. But non-fissile radioactive materials dispersed by a conventional explosive or even released accidentally could cause damage to property and the environment, and cause societal and political disruption.

Examples of non-fissionable radioactive materials seen in press reports are cesium-137, strontium-90, and cobalt-60. These cannot be used in nuclear weapons but could be used to contaminate water supplies, business centers, government facilities, or transportation networks. Although it is unlikely they would cause significant numbers of casualties, they could cause physical disruption, interruption of economic activity, post-incident clean-up, and psychological trauma to a workforce and to a populace. Non-state actors already have attempted to use radioactive materials in recent operations. For example:

- In November 1995, a Chechen insurgent leader threatened to turn Moscow into an "eternal desert" with radioactive waste, according to press reports. The Chechens directed a Russian news agency to a small amount of cesium-137—a highly radioactive material that can be used both for medical and industrial purposes—in a shielded container in a Moscow park, which the Chechens claimed to have placed. Government spokesmen told the press that the material was not a threat, and would have to have been dispersed by explosives to be dangerous. According to Department of Defense assessments, there was only a very small quantity of cesium-137 in the container. If it had been dispersed with a bomb, an area of the park could have been contaminated with low levels of radiation. This could have caused disruption to the populace, but would have posed a minimal health hazard for anyone outside the immediate blast area.

* The Japanese cult Aum Shinrikyo, which attacked Japanese civilians with deadly gas exactly one year ago (March 20, 1995) also tried to mine its own uranium in Australia and to buy Russian nuclear warheads.

Traditional terrorist groups with established sponsors probably will remain hesitant to use a nuclear weapon, for fear of provoking a worldwide crackdown and alienating their supporters. In contrast, a new breed of multinational terrorists, exemplified by the Islamic extremists involved in the bombing of the World Trade Center, might be more likely to consider such a weapon if it were available. These groups are part of a loose association of politically committed, mixed nationality Islamic militants, apparently motivated by revenge, religious fervor, and a general hatred for the West.

The Threat From Organized Crime

Organized crime is a powerful and pervasive force in Russia today. We have no evidence, however, that large organized crime groups, with established structures and international connections, are involved in the trafficking of radioactive materials. The potential exists, though, and Russian authorities have announced arrests of criminals, alleged to be members of organized crime groups, associated with seizures of non-weapons grade nuclear materials.

We estimate that there are some 200 large, sophisticated criminal organizations that conduct extensive criminal operations throughout Russia and around the world. These organizations have established international smuggling networks that transport various types of commodities. Many of these groups have connections to government officials that could provide them access to nuclear weapons or weapons grade materials and enhance their ability to transport them out of the country. In fact, various reports suggest there are vast networks, consisting of organized crime bosses, government officials, military personnel, intelligence and security service officers, as well as legitimate businesses. These networks would have the resources and the know-how to transport nuclear weapons and materials outside the former Soviet Union.

What are the Prospects?

We believe the likelihood of the loss of a nuclear weapon is still slight today. But, the threat from within the Russian military and a deteriorating economy mean that this judgment could change rapidly. Moreover, besides the materials in the weapons program, we are concerned about the possible loss of weapons-usable nuclear materials in research and other facilities that are not controlled by the Ministry of Defense (MOD). We believe the Russians may not know where all their material is located. The fact that some materials from these non-weapons facilities have already made it out of the country shows that these materials are not as well protected as the materials controlled by the military. Finally, we do not know what we are not seeing: significant quantities of fissile materials can be hypothetically as few as four kilograms—quantities easily smuggled with normal commercial transactions.

Assessments of nuclear material security indicate that theft of nuclear material from a weapons program or from facilities belonging to the Ministry of Defense is less likely than thefts from non-MOD sites such as research facilities, scientific institutes, and reactor fuel facilities. However, we are concerned about the possibility of an "inside job" from a nuclear weapons facility. A knowledgeable Russian has told us that, in his opinion, accounting procedures are so inadequate that an officer with access could remove a warhead, replace it with a readily available training dummy, and authorities might not discover the switch for as long as six months. We do not have any evidence corroborating this particular point, but it is an unnerving prospect, which leaves us uncertain as to how quickly we would find out about the actual loss of a warhead.

It is encouraging that the Russians recognize many of the same nuclear security issues we do, even though they may see their importance or risk differently, and may not believe all our concerns are well founded. With upcoming elections in Russia, there could be changes in leadership, but we have no reason to doubt a continued Russian commitment to support past agreements and treaties.

Intelligence Community Response

The mission of the US Intelligence Community in the counterproliferation arena is to support those who make and execute all four aspects of US counterproliferation policy: preventing acquisition; capping or rolling back existing programs; deterring use of WMD; and ensuring US forces' ability to operate against proliferated weapons.

To achieve these ends, the Intelligence Community focuses its efforts on providing accurate, comprehensive, timely, and actionable foreign intelligence. The Community has also searched for new ways and opportunities to add substantial value to counterproliferation policy decisions and activities. This has included:

- Support to those policy makers responsible for implementation of the Treaty on the Non-Proliferation of Nuclear Weapons wherein the US and other signatories have expressed their nonproliferation commitments;
- Support to those implementing the Comprehensive Test Ban Treaty, wherein the US and other signatories have expressed their commitments to end nuclear testing; and
- Examining the entire Russian nuclear weapons cycle to identify areas where transparency measures would be most effective.
- Maintaining a surge capability to quickly deploy specialists outside the United States to the scene of a terrorist nuclear or radiological threat to provide the US Mission and host government advice and guidance on dealing with the threat. During such an event, the specialists would coordinate fully with appropriate United States Government Agencies, keeping them informed and drawing upon their expertise if follow-up action is required.

US Intelligence has instituted a corporate strategic planning and evaluation process for support to counter proliferation. This process contributes to the Intelligence Community's National Needs Process and the National Foreign Intelligence Program (NFIP), the Joint Military Intelligence Program (JMIP), and the Tactical Intelligence and Related Activities (TIARA) program and Planning Guidance. A major benefit of this effort has been the establishment of a significant Department of Defense (DoD) representation within the DCI's Nonproliferation Center. This has helped integrate Intelligence support to DoD counterproliferation needs and actions. The Intelligence Community also has expanded its relations with the law enforcement community and is sharing information and resources in support of the law enforcement community's counterproliferation efforts.

As the threat of proliferation has increased, US Intelligence capabilities to support counterproliferation efforts have been redirected or expanded and now include:

- Assessing the intentions and plans of proliferating nations;
- Identifying nuclear weapons programs and clandestine transfer networks set up to obtain controlled materials or launder money;
- Supporting diplomatic, law enforcement, and military efforts to counter proliferation;
- Providing direct support for multilateral initiatives and security regimes; and
- Overcoming denial and deception practices set up by proliferators to conceal their programs.

These initiatives have enhanced the ability of the Intelligence Community to aggressively pursue efforts to uncover hidden supply lines and stop key materials and technologies from reaching countries of proliferation concern. The US Government, in cooperation with other governments, has been able to halt the transfer of a large amount of equipment that could be used in developing nuclear weapons programs, including mass spectrometers, custom-made cable equipment, graphite materials, aluminum melting furnaces, arc-welding equipment, and a gas jet atomizer.

All of these efforts have proved fruitful thus far, but more can, and must, be done. This is not the time to relax our efforts. Now is the time to prevent countries of proliferation concern from obtaining the materials and technology they need to advance their weapons of mass destruction programs. This is the time to put forth our greatest effort to keep nuclear materials out of the hands of groups or individuals who would inflict damage on the world community. We are at a significant juncture in history. Now is the time for all elements of our Government to pull even closer together and to act in concert with our allies in the world community. Now is the time to reaffirm our commitment to doing the absolute best that we can to combat the proliferation of nuclear materials.

Trial of Defendants in 1998 Bombing of U.S. Embassies

An Attempt to Purchase Uranium: Testimony of Prosecution Witness

Jamal Ahmed Al-Fadl*

UNITED STATES DISTRICT COURT
SOUTHERN DISTRICT OF NEW YORK

———————————————

UNITED STATES OF AMERICA
v.
USAMA BIN LADEN, et al.,
Defendants.

———————————————

New York, N.Y.
February 7, 2001
10:00 a.m.

Before:
HON. LEONARD B. SAND,
District Judge

MARY JO WHITE
United States Attorney for the
Southern District of New York
BY: PATRICK FITZGERALD

JAMAL AHMED AL-FADL,
DIRECT EXAMINATION

* Excerpt for the trial transcript, U.S. v. Usama Bin Laden et al, February 7, 2001. For additional information on bin Laden's terrorist group, see Yonah Alexander and Michael S. Swetnam, *Usama bin Laden's al-Qaida: Profile of a Terrorist Network*. Ardsley, NY: Transnational Publishers, 2001.

BY MR. FITZGERALD:

...

Q. During the time you were involved with al Qaeda, did there come a time when you became involved in an attempt to purchase uranium?

A. Yes.

Q. Can you tell us when that was?

A. That's area of '94 or end of '93.

Q. Can you tell us how you came to be involved in the purchase of uranium?

A. I remember Abu Fadhl al Makkee, he call me and he told me we hear somebody in Khartoum, he got uranium, and we need you to go and study that, is that true or not.

...

Q. What did you do after he told you this?

A. He told me go to Abu Abdullah al Yemeni and he talk more about that with you.

...

Q. Did you go see Abdullah al Yemeni?

A. Yes.

Q. What happened when you saw him?

A. He told me somebody's name, Moqadem Salah Abdel al Mobruk. He is a minister during Numeiri time.

Q. Is he a former president of the Sudan?

A. Yes, '69 to '83.

...

Q Did you go to see this officer named Mobruk?

A. I went to one of my cousins, his name Faisal, and I ask him if he know Moqadam Salah Abdel al Mobruk.

Q. What happened then?

A. He told me, I know him but I don't have relationship with him, but I tell you I know somebody, he know him better than me. And he told me go to al Fadl al Shahideen.

...

Q. Did you have, did you actually have a meeting with Salah Abdel al Mobruk?

A. Yes.

Q. Tell us what happened at the meeting.

A. I went, and this is first time I meet him, and he told me this guy, his name Basheer, he going to help you, and go with him and discuss everything with him.

Q. Had you ever met this person named Basheer before?

A. No.

Q. Did you go with Basheer?

A. Yes.

Q. Tell the jury what you did.

A. We went to another office in Jambouria Street in Khartoum City.

Q. What happened when you went to that street in Khartoum?

A. Basheer, he told me, are you serious? You want uranium? I tell him yes. I know people, they very serious, and they want to buy it. And he told me did the money ready, and I say what they need. They need the information about uranium, they want to know which quality, which the country make it, and after that we going to talk with you about the price. He say I going to give you this information in a paper, and we need $1,500,000, and everything go well we need it outside. We need the money outside of Sudan.

...

Q. What happened then?

A. After that he tell me how you going to check it? I tell him I don't know, I have to go to those people and I tell them what you tell me and I give you answer for that.

Q. What happened that?

A. After that I went to Abdallah al Yemeni and I told him what I got. He told me go to Abu Fadhl al Makkee and told him about what you got, what you have information, and I went to Abu Fadhl al Makkee and I told him, and he say you have to go to Abu Rida al Suri and sit down with him and told him, and he going to go with you after that. I went to Ikhlak company in Baraka building in Khartoum City, and I told him about the whole information, and he say tell him we have our machine, electric machine, we going to check the uranium but first we want to see and we want information. We want to see the cylinder and we want to need information about the quality and which country it make. And he tell me, he give me a little paper and he tell me give him this paper and this information we need. I took the information and I go back to Fadhl Shaheedin and I told him I need meeting with Basheer.

...

Q. Did you go to the meeting?

A. Yes.

...

Q. You went with Fadl al Shaheedin and Abu Rida al Suri in a jeep to Khartoum north to a town called Bait al Mal, with Basheer?

A. And we went over there and we, they took us inside house in Bait al Mal, and after few minutes they bring a big bag and they open it, and it cylinder, like this tall.

Q. For the record, the witness is indicating approximately two to three feet.

A. It's like this tall, I believe. And they give us a paper before that, and Abu Rida al Suri, I remember he took the paper and it's a lot written in the cylinder. It's like —

Q Tell the word that you are saying to the interpreter.

A. (Through the interpreter) The information was like engraved. (Continuing in English) Abu Rida al Suri looked to his paper and he looked to the cylinder, and after that he say

OK, that is good. And he got conversation with Basheer, and we left the house, and few days later he told me —

THE COURT: Who told you?

A. Abu Rida al Suri, he told me go to Fadl al Shaheedin and tell him we want to see Basheer again.

Q. So Abu Rida al Suri told you to go to Fadl al Shaheedin and tell him that who wanted to meet?

A. He told me go to Basheer and tell him we need another meeting, and in the same time he give me the paper we got from Basheer about the information, and he told me I needed to take this paper to Abu Hajer and give him this paper, and whatever he tell you, or if he don't say anything, that's fine.

Q. So he told you to take the paper to Abu Hajer. What did you do?

A. I went to Abu Hajer in his house and I give him the paper and he need it and he say OK.

Q. What was on the paper?

A. It's information, I remember it say South Africa and serial number and quality something. It's all in English. So I don't remember all the what in the paper.

Q. What happened when you gave this paper to Abu Hajer?

A. He read it and he say OK, he say go back to Abu Rida al Suri.

Q. What happened then?

A. After that, I followed, he make a meeting with me and Basheer, and we told Basheer, the people they like to buy the cylinder. And he told me how you going to check it, and I

told him what Abu Rida al Suri tell me, they wait for machine come from outside to check it.

Q. Did Abu Rida al Suri tell you where the machine to test the uranium was coming from?

A He told me going to come from Kenya.

Q. Did you tell that to Basheer?

A. Yes, and he ask me how long is going to take. I tell him I don't know.

Q. What happened that?

A. After that, after few days Abu Fadl al Shahideen, he told me he make meeting between Abu Rida al Suri and Salah Abdel al Mobruk.

Q. So the meeting was between Abu Rida al Suri and Salah Abdel al Mobruk.

A. And I tell him I don't know that, and he say you have to talk with Abu Rida al Suri. And I told him you don't want me no more go for this, and he say yes, everything fine, you did great job, and he give me $10,000.

Q. Did he tell you what the $10,000 he gave you was for?

A. He says this is for what you did, and he told me don't tell Mohamed al Nalfi and don't tell anybody, you did great job, we going to check it and everything be fine.

Q. The person, Mohamed al Nalfi?

A. Yes.

Q. What was your relationship with Mohamed al Nalfi?

A. He is one of our group and he married my sister daughter.

Q. After that, did you take any more role in this attempt to buy uranium? Did you do anything else?

A. No.

Q. Did they ever tell you whether in fact they bought that uranium?

A. No, but I hear they check it in Hilat Koko.

...

Q. Did you ever hear whether or not in fact they checked the uranium in Hilat Koko?

A. No.

.

III.
Ready to Respond

On Keeping America Secure For The 21st Century

William J. Clinton*

In the struggle to defend our people and values and to advance them wherever possible, we confront threats both old and new—open borders and revolutions in technology have spread the message and the gifts of freedom but have also given new opportunities to freedom's enemies. Scientific advances have opened the possibility of longer, better lives. They have also given the enemies of freedom new opportunities.

Last August, at Andrews Air Force Base, I grieved with the families of the brave Americans who lost their lives at our embassy in Kenya. They were in Africa to promote the values America shares with friends of freedom everywhere—and for that they were murdered by terrorists. So, too, were men and women in Oklahoma City, at the World Trade Center, Khobar Towers, on Pan Am 103.

The United States has mounted an aggressive response to terrorism—tightening security for our diplomats, our troops, our air travelers, improving our ability to track terrorist activity, enhancing cooperation with other countries, strengthening sanctions on nations that support terrorists.

Since 1993, we have tripled funding for FBI anti-terrorist efforts. Our agents and prosecutors, with excellent support from our intelligence agencies, have done extraordinary work in tracking down perpetrators of terrorist acts and bringing them to justice. And as our air strikes against Afghanistan—or against the terrorist camps in Afghanistan—last summer showed, we are prepared to use military force against terrorists who harm our citizens. But all of you know the fight against terrorism is far from over. And now, terrorists seek new tools of destruction.

Last May, at the Naval Academy commencement, I said terrorist and outlaw states are extending the world's fields of battle, from physical space to

---

* Except from remarks by President William J. Clinton at the National Academy Of Sciences, Washington, D.C., January 22, 1999.

cyberspace, from our earth's vast bodies of water to the complex workings of our own human bodies. The enemies of peace realize they cannot defeat us with traditional military means. So they are working on two new forms of assault, which you've heard about today: cyber attacks on our critical computer systems, and attacks with weapons of mass destruction—chemical, biological, potentially even nuclear weapons. We must be ready—ready if our adversaries try to use computers to disable power grids, banking, communications and transportation networks, police, fire and health services—or military assets.

The potential for harm is clear. We must be ready if adversaries seek to attack with weapons of mass destruction, as well. Armed with these weapons, which can be compact and inexpensive, a small band of terrorists could inflict tremendous harm. Four years ago, though, the world received a wake-up call when a group unleashed a deadly chemical weapon, nerve gas, in the Tokyo subway. We have to be ready for the possibility that such a group will obtain biological weapons. We have to be ready to detect and address a biological attack promptly, before the disease spreads. If we prepare to defend against these emerging threats we will show terrorists that assaults on America will accomplish nothing but their own downfall.

Let me say first what we have done so far to meet this challenge. We've been working to create and strengthen the agreement to keep nations from acquiring weapons of mass destruction, because this can help keep these weapons away from terrorists, as well. We're working to ensure the effective implementation of the Chemical Weapons Convention; to obtain an accord that will strengthen compliance with the biological weapons convention; to end production of nuclear weapons material. We must ratify the Comprehensive Test Ban Treaty to end nuclear tests once and for all.

As I proposed Tuesday in the State of the Union Address, we should substantially increase our efforts to help Russia and other former Soviet nations prevent weapons material and knowledge from falling into the hands of terrorists and outlaw states. In no small measure we should do this by continuing to expand our cooperative work with the thousands of Russian scientists who can be used to advance the causes of world peace and health and well-being, but who if they are not paid, remain a fertile field for the designs of terrorists.

But we cannot rely solely on our efforts to keep weapons from spreading. We have to be ready to act if they do spread. Last year, I obtained from Congress a 39 percent budget increase for chemical and biological weapons preparedness. This is helping to accelerate our ongoing effort to train and equip fire, police and public health personnel all across our country to deal with chemical and biological emergencies. It is helping us to ready armed forces and National Guard units in every region to meet this challenge; and to improve our capacity to detect an outbreak of disease and save lives; to create the first ever civilian stockpile of medicines to treat people exposed to biological and chemical hazards; to increase research and development on new medicines and vaccines to deal with new threats.

Today, I want to announce the new initiatives we will take, to take us to the next level in preparing for these emerging threats. In my budget, I will ask Congress for $10 billion to address terrorism and terrorist-emerging tools. This will include nearly $1.4 billion to protect citizens against chemical and biological terror—more than double what we spent on such programs only two years ago.

We will speed and broaden our efforts, creating new local emergency medical teams, employing in the field portable detection units the size of a shoe box to rapidly identify hazards; tying regional laboratories together for prompt analysis of biological threats. We will greatly accelerate research and development, centered in the Department of Health and Human Services, for new vaccines, medicines and diagnostic tools.

I should say here that I know everybody in this crowd understands this, but everyone in America must understand this: the government has got to fund this. There is no market for the kinds of things we need to develop; and if we are successful, there never will be a market for them. But we have got to do our best to develop them. These cutting-edge efforts will address not only the threat of weapons of mass destruction, but also the equally serious danger of emerging infectious diseases. So we will benefit even if we are successful in avoiding these attacks.

In all our battles, we will be aggressive. At the same time I want you to know that we will remain committed to uphold privacy rights and other constitutional protections, as well as the proprietary rights of American businesses. It is essential that we do not undermine liberty in the name of liberty. We can prevail over terrorism by drawing on the very best in our free society—the skill and courage of our troops, the genius of our scientists and engineers, the strength of our factory workers, the determination and talents of our public servants, the vision of leaders in every vital sector.

I have tried as hard as I can to create the right frame of mind in America for dealing with this. For too long the problem has been that not enough has been done to recognize the threat and deal with it. And we in government, frankly, weren't as well organized as we should have been for too long. I do not want the pendulum to swing the other way now, and for people to believe that every incident they read about in a novel or every incident they see in a thrilling movie is about to happen to them within the next 24 hours. What we are seeing here, as any military person in the audience can tell you, is nothing more than a repetition of weapons systems that goes back to the beginning of time. An offensive weapons system is developed, and it takes time to develop the defense. And then another offensive weapon is developed that overcomes that defense, and then another defense is built up—as surely as castles and moats held off people with spears and bows and arrows and riding horses, and the catapult was developed to overcome the castle and the moat.

But because of the speed with which change is occurring in our society—in computing technology, and particularly in the biological sciences—we have got to do everything we can to make sure that we close the gap between offense and defense to nothing, if possible. That is the challenge here. We are doing everything we can, in ways that I can and in ways that cannot discuss, to try to stop people who would misuse chemical and biological capacity from getting that capacity. This is not a cause for panic—it is a cause for serious, deliberate, disciplined, long-term concern. And I am absolutely convinced that if we maintain our clear purpose and our strength of will, we will prevail here. And thanks to so many of you in this audience, and your colleagues throughout the United States, and like-minded people throughout the world, we have better than a good chance of success. But we must be deliberate, and we must be aggressive.

Response to Chemical, Biological, and Radiological Attack

The TOPOFF Exercises*

Shortly after the April 1995 bombing of a federal building in Oklahoma City, Oklahoma, President Clinton issued Presidential Decision Directive 39, which enumerated responsibilities for federal agencies in combating terrorism, including domestic incidents. In May 1998, the President issued Presidential Decision Directive 62 that further articulated responsibilities for specific agencies. Both directives call for robust, tailored, and rapidly deployable interagency teams to conduct well-coordinated and highly integrated operations.

In a declared national emergency, the Federal Emergency Management Agency (FEMA) is responsible for managing the consequence management support provided by other federal agencies and coordinating response activities with state and local authorities. Federal agencies provide this support through their response teams or other assets. FEMA coordinates the federal response through a generic disaster contingency plan known as the Federal Response Plan.

Eight federal agencies—the Departments of Defense, Energy, Health and Human Services, Transportation, and Veterans Affairs; the Federal Emergency Management Agency; the Environmental Protection Agency; and the Nuclear Regulatory Commission—have response teams that can deploy to or near the site of a terrorist incident involving a chemical, biological, radiological, or nuclear agent or weapon. Most federal response teams are long-standing and were created for purposes other than combating terrorism such as responding to natural disasters, hazardous material spills, and military crises.

For example, the Department of Energy's Aerial Measuring System is the only team that can fly aircraft over an incident site to rapidly survey large areas for radiological contamination. This team gathers information that is

---

* Excerpt from "Combating Terrorism: Federal Response Teams Provide Varied Capabilities; Opportunities Remain to Improve Coordination," United States General Accounting Office Report to Congressional Requesters, GAO-01-14, November 30, 2000.

used by other responders and decisionmakers to conduct an initial response until further assessments are made. Unlike any other federal teams, the Department of Energy's Radiological Assistance Program teams can respond quickly to a radiological incident, put on protective gear, enter a contaminated area, and take initial measurements of radioactivity. Another federal team with unique capabilities in a radiological incident is the Environmental Protection Agency's Radiological Emergency Response Team. This team, through its two mobile laboratories, can prepare air, soil, and water samples and perform a field analysis on them to detect low levels of radioactivity.

A 1999 congressional mandate required that a national combating-terrorism field exercise be conducted "without notice" and include "the participation of all key personnel." The Department of Justice and FEMA sponsored such an exercise, TOPOFF 2000, in May 2000 that included concurrent responses to a biological terrorist incident in the Denver, Colorado area and a chemical terrorist incident in Portsmouth, New Hampshire. Included, as well, was a previously scheduled radiological terrorist incident exercise in Washington, D.C. and Prince George's County, MD known as NCR-2000 in which mock terrorists used explosive devices to disburse radioactive material. Eighteen federal agencies participated in addition to state and local government agencies. Private voluntary organizations such as the American Red Cross and the Salvation Army also participated in TOPOFF 2000.

TOPOFF 2000 and NCR-2000 included scenarios where crisis and consequence management activities occurred simultaneously. In a terrorist incident, crisis and consequence management activities would overlap, so it is important that federal teams exercise these activities together.

TOPOFF 2000 and NCR-2000 also included transfers of authority among government agencies. For example, a local fire chief transferred authority over the incident site to Federal Bureau of Investigation officials to enable processing of the crime scene. Such transfers are important to practice because the response to a chemical, biological, radiological, or nuclear terrorist incident would likely require a response from multiple agencies at the federal, state, and local levels.

The exercises were conducted as a field exercise rather than a tabletop exercise. Field exercises are more challenging because agency command and response teams actually deploy to practice their skills and coordination in a realistic field setting. Tabletop exercises, on the other hand, do not include the deployment of actual response teams and their equipment.

TOPOFF 2000 and NCR-2000 were designed and executed as a no-

notice exercise. No-notice exercises provide the highest degree of realism to federal response teams and can lead to improvements in deployment procedures to an incident site so that state and local first responders receive federal assistance as soon as possible.

In TOPOFF 2000, a simulated National Pharmaceutical Stockpile was delivered and distributed for the first time to treat victims exposed to aerosolized plague. The delivery of the stockpile during an exercise provided an opportunity for federal, state, and local governments to coordinate their respective responses.

Lessons Learned from a Full-Scale Bioterrorism Exercise Operation TOPOFF in Denver

Richard E. Hoffman and Jane E. Norton*

During May 20-23, 2000, local, state, and federal officials, and the staff of three hospitals in metropolitan Denver, participated in a bioterrorism exercise called Operation Topoff. As a simulated bioterrorist attack unfolded, participants learned that a *Yersinia pestis* aerosol had been covertly released 3 days earlier at the city's center for the performing arts, leading to greater than 2,000 cases of pneumonic plague, many deaths, and hundreds of secondary cases. The exercise provided an opportunity to practice working with an infectious agent and to address issues related to antimicrobial prophylaxis and infection control that would also be applicable to smallpox or pandemic influenza

The sequence of events and the exact date of the exercise were not specified. However, the probable weekend and possible bioagents were suggested, which enabled us to begin preparations approximately 8 weeks ahead. Preparations included temporary appointments to the governor's 19-person Expert Emergency Epidemic Response Committee that was created by enactment of a Bioterrorism and Pandemic Influenza Response Law on March 15, 2000; recruitment of 25 epidemiologic and emergency management personnel from the 1,050 employees of our department, and assignment to disaster response teams (e.g., surveillance, field investigation, and emergency management co-

* Dr. Hoffman is the chief medical officer and state epidemiologist for the Colorado Department of Public Health and Environment. Ms. Norton is the executive director of the Colorado Department of Public Health and Environment.Excerpt from *Emerging Infectious Diseases* Journal, Vol. 6, No. 6, Nov–Dec 2000, National Center for Infectious Diseases, Centers for Disease Control and Prevention.

ordination); and establishment of a command center by reserving conference rooms and installing telephone, computer, and television equipment.

The Colorado Bioterrorism And Pandemic Influenza Response Law was not enacted to prepare for the exercise, but it proved extremely useful. We recommend that state health agencies review their statutory authority and evaluate whether their laws would be adequate to deal with the threats of bioterrorism and pandemic influenza.

During the exercise, we were provided information either from other participating agencies or from exercise controllers, and it was our task to investigate and respond. The staff reviewed mock medical records, analyzed laboratory specimens, interviewed patients, conducted meetings and group conference calls to assess surveillance data and decide on the next steps, drafted public health and executive orders, made written requests to federal officials for specific assistance, participated in news conferences, and packaged mock antibiotics for distribution at a prophylaxis clinic. By the end of day one, 783 cases and 123 deaths from plague had been reported from 16 hospitals (three participating hospitals and 13 simulated facilities). By the end of day two, 1,871 cases and 389 deaths were attributed to pneumonic plague, with 307 patients requiring ventilatory support. Cases were reported from six states outside Colorado. By the end of day three, 3,700 cases and 950 deaths were reported, including at least 780 secondary cases.

The exercise required state health department personnel to develop new working relationships. Although hospitals and local and state health agencies often collaborate with the Centers for Disease Control and Prevention in controlling an epidemic, we were unaccustomed to working closely with the Federal Bureau of Investigation, the U.S. Attorney for the District of Colorado, the Federal Emergency Management Agency, the Regional Office of the U.S. Public Health Service, and the Colorado Office of Emergency Management. Although lines of authority were clear, much time was spent in consultation and debate through scheduled bridge calls. Many persons joined these calls, and decision-making became inefficient, although not impossible. In a true incident, a central location for face-to-face meetings should be large enough to accommodate representatives from all agencies involved, but one difficulty encountered with arranging such meetings was that each agency seemed most comfortable in its own command center.

Another lesson we learned concerned our own organization. In addition to the surveillance, field investigation, and emergency management coordination teams, we needed teams to address laboratory testing, mass fatalities, legal problems, information technology, infection control, public and professional communications, and antibiotic and vaccine administration. During a disaster, no routine agency business can be conducted, as all employees are involved in the public health response. Finally, activities cannot depend on the direction of one or two key persons, such as the executive director and the state epidemiologist; other skilled, informed persons must be able to assume leadership roles. An electronic database documenting events, decisions, and requests for resources should be maintained. These logs enable staff to monitor the epidemic and the public health response rapidly.

In Colorado, where plague is endemic, we are familiar with the public health management of single plague cases, but the magnitude of the simulated epidemic and the fact that infection was spreading from person to person after a short (2- to 3-day) incubation period quickly overwhelmed the available resources. The challenge to our surveillance system was not in detecting the outbreak but rather in maintaining surveillance at each of the 22 acute-care hospitals in metropolitan Denver. Our hospital surveillance system usually relies on reporting by infection control practitioners, but during the exercise these practitioners had many additional responsibilities. In a true bioterrorist attack, emergency response teams of state or local health department employees should be set up and sent to each hospital to monitor cases and provide information to a central command center.

As more cases were identified, an anticipated issue emerged: who should receive antimicrobial prophylaxis? The governor's committee debated whether to limit prophylaxis to close contacts of infectious cases or offer it more widely (e.g., to all health-care workers, first responders, and public safety workers and their families) to gain the support and participation of key workers. The committee decided on the latter approach, but not unanimously.

The process of isolating plague patients until they are no longer contagious and identifying close contacts is typically straightforward. Isolation, however, was not possible during this exercise. The hospitals had too many patients and worried-well persons and too few health-care workers and empty rooms to permit isolation of pneumonic plague patients. Case reporting was delayed, and there were too few trained public health workers to conduct interviews and locate contacts in a timely manner. As a result, an executive order was issued quarantining all persons in metropolitan Denver in their homes. With infection control in the general population supposedly managed by the order, we could turn our attention to securing additional supplies, staff, beds, and equipment for the hospitals.

However, quarantining two million persons is not simple. Essential workers must be identified, be given prophylaxis and protective barriers, and be permitted to do their jobs. Other members of the community can stay in their homes only a few days before they need fresh supplies of food. Therefore, a one-time, blanket quarantine order is unlikely to be successful and cannot be enforced unless these and many other issues are addressed. The hospitals were quite demanding in their requests for reinforcements, and we made great efforts to assist them. However, by day three of the exercise it became clear that unless controlling the spread of the disease and triage and treatment of ill persons in hospitals receive equal effort, the demand for health-care services will not diminish. This was the single most important lesson we learned by participating in the exercise.

Federal Response to Radiological Accidents and Incidents

U.S. Department of Energy*

The Department of Energy (DOE) is prepared to respond immediately to any type of radiological accident or incident anywhere in the world with the following seven radiological emergency response assets:

- AMS (Aerial Measuring System) detects, measures and tracks radio-active material at an emer-gency to determine contamination levels.

- ARAC (Atmospheric Release Advisory Capability) develops predic-tive plots generated by sophisticated computer models.

- ARG (Accident Response Group) is deployed to manage or support the successful resolution of a U.S. nuclear weapons accident anywhere in the world.

- FRMAC (Federal Radiological Monitoring and Assessment Center) coordinates Federal radiological monitoring and assessment activities with those of state and local agencies.

- NEST (Nuclear Emergency Search Team) provides the nation's spe-cialized technical expertise to the Federal response in resolving nuclear/ radiological terrorist incidents.

- RAP (Radiological Assistance Program) is usually the first DOE re-sponder for assessing the emergency situation and deciding what fur-ther steps should be taken to minimize the hazards of a radiological emergency.

- REAC/TS (Radiation Emergency Assistance Center/Training Site) provides treatment and medical consultation for injuries resulting from radiation exposure and contamination, as well as serving as a training facility.

---

*Excerpt from U.S Department of Energy Aerial Monitoring System (AMS) fact sheet.

94

Introduction

The Aerial Measuring System (AMS) is based and operated out of Nellis Air Force Base in Las Vegas, Nevada with additional operational capability at Andrews Air Force Base near Washington, DC. The AMS aircraft carry radiation detection systems which provide real-time measurements of extremely low levels of ground and airborne contamination. AMS can also provide detailed aerial photographs and multi-spectral imagery and analysis of an accident site.

In addition to responding to emergencies, AMS operates on a multi-year survey schedule that includes work for DOE and other Federal agencies, such as the Nuclear Regulatory Commission. AMS conducts regularly scheduled surveys to create a baseline of radiological, multispectral analysis, thermal imagery, and other remotely sensed data. AMS has performed baseline radiation surveys of most nuclear facilities in the country. In an emergency situation, this baseline information can be compared to current emergency data to help in assessing the amount of contamination. The AMS capability can also be used to locate lost or stolen radiological materials.

Emergency Response

The AMS mission is to provide rapid response to radiological emergencies with helicopters and fixed-wing aircraft equipped to detect and measure radioactive material deposited on the ground and to sample and track airborne radiation. The AMS team of scientists, technicians, pilots, and ground support personnel combine their talents and expertise to keep AMS in a constant state of readiness to respond to a major radiological emergency.

AMS uses a sophisticated radiation detection system to gather radiological information and store it on computers. These computers are used to produce maps of radiation exposure and concentrations. Detecting, tracking, and modeling of radiation is one of the first tools used to decide where to send state, or Federal agency ground monitoring teams.

In the event of an accident or incident involving radiological materials, DOE in consultation with state and other Federal partners will deploy AMS immediately to the accident site. A fixed-wing aircraft will normally arrive first. The fixed-wing aircraft is used to determine the path of the radioactive plume and to determine the location of any ground contamination. The helicopters are used to perform detailed surveys of any ground contamination. A four-wheel drive vehicle-based radiation detection system, named KIWI, can be used to develop highly detailed maps of any ground contamination.

DOE scientists are then able to rapidly develop maps of the air-borne and ground hazards. This enables the scientists to determine ground deposition of radiological materials and to project the radiation dose to which people and the environment are exposed. This information gives officials the information they need to effectively respond to the emergency.

Each type of aircraft has its own specialization. Fixed-wing (Beechcraft B-200 or Cessna Citation) aircraft are faster, so they can arrive at the emergency scene sooner. They provide rapid mapping of the extent and levels of contamination. Helicopters (BO-105 or Bell 412) are slower and are able to travel at lower altitudes, typically 150 feet. This allows more detail to complete the picture than with fixed-wing aircraft. They provide detailed and highly sensitive quantitative ground data mapping of contamination. Helicopters may be brought in to the emergency scene after the fixed-wing aircraft have gathered the qualitative data to get a closer assessment.

Combating Nuclear Terrorism NEST Response

Lisa E. Gordon-Hagerty*

Growing concerns about the availability of materials for nuclear weapons has brought increased attention to the problem of responding to the threat presented by an adversary who employs an improvised nuclear device, a radiological dispersal device, or a nuclear weapon stolen from another nation's stockpile. The common denominator in terrorism is the use of tactics that fall outside of traditionally recognized military methods. Typical approaches that have been used by terrorists include civilian bombings, assassination, smuggling and extortion. The motives behind such acts most often include a broad mixture of terror, ethnic or religious fanaticism, and revenge. These types of threats strain the detection capability of the intelligence and the law enforcement communities ability to intervene, witnessed by the lack of success in preventing the 1993 bombing of the New York World Trade Center.

When the destructive potential of a nuclear device is taken into account, successful intervention and neutralization of this threat is paramount to ensuring the safety of U.S. citizens and national security interests.

Resident Technical Nuclear Expertise

As a result of the Department of Energy's responsibility to maintain the nuclear weapon complex, it is both logical and prudent that DOE provide the technical expertise to respond to malevolent nuclear incidents. This unique technical expertise exists exclusively at the DOE nuclear weapon laboratories: Los Alamos, Sandia, and Lawrence Livermore National Laboratories.

---

* Director, Office of Emergency Response; Acting Director, Office of Weapons Surety; Defense Programs, Department of Energy. From statement before the House National Security Committee Subcommittee on Military Research and Development, October 1, 1997.

As a result of the moratorium on underground nuclear weapon testing, the Department of Energy has developed the Stockpile Stewardship and Management Program (SSMP) to ensure the continued safety and reliability of the nation's nuclear weapons stockpile, and to preserve the core intellectual and technical competencies of the United States in nuclear weapons design production, and dismantlement.

It is precisely this nuclear weapon expertise and the computational simulations and experimental validation provided by the Stockpile Stewardship and Management Program that are required to identify and assess the nature and seriousness of a nuclear terrorist device. The effectiveness of many technical operations can only be validated by the laboratory's technical staffs supported by computer simulations and experimental validation programs supported by SSMP.

DOE's Technical/Operational Capabilities to Combat Nuclear Terrorism

If a nuclear terrorist incident occurs in the United States, the lead Federal agency responsibility resides with the Federal Bureau of Investigation. The Department of State would take the lead should the incident occur overseas. The DOE Emergency Response Program is responsible for day-to-day program management of the Department's nuclear counter terrorism program. The Department of Energy's Nuclear Emergency Search Team, more commonly known as NEST, provides the technical expertise and support to other Federal agencies, as needed.

Made up of several components, NEST capabilities include search and identification of nuclear materials, diagnostics and assessment of suspected nuclear devices, and disablement and containment programs. NEST personnel and equipment are deployable at all times. They can be quickly transported by military or commercial aircraft to any location worldwide.

NEST possesses the capability to render a rogue device safe and package it for transport to a secure location for follow-on disassembly operations. This program consists of an all-volunteer community composed of scientists, engineers, and technicians from the nuclear weapons design laboratories. The operational capability deployed in response to an incident of nuclear terrorism varies in size from a five person advisory team that supports specialized classified programs, to a NEST deployment with as many as 800 searchers and scientists, complemented by their technical and logistical equipment. We have developed operational programs tailored to meet the needs of our interagency partners: the FBI, and the Departments of State and Defense. We have continuously updated and modified those operational programs as the threat and needs of the supported agencies have evolved.

Our capabilities must constantly evolve commensurate with the available technology. Further, we must ensure that our operational capabilities are not limited by the capabilities of our computational or experimental testing programs.

History of NEST

Established in the mid-seventies, NEST was designed to respond to incidents of nuclear extortion in support of the FBI. The extortion scenario allowed for planning and operations to be conducted over a period of several days because the intelligence and law enforcement communities believed that the extortionist would allow time for negotiations. The idea that a nuclear device would fall into the hands of terrorists and be detonated without notice was not deemed credible at that time. Consequently, the NEST capabilities were developed and based on large-scale deployments. This process was slow but very thorough, because it was assumed there would be sufficient time to deploy all NEST assets to meet the technical challenge.

In August, 1980, a sophisticated improvised explosive device was detonated in Harvey's Casino in State Line, Nevada. The device was exploded by a failed attempt to render it safe. While this particular device was not nuclear, it offered many of the problems that our scientists and analysts feared could be encountered in a nuclear device. It was the most sophisticated device of its type that the U.S. had encountered to date and thus became a benchmark for the development of new equipment and techniques to render safe similar devices.

In the years that followed, the nuclear threat remained relatively constant and the capabilities of the NEST program continued to be enhanced. Nonetheless, the NEST organization continued to believe that time was on their side when responding to nuclear threats.

Current Counter Terrorism Strategy

In early 1992, based on intelligence estimates, the Department's operational planners re-evaluated the nuclear incident scenarios. While the threat of nuclear extortion did not go away, a new threat had emerged: nuclear terrorism. We now know that terrorists are willing to use large explosive devices, and devices that disburse chemical agents, without warning. We must therefore assume that nuclear terrorist devices could be placed and detonated without warning.

As a result of this assumption, the focus of DOE's efforts to combat terrorism has broadened. While DOE has not given up its technical capability to respond to an extortion scenario, we have re-directed deployment readiness and training requirements to respond more rapidly to an act of terrorism where time is not on our side. It is now commonplace for the Office of Emergency Response to plan and execute no-notice deployments of NEST assets. These deployment challenges are designed to provide a realistic technical exercise and the ability to mobilize rapidly. The training program has been expanded to include exercising our capabilities against a non-U.S. nuclear weapon that falls into terrorist hands or against a homemade nuclear device.

The Department's current counter terrorism strategy is to tailor our operational assets, as necessary, to respond where nonproliferation measures fail. This strategy employs a wide variety of our scientific and technical expertise to neutralize nuclear weapons or devices aimed at United States interests by rogue states, extra-national entities, and terrorist groups. DOE's substantial capability includes detecting, locating, identifying, diagnosing, and disabling such weapons. DOE also has the capability to mitigate the blast effects of non-nuclear disablement activity.

NEST teams now practice a wide variety of deployment scenarios from table-top exercises to long-range deployments to remote locations. In conjunction with the FBI, State and DOD, we conduct smaller and more focused terrorism related exercises more frequently than in the past. The NEST exercise program has re-focused its efforts to support rapid and customized deployment to a wide range of nuclear threats. As a result of these exercises, we have enhanced interagency coordination and streamlined command and control during an incident.

NEST is perhaps the most important national technical capability available to counter the potential threat of nuclear terrorism.

Biological and Chemical Terrorism: CDC Strategic Plan for Preparedness and Response*

Centers for Disease Control and Prevention

Introduction

An act of biological or chemical terrorism might range from dissemination of aerosolized anthrax spores to food product contamination, and predicting when and how such an attack might occur is not possible. However, the public health infrastructure must be prepared to prevent illness and injury that would result from biological and chemical terrorism, especially a covert terrorist attack. As with emerging infectious diseases, early detection and control of biological or chemical attacks depends on a strong and flexible public health system at the local, state, and federal levels. In addition, primary health-care providers throughout the United States must be vigilant because they will probably be the first to observe and report unusual illnesses or injuries.

U.S. Vulnerability To Biological And Chemical Terrorism

Terrorist incidents in the United States and elsewhere involving bacterial pathogens, nerve gas, and a lethal plant toxin (i.e., ricin) have demonstrated that the United States is vulnerable to biological and chemical threats as well as explosives. Recipes for preparing "homemade" agents are readily available, and reports of arsenals of military bioweapons raise the possibility that terrorists might have access to highly dangerous agents, which have been engineered for mass dissemination as small-particle aerosols. Such agents as the variola virus, the causative agent of smallpox, are highly contagious and often fatal. Responding to large-scale outbreaks caused by these agents will require the rapid mobilization of public health workers, emergency responders, and private health-care providers. Large-scale outbreaks will also require rapid procurement and distribution of large quantities of drugs and vaccines, which must be available quickly.

---

* Excerpt from Recommendations of the CDC Strategic Planning Workgroup, Centers for Disease Control and Prevention, April 21, 2000.

Overt Versus Covert Terrorist Attacks

In the past, most planning for emergency response to terrorism has been concerned with overt attacks (e.g., bombings). Chemical terrorism acts are likely to be overt because the effects of chemical agents absorbed through inhalation or by absorption through the skin or mucous membranes are usually immediate and obvious. Such attacks elicit immediate response from police, fire, and EMS personnel. In contrast, attacks with biological agents are more likely to be covert. They present different challenges and require an additional dimension of emergency planning that involves the public health infrastructure.

Local public health agency preparedness

- Because the initial detection of a covert biological or chemical attack will probably occur at the local level, disease surveillance systems at state and local health agencies must be capable of detecting unusual patterns of disease or injury, including those caused by unusual or unknown threat agents.
- Because the initial response to a covert biological or chemical attack will probably be made at the local level, epidemiologists at state and local health agencies must have expertise and resources for responding to reports of clusters of rare, unusual, or unexplained illnesses.

In 1999, the vulnerability of the food supply was illustrated in Belgium, when chickens were unintentionally exposed to dioxin-contaminated fat used to make animal feed.

Focusing Preparedness Activities

Early detection of and response to biological or chemical terrorism are crucial. Without special preparation at the local and state levels, a large-scale attack with variola virus, aerosolized anthrax spores, a nerve gas, or a foodborne biological or chemical agent could overwhelm the local and perhaps national public health infrastructure.

The epidemiologic skills, surveillance methods, diagnostic techniques, and physical resources required to detect and investigate unusual or unknown diseases, as well as syndromes or injuries caused by chemical accidents, are similar to those needed to identify and respond to an attack with a biological or chemical agent. However, public health agencies must prepare also for the special features a terrorist attack probably would have (e.g., mass casualties or the use of rare agents).

Steps in Preparing for Biological Attacks

- Enhance epidemiologic capacity to detect and respond to biological attacks.
- Supply diagnostic reagents to state and local public health agencies.
- Establish communication programs to ensure delivery of accurate information.
- Enhance bioterrorism-related education and training for health-care professionals.
- Prepare educational materials that will inform and reassure the public during and after a biological attack.
- Stockpile appropriate vaccines and drugs.
- Establish molecular surveillance for microbial strains, including unusual or drug- resistant strains.
- Support the development of diagnostic tests.
Encourage research on antiviral drugs and vaccines.

Steps in Preparing for Chemical Attacks

- Enhance epidemiologic capacity for detecting and responding to chemical attacks.
- Enhance awareness of chemical terrorism among emergency medical service personnel, police officers, firefighters, physicians, and nurses.
- Stockpile chemical antidotes.
- Develop and provide bioassays for detection and diagnosis of chemical injuries.
- Prepare educational materials to inform the public during and after a chemical attack

Because of the hundreds of new chemicals introduced internationally each month, treating exposed persons by clinical syndrome rather than by specific agent is more useful for public health planning and emergency medical response purposes.

Key Focus Areas

CDC's strategic plan is based on the following five focus areas, with each area integrating training and research:

- preparedness and prevention;
- detection and surveillance;
- diagnosis and characterization of biological and chemical agents;
- response; and
- communication.

Preparedness and Prevention

Detection, diagnosis, and mitigation of illness and injury caused by biological and chemical terrorism is a complex process that involves numerous partners and activities. Meeting this challenge will require special emergency preparedness in all cities and states. CDC will provide public health guidelines, support, and technical assistance to local and state public health agencies as they develop coordinated preparedness plans and response protocols.

Detection and Surveillance

Early detection is essential for ensuring a prompt response to a biological or chemical attack, including the provision of prophylactic medicines, chemical antidotes, or vaccines. CDC will integrate surveillance for illness and injury resulting from biological and chemical terrorism into the U.S. disease surveillance systems, while developing new mechanisms for detecting, evaluating, and reporting suspicious events that might represent covert terrorist acts. As part of this effort, CDC and state and local health agencies will form partnerships with front-line medical personnel in hospital emergency departments, hospital care facilities, poison control centers, and other offices to enhance detection and reporting of unexplained injuries and illnesses as part of routine surveillance mechanisms for biological and chemical terrorism.

Diagnosis and Characterization of Biological and Chemical Agents

CDC and its partners will create a multilevel laboratory response network for bioterrorism (LRNB) that will link clinical labs to public health agencies in all states, districts, territories, and selected cities and counties and to state-of-the-art facilities that can analyze biological agents.

Response

A comprehensive public health response to a biological or chemical terrorist event involves epidemiologic investigation, medical treatment and prophylaxis for affected persons, and the initiation of disease prevention or environmental decontamination measures. CDC will assist state and local health agencies in developing resources and expertise for investigating unusual events and unexplained illnesses. In the event of a confirmed terrorist attack, CDC will coordinate with other federal agencies. PDD 39 designates the Federal Bureau of Investigation as the lead agency for the crisis plan and charges the Federal Emergency Management Agency with ensuring that the federal response management is adequate to respond to the consequences of terrorism. CDC will maintain a national pharmaceutical stockpile.

Communication Systems

U.S. preparedness to mitigate the public health consequences of biological and chemical terrorism depends on the coordinated activities of well-trained health-care and public health personnel throughout the United States who have access to up-to-the minute emergency information. Effective communication with the public through the news media will also be essential to limit terrorists' ability to induce public panic and disrupt daily life.

During the next 5 years, CDC will work with state and local health agencies to develop a) a state-of-the-art communication system that will support disease surveillance; b) rapid notification and information exchange regarding disease outbreaks that are possibly related to bioterrorism; c) dissemination of diagnostic results and emergency health information; and d) coordination of emergency response activities. Through this network and similar mechanisms, CDC will provide terrorism-related training to epidemiologists and laboratorians, emergency responders, emergency department personnel and other front-line health-care providers, and health and safety personnel.

Conclusion

Recent threats and use of biological and chemical agents against civilians have exposed U.S. vulnerability and highlighted the need to enhance our capacity to detect and control terrorist acts. The U.S. must be protected from an extensive range of critical biological and chemical agents, including some that have been developed and stockpiled for military use. Even without threat of war, investment in national defense ensures preparedness and acts as a deterrent against hostile acts. Similarly, investment in the public health system provides the best civil defense against bioterrorism.

Bioterrorism: Our Front Line Response Evaluating U.S.Public Health and Medical Readiness

Donald A. Henderson*

Over the past four years, concerns about terrorism, and bioterrorism in particular, have increased sharply. Three events, in particular, are seen as having been of special significance. First was the sarin gas attack in Tokyo in 1995 perpetrated by the apocalyptic religious cult, Aum Shinrikyo only after several failures in efforts to disseminate anthrax and botulinum toxin. Second was the discovery in 1995 that, however threatening Iraq's bioweapons capability had been thought to be, new documents revealed that it was far more advanced and extensive than had been appreciated. Finally, an appreciation of the scope and sophistication of a Soviet bioweapons program became increasingly available during the 1990s with the defection of senior bioweapons officials.

A Presidential Decision Directive (PDD-39) in June 1995 provided for a broad mobilization within federal agencies to begin to counter the threat; substantial special funding was provided in the 1997 Defense Against Weapons of Mass Destruction Act. Only recently have the civilian medical and public health communities begun to be engaged in examining the practical challenges posed by this threat.

The Unique Nature of the Biological Threat

Of the weapons of mass destruction, the biological ones are the most greatly feared but the country is least well prepared to deal with them. So far,

* Dr. Henderson is Professor of Epidemiology and International Health and Director of the Center for Civilian Biodefense Studies at Johns Hopkins University. Excerpt from testimony before the Senate Committee On Health, Education, Labor And Pensions, Subcommittee on Public Health, March 25, 1999.

virtually all federal efforts in strategic planning and training have been directed toward crisis management after a chemical release or an explosion. Should such an event occur, plans appropriately call for so-called "first responders"—fire, police, and emergency rescue workers—to proceed to the scene. There, with the FBI assuming lead responsibility, they are expected to stabilize the situation, to deal with casualties, to decontaminate, and to collect evidence for identification of a perpetrator

A bioterrorist event presents an entirely different scenario, one that is alien to civil authorities. Epidemics of serious diseases such as could be anticipated are wholly unknown to American cities. Unlike an explosive or chemical event, the bioweapons release would be silent and almost certainly undetected. The aerosol cloud would be invisible, odorless and tasteless. It would behave much like a gas in penetrating interior areas. No one would know until days or weeks later that anyone had been infected. Then, patients would begin appearing in emergency rooms and physicians' offices with symptoms of a strange disease that few physicians had ever seen. There would be no sudden alarm calling for action within minutes to hours on the part of "first responders". In fact, the "first responders" would not be fire and law enforcement staff but public health and medical personnel.

Responses Following a Bioweapons Attack

Special measures would be needed for patient diagnosis, care and hospitalization, for laboratory confirmation regarding the identity of microbes unknown to most laboratories, for providing vaccine and perhaps antibiotics to large portions of the population, and for identifying and possibly quarantining patients. Trained epidemiologists would be needed to identify where and when infection had occurred, so as to identify how and by whom it may have been spread. Public health administrators would be challenged to undertake emergency management of a problem alien to their experience, in a public environment where epidemics of pestilential disease are unknown, and in an environment where the potential for panic is high.

In brief, the personnel that are required, the skills that they must have and the strategies to be employed are unique. The common assumption that chemical and biological threats are generically so similar that they can be readily handled by multi-purpose "chembio" experts is clearly absurd.

However, until very recently, none of the relevant medical and public health groups had been meaningfully involved in assessing risks, nor in planning for appropriate civilian responses, nor in training, nor in defining research and development needs.

The National Initiative

An augmented full-time cadre of professionals at the state and local level would represent, for biological weapons, a counterpart to the National Guard Rapid Assessment and Initial Detection Teams for chemical weapons.

The Major Threats

An assessment of the relative threats posed by different agents by a working group under the aegis of the Johns Hopkins Civilian Biodefense Studies Center comprised of experts from federal, state and local institutions as well as academia identified six organisms as posing a sufficiently serious threat as to potentially cause major medical problems and social disruption throughout a large community. These were smallpox, anthrax, plague, botulinum toxin, tularemia and a hemorrhagic fever agent such as the Ebola or Marburg virus.

By far, the two of greatest concern are smallpox and anthrax. Both are associated with high case fatality rates when dispersed as an aerosol. For smallpox, the case-fatality rate is 30%; for anthrax, above 80%. There is no immunity against anthrax in the population and virtually none against smallpox. Both agents have other advantages in that they can be grown reasonably easily and in large quantities and are sturdy organisms that are resistant to destruction. They are thus especially suited to aerosol dissemination to reach large areas and numbers of people. Smallpox has the added attribute of being able to spread further from person to person.

The working group supported the view that reserve stockpiles both of anthrax and smallpox vaccines should be produced, that a stockpile of antibiotics should be created to deal with anthrax, and that the possible development of second generation vaccines for both diseases should be explored as a matter of urgency.

A Look to the Future

Biologists, especially those in medicine and public health, are as critical to confronting the problems posed by biological weapons as are physicists in dealing with nuclear threats and chemists with chemical weapons. There is a need to expand the discussion regarding the salient issues both at national and local levels, to recruit the interest and commitment of scientists in devising strategy, in undertaking needed research and in the complex planning process which is needed to blend together the very diverse array of institutions, both public and private in coherent local, state and federal plans.

Plans for dealing with large numbers of patients, including those who require isolation will have to be elaborated on a regional basis and plans developed for emergency care facilities, for decontamination procedures, for dispensing rapidly large quantities of vaccine and antibiotics, for rapid and secure communications, for informing the media and the public in a timely manner, for provision of mental health services and for emergency mortuaries.

Developing the experts and expertise will require a major educational effort, given the variety of specialists that are needed and the now virtual absence of knowledgeable and experienced specialists. There is a need to train primary care physicians and emergency room personnel in early recognition of the most important disease threats. Infectious disease specialists and hospital epidemiologists must also become versed in case recognition and in steps to take if a suspicious case is detected. There is a need for trained laboratory directors and key staff in laboratories with designated responsibilities for lab diagnoses. Moreover, state and local health officers and epidemiologists require training in, among other things, detection, surveillance and management of epidemic disease. Such an effort will require the full participation of professional organizations as well as those in the public sector and in academia.

Last but not least, it will be important to recruit the help of the medical and public health community in longer-term measures that may prevent acts of terrorism. This would include strengthening the provisions of the Biological Weapons Convention Treaty and expanding our intelligence capabilities so as to anticipate and perhaps interdict terrorists. The fostering of international cooperative research programs to encourage openness and dialogue as is now being done with Russian laboratories is also important.

The possible role of the medical community in educating people and policymakers everywhere about the dread realities of bioterrorism has also been proposed as a parallel effort to an earlier initiative that proved so effective in clarifying the disastrous consequences of a nuclear war.

Countering Terrorism Abroad

Madeleine K. Albright*

The President has designated the Department of State as the lead agency for coordination of our counterterrorism policy and operations abroad, while the FBI is the lead agency for countering terrorism in the United States.

The Five-Year Interagency Counterterrorism and Technology Crime Plan serves as a baseline strategy for coordinating our response to terrorism in the United States and against American targets overseas.

I will begin by discussing the threat posed to the United States and the world by the forces of international terror.

Our adversaries are likely to avoid traditional battlefield situations because, there, American dominance is well established. They may resort instead, to weapons of mass destruction and the cowardly instruments of sabotage and hidden bombs. As we know from explosions over the past decade in Africa, the Khobar apartment complex, the World Trade Center and Pan Am 103, these unconventional threats endanger both Americans and others around the world.

Accordingly, we must be vigilant in protecting against the terrorist triple threat posed, first, by the handful of countries that actively sponsor terrorism; second, by long active terrorist organizations; and third, by loosely affiliated extremists such as, among others, Osama bin Laden, who has urged his followers to kill Americans when and wherever they can.

The advance of technology has given us new means to counter terrorists. But it has also enabled terrorists to develop more powerful weapons and to travel, communicate, recruit, and raise funds on a global basis.

To counter this plague, law-abiding peoples everywhere must close ranks to detect, deter, prevent and punish terrorist acts. It is not enough for Americans to be concerned only about attacks against Americans. We must reach out to all those victimized or threatened by terror. The victims of the attacks

---

* Secretary of State. Excerpt from testimony of Dr. Albright before the Senate Appropriations Subcommittee on Commerce, State, the Judiciary and Related Agencies, February 4, 1999.

orchestrated in Africa by Osama bin Laden, after all, were predominately African, including many practitioners of Islam. Terrorism is a highly indiscriminate form of violence. It must be opposed not simply as a matter of national interest, but as a fundamental question of right and wrong.

Fighting Back

Following the embassy attacks last August, President Clinton ordered military strikes to disrupt terrorist operations and deter new bombings.

The message he conveyed is that, in this battle, we will not simply sit back and wait. We will take the offensive. We will do all we can to limit terrorist movements, block terrorist funds and prevent terrorist acts.

As the President's decision demonstrated, we will not hesitate, where necessary, to use force to respond to or defend against acts of terrorism. But force is only one element in our strategy.

Every day, in every part of the world, we use a full array of foreign policy tools in our zero tolerance campaign against international terror.

For example, we place the highest priority on measures to prevent weapons of mass destruction from falling into the wrong hands. This imperative is on our agenda with virtually every nation and figures in almost every major meeting I have.

We constantly exchange information with friendly governments concerning terrorist activities and movements, thereby preventing attacks and facilitating arrests.

We work with other agencies and other countries to strengthen screening procedures and increase intelligence sharing on visa applications.

We are expanding our Anti-terrorism Training Assistance Program, which has already instructed more than 20,000 law enforcement officers from more than 90 countries, in subjects such as airport security, bomb detection, maritime security, VIP protection, hostage rescue and crisis management.

We are engaged, through the State Department-chaired Technical Support Working Group, in a vigorous research and development program to improve our ability to detect explosives, counter weapons of mass destruction, protect against cyber sabotage and provide physical security. In the technological race with terror, we are determined to gain and maintain a decisive strategic edge.

The Rule of Law

At home, we have changed our statutes to block the financial assets of terrorist groups, prevent them from raising funds in the United States, and allow us to bar foreigners who support such groups.

Around the world, we couple law enforcement with diplomacy in order to bring suspected terrorists before the bar of justice. As the Subcommittee knows, we have done this successfully in the World Trade Center case, the CIA killings and to a very considerable extent, in the Africa embassy bombings—which triggered a worldwide manhunt for bin Laden and his associates in murder.

Our effort to strengthen the rule of law against terrorism is global. At its heart is the message that every nation has a responsibility to arrest or expel terrorists, shut down their finances and deny them safe haven.

Our purpose is to weave a web of law, power, intelligence, and political will that will entrap terrorists and deny them the mobility and sustenance they need to operate.

It is right for nations to bring terrorists to justice and those who do so should be recognized and rewarded appropriately.

It is wrong to finance terrorist groups, whether or not specific contributions are for terrorist purposes. It is cowardly to give terrorist groups money in return for not being targeted. It is irresponsible simply to look the other way when terrorists come within one's jurisdiction. And it fools no one to pretend that terrorist groups are something they are not.

Diplomatic Force Protection

The measures we take to provide physical protection for our diplomatic personnel overseas play a major role in our strategy for countering terror. In the aftermath of the embassy bombings last August, I established Accountability Review Boards, chaired by Admiral William Crowe, to investigate and recommend improved security systems and procedures. I received their report last month

The Boards identified what they termed "a collective failure" by the Executive and Legislative branches of our government over the past decade "to provide adequate resources to reduce the vulnerability of U.S. diplomatic missions."

The report cites some of the steps we have taken, particularly since August, to strengthen perimeter defense, increase security personnel and speed necessary construction and repairs.

The Accountability Review Boards concluded, however, and I agree, that these measures must be viewed as just an initial deposit towards what is required to provide for the security of our posts overseas.

According to the report, "We must undertake a comprehensive and long-term strategy ... including sustained finding for enhanced security measures, for long-term costs for increased security personnel and for a capital building program based on an assessment of requirements to meet the new range of global terrorist threats."

Under international law, the host country is responsible for protecting diplomatic missions. We hold every nation to that standard, and will assist, where we can, those who need and want help in fulfilling that duty. In an age of advanced technology and suicide bombers, no one can guarantee perfect security. But our embassies represent America. They should not be easy targets for anyone. We owe our people and all who use or visit our facilities the best security possible.

I cannot detail in public everything that we are doing, often in partnership with others, to prevent and prepare for potential terrorist strikes. I am able to say, however, that we will continue to implement additional physical protection measures as rapidly as we can. We are improving our programs for dealing with vehicle-bomb attacks, such as those experienced in Africa. We see the need for additional crisis management training and have begun such a project at the Foreign Service Institute.

We are engaged, with other agencies, in a review of equipment and procedural needs related to the possibility of a terrorist incident involving the use of chemical or biological weapons.

Security and Diplomacy

Finally, we agree fully with the Accountability Review Boards on the need to demonstrate the high priority we attach to security issues. No assumptions should be made about when, where, why, how or by whom, a terrorist strike might be perpetrated. Literally nothing should be taken for granted.

Security Improvements at U.S. Embassies Response to Recommendations of the Accountability Review Boards on the August 1998 Bombings in Nairobi and Dar es Salaam*

Systems/Procedures: Recommendation I
Alarms and Drills

The Boards noted that vehicle bombs have become the weapon of choice of transnational terrorists. The Boards believed that training our personnel in steps to take in the event of a car bomb attack can reduce injuries and save lives. Notwithstanding the long history of car bombings, the Boards pointed out that the Department of State did not include vehicular bomb scenarios in posts' Emergency Action Plans (EAPs). The Boards stated that, given the probability of more car bombs in the future, such contingencies should be provided for in all EAPs, accompanied by the necessary training and drills. The Boards also recommended additional alarm equipment to be used by perimeter guards.

Recommendation 1: Emergency Action Plans for all posts should be revised to provide a "special alarm signal" for large exterior bombs and duck-and-cover practice drills in order to reduce casualties from vehicular bombs. Special equipment should be provided to perimeter guards.

The Department agrees and is implementing this recommendation. Posts have received additional guidance on large exterior bombs, including vehicle

---

* From "Response to the Congress on Actions Taken by the Department of State in Response to the Program Recommendations of the Accountability Review Boards on the Embassy Bombings in Nairobi and Dar es Salaam," U.S. Department of State, April 1999. The Nairobi and Dar es Salaam Accountability Review Boards, chaired by Adm. William J Crowe, issued their findings and recommendations on January 8, 1999.

bombs, for their Emergency Action Plans. They have also been advised that drills should involve all mission personnel and encompass all scenarios. The Selectone system installed at all embassies and consulates alerts personnel of emergencies. A specific tone notifies personnel to take cover immediately in the event of a terrorist attack to include a vehicle bomb attack. This is accompanied by verbal announcements. The Department has completed evaluation and testing of new equipment, including how it can be integrated with existing equipment to enhance its warning and communications capacity. The Department is currently working on an effective means of putting these systems in place as quickly as possible.

In addition, the Department has issued instructions both abroad and at home on personal security practices that could save lives. The widely publicized admonition not to go to windows during outside commotions may have already averted tragedy in Tashkent when mission employees, hearing gunfire at a nearby government building, took cover just before a car bomb exploded and the windows blew in.

Systems/Procedures: Recommendation 8
Better Training for Security Officers

The Boards found that one of the critical lessons to be learned from the Nairobi and Dar es Salaam bombings is that security personnel need to understand the modus operandi of terrorists. Security officers need not only intelligence about terrorists, but they need to appreciate and to understand offensive operations and the many ingredients that make for a successful mission. They need to know terrorist intelligence requirements and methods of collection, local support needs, logistical problems and weapons.

The Boards commented that it is not enough for an RSO to receive two to four hours of exposure to explosives and to learn how to fire a weapon in self-defense. In the Boards' view, RSOs need to understand what the terrorist knows about explosives, explosive effects, mortars, rockets, assassination devices, and chemical/biological weapons. The Boards stressed that security officers need to look at their area of responsibility with the eyes of the attacker.

Recommendation 8: The Department of State should provide all Regional Security Officers comprehensive training on terrorism, terrorist methods of operation, explosive devices, explosive effects, and other terrorist weapons to include weapons of mass destruction such as truck bombs, nuclear devices and chemical/biological weapons. The training

must also provide RSOs with the ability to examine their areas of responsibility from the offensive point of view, to look for vulnerabilities as
seen through the eyes of the attacker.

The Department is conducting a comprehensive curriculum review of
the Regional Security Officer (RSO) Training Program and is implementing
the recommendations of the Boards during this process. Training in counterterrorism methodology, explosive ordnance disposal, chemical/biological
warfare, surveillance detection, and other related topics are being included in
the syllabi for the Diplomatic Security Training Center's Basic Special Agent
Course, Special Agent In-Service Course, Regional Security Officer Basic
Course, and Regional Security Officer In-Service Course. The Diplomatic
Security Training Center (DSTC) has doubled the amount of time spent training RSOs on explosive ordnance disposal from one to two days, and plans to
expand this training to five days for subsequent classes. The DSTC's Mobile
Security Division (MSD) has developed a comprehensive training module for
surveillance detection techniques which is being incorporated into the above
courses and others. The MSD has also developed a training syllabus for chemi-
cal/biological warfare that will be included in overseas training and will also
be taught to appropriate domestic personnel. The DSTC is also working with
the Counterterrorist Center (CTC) to incorporate elements of CTC's vulnerability and threat assessment methodology into the physical security training
provided in RSO courses. Efforts to identify and develop other, appropriate
course work are ongoing.

Systems/Procedures: Recommendation 15
Prepare for Chemical, Biological, Nuclear Terror

In the Boards' review of security and counter-terrorism guidance provided to Embassies Nairobi and Dar es Salaam, as well as the Department's
terrorism threat analysis system and Emergency Action Plan (EAP) guidelines applicable to all posts, they found no reference to the potential threat of
terrorism using biological, chemical or nuclear weapons or materials. The
Boards observed that the Administration and Congress have focused considerable attention and resources on defending against and preparing for terrorist attacks in the United States by both domestic and international terrorists
using such weapons of mass destruction. The Boards noted, however, that the
recent emergency security supplemental appropriation passed in the wake of
the East African bombings made no provision for addressing this problem
abroad.

While the attacks on Nairobi and Dar es Salaam offered no direct in-
sights for dealing with such emergencies, the Boards concluded that, if Ameri-

cans are threatened by such attacks at home, our missions abroad would appear to be equally or even more exposed. The Boards recommended that the Department's threat analysis, protective security systems, EAP guidelines, training and contingency planning systems should be broadened to address the threat of terrorists using materials of mass destruction.

Recommendation 15: The Department of State, in coordination with the intelligence community, should advise all posts concerning potential threats of terrorist attacks from the use of chemical, biological or nuclear materials, should establish means of defending against and minimizing the effect of such attacks through security measures and the revision of EAP procedures and exercises, and should provide appropriate equipment, medical supplies, and first responder training.

We agree. The task of devising effective responses to these threats presents major technical and financial challenges. Although we must begin to respond immediately—and have done so—we must also recognize that this will remain a difficult work in progress, reflecting changing threat information and the best and most recent scientific and technical knowledge.

The Department of State has been seriously concerned with the threat of chemical, biological, radiological, and nuclear warfare (CBRN) since the Iran and Iraq war. The expressed interest in chemical and biological weapons by several foreign groups and the changing nature of terrorism increase concerns that such weapons may be used for terrorist purposes.

Looking to the future, State has worked aggressively to improve its posture world-wide vis a vis potential CBRN terrorist attacks. All Department elements working together have established an expanded CBRN protection program, which has components including detection, prevention, training, protection, and consequence management. We will also revise the *Emergency Planning Handbook* to incorporate CBRN incident response, protection, and evacuation. This is a resource intensive program. The Department will identify the resources needed and request additional funds for its implementation, based on the best current threat information and the best and most recent scientific and technical knowledge.

In addition, the Department is bolstering the "front line" of defense by developing training courses in its Antiterrorism Assistance (ATA) program for first responders and crisis management officials in host countries.

The Consequence Management Response Team (CMRT) is the only interagency response team that provides the coordination and connectivity for planning and execution of a combined USG-Host Nation response to the consequences of incidents involving chemical, biological, radiological, or nuclear contaminates. The CMRT members are the on-the-ground USG co-ordinators and work directly with the country team, the host nation's crisis managers, and the incident site response team. CMRT members are also represented on the State Department's Task Force in Washington, D.C. From these various locations, CMRT members are able to coordinate response requirements at or near real time, using state-of-the-art, secure communications. The CMRT is designed to provide timely status reports and identify essential requirements for interagency response.

Military Threats and Security Challenges Through 2015

Thomas R. Wilson*

The Global Security Environment

To paraphrase the ancient Chinese curse ... 'we are living in very inter-esting times.' More than a decade has passed since the end of the Cold War, yet we seem no closer to the emergence of a new, stable international order. Rather, the complex mix of political, economic, military, and social factors that have undermined stability during much of the 1990s remain at play.— Large regional military threats.

The Growing Asymmetric Threat

Most of the rest of the world believes the United States will remain the dominant global power during the next 15 years. Foreign assessments gener-ally point to the following US strengths: our economy weathered the recent global financial crisis in excellent shape and is uniquely positioned to capital-ize on the coming 'high-tech boom;' we are among the world's leaders in the development and use of the most important technologies (both civilian and military); we have the world's best university system and the most fluid and effective capital markets; we spend nearly half of what the advanced indus-trial world spends on all types of research and development each year; we retain strong alliances with key nations; and we enjoy unrivaled 'soft power'— the global appeal of American ideas, institutions, leadership and culture.

Adversary anticipation of continued US military superiority is the gen-esis of the asymmetric challenge. Potential US opponents (from druglords and terrorists to criminal gangs, insurgents, and the civilian and military lead-

* Vice Admiral Wilson is Director of the Defense Intelligence Agency. From statement before the Senate Select Committee on Intelligence, February 2, 2000.

ership of opposing states) do not want to engage the US military on its terms. They are more likely to pursue their objectives while avoiding a US military confrontation, and/or to develop asymmetric means (operational and technological) to reduce US military superiority, render it irrelevant, or exploit our perceived weaknesses. Asymmetric approaches are imperative for US adversaries and are likely to be a dominant component of most future threats.

The asymmetric problem is extremely complex because adversaries, objectives, targets, and means of attack can vary widely from situation to situation. Moreover, some developments—such as WMD and missile proliferation, counter-space capabilities, denial and deception operations, etc.—could have both symmetric and asymmetric applications, depending on the context. Recognizing these potential ambiguities, and understanding that many different approaches are possible, I am most concerned about the following 'asymmetric' trends, developments, and capabilities.

Terrorism. Terrorism remains a very significant asymmetric threat to our interests at home and abroad. The terrorist threat to the US will grow as disgruntled groups and individuals focus on America as the source of their troubles. Most anti-US terrorism will be regional and based on perceived racial, ethnic or religious grievances. Terrorism will tend to occur in urban centers, often capitals. The US military is vulnerable due to its overseas presence and status as a symbol of US power, interests, and influence. However, in many cases, increased security at US military and diplomatic facilities will drive terrorists to attack 'softer' targets such as private citizens or commercial interests.

Terrorism will be a serious threat to Americans especially in most Middle Eastern countries, North Africa, parts of Sub-Saharan Africa, Turkey, Greece, the Balkans, Peru, and Colombia. The characteristics of the most effective terrorist organizations—highly compartmented operations planning, good cover and security, extreme suspicion of outsiders, and ruthlessness—make them very hard intelligence targets. Middle East-based terrorist groups will remain the most important threat. State sponsors (primarily Iran) and individuals with the financial means (such as Usama bin Ladin) will continue to provide much of the economic and technological support needed by terrorists. The potential for terrorist WMD use will increase over time, with chemical, biological, and radiological agents the most likely choice.

WMD Proliferation. Several rogue states will likely acquire nuclear weapons during the next decade or so, and some existing nuclear states will undoubtedly increase their inventories. As these trends unfold, the prospects for limited nuclear weapons use in a regional conflict will rise. So too will the potential for a terrorist or some other sub-national group to acquire and use a weapon.

Chemical and biological weapons are generally easier to develop, hide, and deploy than nuclear weapons and will be readily available to those with the will and resources to attain them. I expect these weapons to be widely proliferated, and they could well be used in a regional conflict over the next 15 years. I am also concerned that sub-national groups or individuals will use chemical or biological agents in a terrorist or insurgent operation. Such an event could occur in the United States or against US-allied forces and facilities overseas. The planning for such 'smaller-scale' incidents would be extremely difficult to detect, and consequently, to deter or warn against.

The Foreign Intelligence Threat. Adversaries hoping to employ asymmetric approaches against the United States desire detailed intelligence on US decision-making, operational concepts, capabilities, shortcomings, and vulnerabilities. Consequently, we continue to face extensive intelligence threats from a large number of foreign nations and sub-national entities including terrorists, international criminal organizations, foreign commercial enterprises, and other disgruntled groups and individuals. These intelligence efforts are generally targeted against our national security policy-making apparatus, our national infrastructure, our military plans, personnel, and capabilities, and our critical technologies. While foreign states—particularly Russia and China—present the biggest intelligence threat, all our adversaries are likely to exploit technological advances to expand their collection activities. Moreover, the open nature of our society, and increasing ease with which money, technology, information, and people move around the globe in the modern era, make effective counterintelligence and security that much more complex and difficult to achieve.

Cover, Concealment, Camouflage, Denial and Deception (C3D2). Many potential adversaries—nations, groups, and individuals—are undertaking more and increasingly sophisticated C3D2 activities against the United States. These operations are generally designed to hide key activities, facilities, and capabilities (e.g. mobilization or attack preparations, WMD programs, advanced weapons systems developments, treaty noncompliance, etc.) from US intelligence, to manipulate US perceptions and assessments of those programs, and to protect key capabilities from US precision strike platforms. Foreign knowledge of US intelligence and military operations capabilities is essential to effective C3D2. Advances in satellite warning capabilities, the growing availability of camouflage, concealment, deception, and obscurant materials, advanced technology for and experience with building underground facilities, and the growing use of fiber optics and encryption, will increase the C3D2 challenge.

USS Cole Commission Report*

William W. Crouch and Harold W. Gehman Jr.

Since the attack on Khobar Towers in June 1996, the Department of Defense (DoD) has made significant improvements in protecting its service members, mainly in deterring, disrupting and mitigating terrorist attacks on installations. The attack on USS COLE (DDG 67), in the port of Aden, Yemen, on 12 October 2000, demonstrated a seam in the fabric of efforts to protect our forces, namely in-transit forces. Our review was focused on finding ways to improve the US policies and practices for deterring, disrupting and mitigating terrorist attack on US forces in transit.

Overseas Presence since the End of the Cold War

Our review was based on the premise that worldwide presence and continuous transit of ships, aircraft and units of the United States military support the engagement elements of both the National Security Strategy and the National Military Strategy and are in the nation's best interest. The US military is conducting overseas operations in a new post-Cold War world environment characterized by unconventional and transnational threats. Operating in this new world exposes US forces to terrorist attacks and requires a major effort in force protection. This major effort will require more resources and, in some cases, a better use of existing resources for protecting transiting units. The net result of our recommendations is a form of operational risk management applied at both the national and operational levels to balance the benefits with the risks of overseas operations. We determined that the "fulcrum" of this balance is usually the Unified Commander-in-Chief's (CINC) Service Component Commander; therefore, a significant number of our recommendations are designed to improve that commander's antiterrorism/force protection (AT/FP) capabilities.

---

* Excerpts from the Executive Summary, January 9, 2001. Defense Secretary William S. Cohen appointed retired Army Gen. William W. Crouch and retired Navy Adm. Harold W. Gehman Jr. as co-chairs of the Commission on Oct. 19, 2000 to investigate the terrorist bombing of the destroyer USS Cole as it was refueling in the Yemeni port of Aden. Seventeen sailors died as a result of the attack and 39 were wounded.

Unclassified Findings

Organizational

Finding: Combating terrorism is so important that it demands complete unity of effort at the level of the Office of the Secretary of Defense.

Finding: The execution of the engagement element of the National Security Strategy lacks an effective, coordinated interagency process, which results in a fragmented engagement program that may not provide optimal support to in-transit units.

Finding: DoD needs to spearhead an interagency, coordinated approach to developing non-military host nation security efforts in order to enhance force protection for transiting US forces.

Antiterrorism/Force Protection (AT/FP)

Finding: Service manning policies and procedures that establish requirements for full-time Force Protection Officers and staff billets at the Service Component level and above will reduce the vulnerability of in-transit forces to terrorist attacks.

Finding: Component Commanders need the resources to provide in-transit units with temporary security augmentation of various kinds.

Finding: Service AT/FP programs must be adequately manned and funded to support threat and physical vulnerability assessments of ports, airfields and inland movement routes that may be used by transiting forces.

Finding: More responsive application of currently available military equipment, commercial technologies, and aggressive research and development can enhance the AT/FP and deterrence posture of transiting forces.

Finding: The Geographic Commander in Chief should have the sole authority for assigning the threat level for a country within his area of responsibility.

Finding: AT/FP will be enhanced by improvements to the THREATCON system.

Recommendations:

- *Secretary of Defense change the term "THREATCONs" to "Alert States," "FP Conditions," or some other term.*

- *Secretary of Defense direct the CINCs and Services to give Component Commanders the responsibility and resources to direct tailored force protection measures to be implemented at specific sites for in-transit units.*

- *Secretary of Defense direct that the AT/FP plan and the particular measures that are triggered by a specific THREATCON be classified.*

Finding: The CJCS Standing Rules of Engagement for US forces are adequate against the terrorist threat.

Finding: We need to shift transiting units from an entirely reactive posture to a posture that more effectively deters terrorist attacks.

Finding: The amount of AT/FP emphasis that units in-transit receive prior to or during transfer between CINCs can be improved.

Finding: Intra-theater transiting units require the same degree of attention as other transiting units to deter, disrupt and mitigate acts of terrorism.

Finding: Using operational risk management standards as a tool to measure engagement activities against risk to in-transit forces will enable commanders to determine whether to suspend or continue engagement activities.

Finding: Incident response must be an integral element of AT/FP planning.

Intelligence

Finding: In-transit units require intelligence support tailored to the terrorist threat in their immediate area of operations. This support must be dedicated from a higher echelon (tailored production and analysis).

Finding: If the Department of Defense is to execute engagement activities related to the National Security Strategy with the least possible level of risk, then Services must reprioritize time, emphasis, and resources to prepare the transiting units to perform intelligence preparation of the battlespace–

like processes and formulate intelligence requests for information to support operational decision points.

Finding: DoD does not allocate sufficient resources or all-source intelligence analysis and collection in support of combating terrorism.

Finding: Service counterintelligence programs are integral to force protection and must be adequately manned and funded to meet the dynamic demands of supporting in-transit forces.

Finding: Clearer DoD standards for threat and vulnerability assessments, must be developed at the joint level and be common across Services and commands.

Training

Finding: Military Services must accomplish AT/FP training with a degree of rigor that equates to the unit's primary mission areas.

Finding: Better force protection is achieved if forces in transit are trained to demonstrate preparedness to deter acts of terrorism.

Finding: DoD must better support commanders' ability to sustain their antiterrorism/force protection program and training regimens.

IV.
Is the Homeland Safe?

Organization of the Federal Government to Prevent and Respond To Terrorism

Janet Reno*

Since the issuance of Presidential Decision Directive 39 (PDD-39) on June 21, 1995, substantial steps have been taken to develop an effective capability to address the threat posed by chemical and biological terrorism. The objective is to do everything possible to deter and prevent such terrorist acts. At the same time, however, we are working to ensure that the necessary capabilities and procedures are in place to respond to such an act, so that we can effectively manage the crisis and mitigate its consequences.

A key aspect of our efforts under PDD-39 has been to enlist the involvement of all federal agencies which have relevant expertise and to develop mechanisms for effective coordination among those agencies. Similarly, we are reaching out to state and local authorities in an effort to ensure that their resources and capabilities are effectively integrated into the overall crisis response and consequence management plans and preparations.

The Conference Committee Report accompanying the 1998 Appropriations Act for the Departments of Commerce, Justice, and State, the Judiciary, and Related Agencies directs me to develop a Five-Year Counterterrorism and Technology Plan by December 31, 1998, to serve as a baseline for coordination of national policy and operational capabilities to combat terrorism. The plan is to be representative of all agencies involved in the government's counterterrorism effort and to draw upon the expertise of academia, the private sector, and state and local law enforcement.

---

* Attorney General of the United States. Excerpt from statement before the Subcommittee on Technology, Terrorism and Government Information, U. S. Senate Committee on the Judiciary, and before the Senate Select Committee on Intelligence, April 22, 1998.

I would like to focus first on how the federal government has organized its resources and its decision-making processes to respond to terrorist threats and events.

Intelligence Collection and Assessment

The paramount objective is to prevent terrorist acts before they occur. This is, of course, particularly critical where the planned terrorist act involves use of a weapon of mass destruction, such as a chemical or biological weapon. Intelligence is the lifeblood of prevention, as it provides timely information about the identity, motives, movements, plans, resources, and possible allies of the perpetrators. The CIA is responsible for the collection, analysis, and dissemination of foreign intelligence regarding terrorist groups. Its efforts are coordinated by its Counterterrorist Center (CTC). Whenever information is developed concerning a possible terrorist attack within the United States, it is furnished to the FBI.

The FBI collects, analyzes, and disseminates intelligence on the activities of international terrorists targeting interests within the United States and terrorist groups operating in this country. The resulting information, whether derived from the CIA or developed by the FBI, is used to assist in the development of on-going investigations or in the initiation of new ones. Further, the information is used to disseminate early warnings to all pertinent federal, state, and local law enforcement agencies and, where appropriate, to potential targets of terrorist activity.

Senior Level Interagency Coordination

Information concerning the possibility of an imminent terrorist attack within the United States may be developed by any one of a variety of federal agencies. When credible information is developed, the government has specific procedures to facilitate a prompt, coordinated interagency response.

When the threat involves an act by international terrorists, coordination of issues requiring senior level interagency review is handled through the Coordinating Sub-Group (CSG) of the Deputies Committee. That Committee is comprised of the Deputy Secretaries, or their equivalents, of the Cabinet agencies involved in counterterrorism.

The agency coming into possession of credible information relating to an international terrorist threat immediately notifies the office of the NSC official who chairs the CSG, which has the capability of convening an emergency meeting of that group, via teleconference, in a matter of minutes. For potential acts of terrorism within the United States that are not of an international nature, the same expeditious coordination mechanism is available, except that the Department of Justice, through the FBI, is the organization which convenes and chairs the meetings.

The regular CSG members include the NSC, State Department, Defense Department, CIA, the Department of Justice and the FBI. The CSG is also able to notify and involve established points of contact in a variety of other federal agencies when the circumstances of the particular terrorist threat warrant the inclusion of one or more of those agencies. They include the Departments of Energy, Transportation, Treasury, Health and Human Services, and Agriculture, as well as FEMA, EPA, and the NRC. For a threatened terrorist act involving a chemical or biological weapon, the CSG meeting would include, in addition to the regular members of the CSG, representatives of the Department of Health and Human Services (DHHS), the EPA, and FEMA.

Among the actions which the CSG can recommend to the Deputies Committee is deployment of a Domestic Emergency Support Team (DEST). A specialized module of this team is available as needed to address chemical and biological threats or acts of terrorism. When activated, a DEST team can assemble its components and equipment within a few hours for airlift to the incident area. Once on site, the DEST team is available to provide expert, highly specialized advice and guidance concerning the most appropriate response to the terrorist threat or incident. This on-site information, in turn, provides an informed basis for further decision making concerning the deployment of additional federal resources.

C. Operational Coordination Mechanisms

PDD-39 sets forth lead agency responsibilities for combating terrorism. The Department of Justice, acting through the FBI, has lead responsibility for responding to terrorist threats and incidents occurring within the United States.

As described in PDD-39, the federal response to terrorism includes two components:

—The crisis management component is led by the Department of Justice through the FBI, and includes measures to identify, acquire, and plan the use of resources needed to anticipate, prevent, and resolve a threat or act of terrorism. It is primarily a law enforcement response.

—The consequence management component is coordinated by FEMA, in support of state and local governments, and includes measures to protect public health and safety, restore essential government services, and provide emergency relief to governments, businesses, and individuals affected by the consequences of an act of terrorism.

Let me address briefly the issue of using military personnel as part of the Government's response to a threat or incident of chemical or biological terrorism, as it appears to be the subject of substantial misunderstanding.

The "posse comitatus" restriction on the use of U.S. military forces to enforce laws within the United States is not contained in the Constitution but rather in a post-reconstruction era Act of Congress. That Act expressly recognizes that Congress can enact statutes authorizing military involvement in law enforcement. Further, its provisions have been construed by the courts to be limited to activities that involve the direct execution of laws, e.g., making arrests. In contrast, the Posse Comitatus Act has not been construed to preclude the military from providing logistical, technical, and other forms of assistance to law enforcement. For example, the military has traditionally provided assistance to law enforcement in explosive ordnance disposal.

As part of Nunn-Lugar-Domenici, Congress enacted statutes specifically addressing the use of the military in response to terrorist incidents involving chemical and biological weapons of mass destruction. Further, more generic statutes authorize the President to use military forces to resolve domestic emergencies.

Although the FBI's WMD Operations Unit functions broadly in coordinating the national response to a chemical or biological terrorist incident, it plays a particularly critical role in the initial assessment of a WMD threat.

Pursuant to the 1997 National Defense Authorization Act, DOD has established a telephone hotline to provide relevant data and expert advice to state and local officials responding to emergencies involving a weapon of mass destruction. The assigned DOD component, the Army's Chemical and Biological Defense Command (CBDCOM), works closely with the FBI to ensure effective coordination.

FEMA is assigned the leadership role in the area of consequence management and exercises its responsibilities through the structure established under the Federal Response Plan (FRP). The FRP defines the relationships and roles of 28 federal departments and agencies and the American Red Cross in the consequence management of any disaster or emergency in which FEMA is called on to respond.

Responding to a Chemical or Biological Event Within the United States

I. Crisis Deployment Strategy

In the event of a threatened terrorist act utilizing a chemical or biological weapon, the FBI field office would contact the FBI's WMD Operations Unit for an assessment of the threat. That Unit would activate an interagency team, which would collaborate by conference call and prepare an aggregate assessment of the credibility of the threat using the three criteria discussed above. Assuming that the threat is deemed to be one which must be taken seriously, the FBI Special Agent in Charge (SAC), would undertake coordination of the federal response.

To accomplish the objectives, the SAC would undertake a number of actions, including the following:

- Coordinate with local emergency responders, and as appropriate with elements of HHS and DOD, in an effort to ensure optimal efforts to save lives and prevent additional risk to life, while avoiding any unnecessary disruption of evidence that may be important to a later prosecution.
- Initiate an assessment of the scene of the incident to evaluate the presence of a continuing danger and to develop preliminary information on the relevant forensic aspects of the crime.
- Consult with the FBI's Hazardous Materials Response Unit to assess the capabilities of local and state authorities to identify, package, transport and analyze a sample of the chemical or biological substance.

While these activities are underway in the field, DOJ and FBI Headquarters act immediately to bring together the pertinent Headquarters support apparatus. The FBI Strategic Information and Operations Center (SIOC) is immediately activated and staffed on a 24-hour basis with agents and prosecutors who have terrorism experience. The Counterterrorism Center, which combines the resources and expertise of representatives of 18 federal agencies, supports this effort, and representatives of pertinent agencies are integrated into the SIOC operation.

In the event the chemical or biological aspects of the terrorist incident exceed the staffing or capabilities of the FBI's Hazardous Materials Response Unit and other available civilian components, the Attorney General is authorized by statute to request that the Secretary of Defense supply military assets to handle the deactivation and transport of a weapon of mass destruction.

2. Consequence Management

FEMA is responsible to prepare for, coordinate, and respond to the aftermath of a terrorist attack. FEMA is responsible for working with state and local governments to restore order and to deliver emergency assistance. During a terrorism crisis within the United States, FEMA acts in support of the FBI until the Attorney General is satisfied that addressing the consequences of the act should assume primacy over dealing with the immediate crisis situation. The "Domestic Guidelines" address the procedures for the transfer of such responsibility

3. Prosecution of Terrorists

We have created an Attorney Critical Incident Response Group, or ACIRG, composed of expert federal lawyers in Washington and around the country, whose job it is to provide the Department's leadership with an improved capacity to manage the incident and, on occasion, support the United States Attorney in the on-scene response to the crisis.

As we strengthen our capabilities to prevent, respond to, and manage the consequences of emerging terrorist threats such as chemical and biological weapons, we must achieve even greater coordination of the counterterrorism plans, resources, and programs of the many departments and agencies that have counterterrorism responsibilities. It is also important for us to focus on coordinating government efforts in partnership with the private sector to protect our critical infrastructures against these and other threats.

Securing the National Homeland

Hart-Rudman Commission Phase III Report*

One of this Commission's most important conclusions in its Phase I report was that attacks against American citizens on American soil, possibly causing heavy casualties, are likely over the next quarter century. This is because both the technical means for such attacks, and the array of actors who might use such means, are proliferating despite the best efforts of American diplomacy.

These attacks may involve weapons of mass destruction and weapons of mass disruption. As porous as U.S. physical borders are in an age of burgeoning trade and travel, its "cyber borders" are even more porous—and the critical infrastructure upon which so much of the U.S. economy depends *can* now be targeted by non-state and state actors alike. America's present global predominance does not render it immune from these dangers. To the contrary, U.S. preeminence makes the American homeland more appealing as a target, while America's openness and freedoms make it more vulnerable.

Notwithstanding a growing consensus on the seriousness of the threat to the homeland posed by weapons of mass destruction and disruption, the U.S. government *has not* adopted homeland security as a primary national security mission. Its structures and strategies are fragmented and inadequate. We need orders-of-magnitude improvements in planning, coordination, and exercise. This will necessitate new priorities for the U.S. armed forces and particularly, in our view, for the NationalGuard.

The United States *is today very poorly organized to design and implement any comprehensive strategy to protect the homelan*d. The assets and organizations that now exist for homeland security are scattered across more than two dozen departments and agencies, and all fifty states. The Executive Branch,

---

* Excerpt from "Road Map for National Security: Imperative for Change," Phase III Report of the U.S. Commission on National Security/21st Century, Sen. Gary Hart and .Sen.Warren B. Rudman, Co-Chairs, February 15, 2001. Commissioners: Anne Armstrong, John Dancy, Leslie H. Gelb, Lee H. Hamilton, Donald B. Rice , Harry D. Train, Norman R. Augustine, John R. Galvin, Newt Gingrich, Lionel H. Olmer, James Schlesinger, Andrew Young.

with the full participation of Congress, needs to realign, refine, and rational-ize these assets into a coherent whole, or even the best strategy will lack an adequate vehicle for implementation.

We are confident that the U.S. government can enhance national secu-rity without compromising established Constitutional principles. But in or-der to guarantee this, *we must plan ahead*. In a major attack involving conta-gious biological agents, for example, citizen cooperation with government authorities will depend on public confidence that those authorities can man-age the emergency. If that confidence is lacking, panic and disorder could lead to insistent demands for the temporary suspension of some civil liber-ties. That is why preparing for the worst is essential to protecting individual freedoms during a national crisis.

1: The President should develop a comprehensive strategy to heighten America's ability to prevent and protect against all forms of attack on the homeland, and to respond to such attacks if prevention and protection fail.

2: The President should propose, and Congress should agree to create, a National Homeland Security Agency (NHSA) with responsibility for plan-ning, coordinating, and integrating various U.S. government activities involved in homeland security. The Federal Emergency Management Agency (FEMA) should be a key building block in this effort.

3: The President should propose to Congress the transfer of the Customs Service, the Border Patrol, and Coast Guard to the National Homeland Security Agency, while preserving them as distinct entities.

Steps must be also taken to strengthen these three individual organizations themselves. Therefore, this Commission believes that *an improved computer information capability and tracking system—as well as upgraded equipment that can detect both conventional and nuclear explosives, and chemical and biological agents—would be a wise short-term investment with important long-term ben-efits.*

FEMA has adapted well to new circumstances over the past few years and has gained a well-deserved reputation for responsiveness to both natural and manmade disasters. While taking on homeland security responsibilities, the proposed NHSA would strengthen FEMA's ability to respond to such disasters. It would streamline the federal apparatus and provide greater support to the state and local officials who, as the nation's first responders, possess enormous expertise. To the greatest extent possible, federal programs should build upon the expertise and existing programs of state emergency preparedness systems and help promote regional compacts to share resources and capabilities.

To help simplify federal support mechanisms, *we recommend transferring the National Domestic Preparedness Office (NDPO), currently housed at the FBI, to the National Homeland Security Agency.* The Commission believes that this transfer to FEMA should be done at first opportunity, even before NHSA is up and running.

Intelligence Community. Good intelligence is the key to preventing attacks on the homeland and homeland security should become one of the intelligence community's most important missions.15 Better human intelligence must supplement technical intelligence, especially on terrorist groups covertly supported by states. As noted above, fuller cooperation and more extensive information-sharing with friendly governments will also improve the chances that would-be perpetrators will be detained, arrested, and prosecuted before they ever reach U.S. borders.

4: The President should ensure that the National Intelligence Council: include homeland security and asymmetric threats as an area of analysis; assign that portfolio to a National Intelligence Officer; and produce National Intelligence Estimates on these threats.

5: The President should propose to Congress the establishment of an Assistant Secretary of Defense for Homeland Security within the Office of the Secretary of Defense, reporting directly to the Secretary.

6: The Secretary of Defense, at the President's direction, should make homeland security a primary mission of the National Guard, and the Guard should be organized, properly trained, and adequately equipped to undertake that mission.

At present, the Army National Guard is primarily organized and equipped to conduct sustained combat overseas. In this the Guard fulfills a strategic reserve role, augmenting the active military during overseas contingencies. At the same time, the Guard carries out many state-level missions for disaster and humanitarian relief, as well as consequence management. For these, it relies upon the discipline, equipment, and leadership of its combat forces. The National Guard should redistribute resources currently allocated predominantly to preparing for conventional wars overseas to provide greater support to civil authorities in preparing for and responding to disasters, especially emergencies involving weapons of mass destruction.

7: Congress should establish a special body to deal with homeland security issues, as has been done effectively with intelligence oversight. Members should be chosen for their expertise in foreign policy, defense, intelligence, law enforcement, and appropriations. This body should also include members of all relevant Congressional committees as well as ex-officio members from the leadership of both Houses of Congress.

A sound homeland security strategy requires the overhaul of much of the legislative framework for preparedness, response, and national defense programs. Congress designed many of the authorities that support national security and emergency preparedness programs principally for a Cold War environment. The new threat environment—from biological and terrorist attacks to cyber attacks on critical systems—poses vastly different challenges. *We therefore recommend that Congress refurbish the legal foundation for homeland security in response to the new threat environment.*

National Domestic Preparedness Office

Federal Bureau of Investigation*

Introduction

Success in preventing, preparing for and responding to a terrorist attack in the United States involving conventional or non-conventional weapons of mass destruction (WMD) will depend upon the establishment and maintenance of a coordinated crisis and consequence management infrastructure. Emergency responders who arrive first on the scene, as well as those in the medical profession who provide interim treatment, must be adequately trained, equipped, and exercised to ensure their ability to effectively respond and conduct relief and recovery operations as part of a multi-agency team.

The federal agencies recognize that the response to bioterrorism will be qualitatively different from a chemical event and will primarily involve the public health and medical communities.

Events within the United States and against Americans abroad have demonstrated the need to enhance the nation's domestic preparedness activities. The United States Congress and the President have recognized the need for federal programs to assist state and local jurisdictions in preparing for the threat of WMD terrorism.

In 1996, the Defense Against Weapons of Mass Destruction Act was passed directing the Department of Defense (DoD) to enhance domestic preparedness for responding to and managing the consequences of a terrorist attack using WMD. Under this Act, DoD was directed to provide training, exercises and expert advice to emergency response personnel, and to provide emergency response training equipment to local jurisdictions on a loan basis. In implementing its domestic preparedness program, DoD, in coordination with its interagency partners, selected 120 of the nation's largest cities based upon census population figures, special events, and a balanced distribution throughout the nation. The Act also authorized the Department of Health and Human Services (HHS) to develop Metropolitan Medical Response Systems (MMRS) in local jurisdictions across the country.

---

* Excerpt from "Blueprint for the National Domestic Preparedness Office," NPDO.

In 1996, Congress also passed the Anti-Terrorism and Effective Death Penalty Act, which authorized the Federal Emergency Management Agency (FEMA) and the Department of Justice's Office of Justice Programs (OJP) to fund and develop an emergency response to terrorism training program for fire, emergency medical service, and public safety personnel. Furthermore, the 1998 Commerce, Justice, and State Appropriations Act provided for the creation of an equipment acquisition grant program, as well as training centers for emergency responders at Fort McClellan, Alabama and the New Mexico Institute of Mining and Technology. The equipment acquisition grant program, administered by OJP, offers grants to metropolitan jurisdictions for the purchase of operational equipment. The OJP grant and training programs target the Nation's 120 largest metropolitan jurisdictions, a separate list which partially overlaps the list of 120 cities

The FY1999 Departments of Labor, Health and Human Services and Education appropriation authorized funding for HHS to renovate and modernize the Nobel Army Hospital located at Fort McClellan for the purpose of providing training in the health response to bioterrorism.

In addition to these programs, a multitude of other federal departments and agencies also conduct training programs, or possess relevant expertise and resources for enhancing the capabilities of state and local authorities to respond to acts of WMD terrorism. However, federal efforts to date in this regard have been fragmented. A single office within the Federal government is needed to coordinate domestic preparedness programs.

Domestic Preparedness Assistance from the Federal Government

In response to calls from members of the emergency responder community across the country, the Attorney General proposed the establishment of a National Domestic Preparedness Office (NDPO), to coordinate and serve as an information clearinghouse for federal programs supporting state and local emergency responder communities in the area of WMD-related domestic preparedness planning, training, exercises, and equipment research and development. Forming a partnership between the Federal Government and the nation's emergency responder community (of state, local and tribal governments) is the goal of the NDPO.

Fostering cooperation among federal, state and local agencies is consistent with the Five-Year Interagency Counter-terrorism and Technology Crime Plan (The Five-Year Plan), which sets challenging milestones for a newly established NDPO. In August 1998, during preparations for the Five-Year

Plan, the Attorney General directed the Department of Justice (DOJ)/Office of Justice Programs to host a meeting of the nation's "stakeholders" of the emergency response community. Collectively, the 200 stakeholders represented all of the response disciplines, including fire services, hazardous materials (HAZMAT), law enforcement, emergency management, and health and safety communities, as well as national representatives of various professional associations and organizations. The stakeholders reported their recommendations to the Attorney General at the culmination of a two-day forum.

Responding to Stakeholder Concerns

The principal recommendation that emerged from the meeting of the stakeholders was for the establishment of a single federal coordinating office for the many federal programs providing domestic preparedness assistance to state and local jurisdictions. The NDPO responds to that recommendation. Other recommendations cited by the stakeholders encompass six broad issue areas requiring federal coordination and assistance. These areas are: Planning; Training; Exercises; Equipment Research and Development; Information Sharing; and Public Health and Medical Services. The stakeholders cited the need for federal coordination and assistance in all these areas. They also recommended the creation of a state and local Advisory Group to provide a mechanism for regular input and guidance from the emergency responder community into federal domestic preparedness programs.

In October 1998, after consultation with the National Security Council (NSC), the Federal Bureau of Investigation (FBI), and others, the Attorney General directed the FBI to lead an interagency coordination initiative now known as the NDPO.

Federal participants in the NDPO will include: HHS, DoD, Department of Energy (DOE), the Environmental Protection Agency (EPA), the DOJ/Office of Justice Programs, and FEMA. Other agencies, such as the U.S. Coast Guard, Veteran's Administration, and the Nuclear Regulatory Commission, have expressed interest in participating. The principal federal agencies with responsibilities and resources for domestic preparedness have pledged their support for the establishment of the NDPO to serve as a single office for coordinating federal domestic preparedness programs. The NDPO will address stakeholders' concerns by providing a single point of contact among federal programs, reducing duplication, and improving the quality of federal support provided to the emergency response and health care community.

Emergency Management—FEMA Responsibilities

Catherine H. Light*

The basis for the domestic preparedness and response activities of the Federal Emergency Management Agency (FEMA) derives from two Presidential Decision Directives. Under PDD-39 and reinforced under PDD-62, FEMA is responsible for the consequence management of domestic terrorist incidents involving weapons of mass destruction (WMD). Under PDD-39, FEMA was given the responsibility to ensure that the Federal Response Plan (FRP) is adequate for consequence management activities in response to domestic terrorist attacks involving WMD. Also, FEMA was tasked to ensure that State response plans and capabilities are adequate and tested.

Crisis Management and Consequence Management

Crisis management focuses on causes and involves activities to address the threat or occurrence of a terrorist incident. It is predominantly a law enforcement function that includes measures to anticipate, prevent and/or resolve a threat or act of terrorism. The lead agency for crisis management is the FBI. Consequence management addresses the effects of an incident on lives and property. It includes measures to protect public health and safety, restore essential government services, and provide emergency relief to governments, businesses, and individuals affected by a terrorist incident. FEMA is the lead agency for consequence management.

---

* Director, Office of National Security Affairs, Federal Emergency Management Agency. Excerpt from statement before the Subcommittee on Oversight, Investigations, and Emergency Management, Committee on Transportation and Infrastructure, U.S. House of Representatives, June 9, 1999.

Federal Response Plan

In an actual or potential terrorist incident, FEMA uses the structures and resources of the Federal Response Plan (FRP) to manage the Federal consequence management response. The FRP, first published in 1992 and recently updated, has been used in the past several years to respond to numerous disasters and emergencies declared by the President, including the Oklahoma City bombing in 1995, as well as hurricanes, tornadoes, floods and earthquakes. The Plan brings together twenty-six Federal departments and agencies and the American Red Cross to organize Federal disaster response and recovery efforts and coordinate them with an affected State. Most importantly, it provides a known and flexible framework under which local, State and Federal officials can orchestrate their response to a disaster or emergency and make the most effective use of all available resources. FEMA has developed a special annex to the FRP to address the unique requirements involved in responding to a terrorist incident.

Domestic Preparedness Activities

Although the general threat of a terrorist attack exists, FEMA is not in a position to identify the likelihood of a particular incident or the geographic location where an attack may take place. To ensure the broadest coverage in implementing domestic terrorism preparedness activities, we are emphasizing the following key considerations to ensure that:
- State and local first responders and emergency management personnel are the focus of Federal programs.
- Needs of the balance of the nation, particularly local jurisdictions beyond the largest cities and metro areas, are addressed with plans, training, exercises and equipment.
- Initial training is reinforced and sustained with refresher information and updated instruction.
- Existing plans, capabilities and systems are utilized as the foundation for addressing the unique requirements of WMD.

Planning

The responsibility for developing plans and implementing response falls heavily on the States and the local governments. FEMA is applying its experience gained in responding to natural disasters to guide the development of terrorism consequence management preparedness plans and procedures at the local, State and Federal levels. A fundamental goal of the planning effort is to assist in the development of State and local plans for dealing with WMD contingencies. FEMA grant assistance is being used to enhance planning resources and capabilities at the State and local levels of government. The planning effort is being coordinated with the FBI utilizing existing plans and associated planning structures whenever possible to help ensure that crisis and consequence management plans are in place across the nation.

Training

FEMA has developed and delivered a number of terrorism-related courses for State and local emergency management personnel and first responders. FEMA is utilizing existing programs, networks and facilities to help support the training delivery. In particular, we are using the National Emergency Training Center, which includes the National Fire Academy and the Emergency Management Institute, as well as State fire and emergency management training systems to deliver terrorism-related training to State and local responders. FEMA continues to emphasize the "train-the-trainer" approach to leverage existing capabilities with performance objectives to accomplish training goals.

The National Fire Academy (NFA) has developed courses for first responders in the fire community and other areas. Other courses in the curriculum deal with Basic Concepts; Incident Management; and Tactical Considerations for Emergency Medical Services (EMS), Company Officers, and HAZMAT Response. In addition, FEMA is using the Emergency Management Institute (EMI) to develop and deliver courses such as the Integrated Emergency Management Course on Terrorism that uses a terrorist attack scenario.

Exercises

FEMA is working closely with the National Domestic Preparedness Office (NDPO), the FBI and the States to ensure the development of a comprehensive exercise program that meets the needs of the first responder communities and other response elements. The FBI, in coordination with FEMA, DOD, DOE, HHS, and EPA, and other departments and agencies, will ensure the implementation of a comprehensive terrorism exercise program. State and local involvement in the planning, scheduling, and conduct of coordinated exercises will be a key component of the exercise effort.

Equipment

The NDPO has assumed the lead for developing a list of standardized equipment for the first responder community. FEMA, along with other Federal agencies and first responder communities, is helping to develop the required Standard Equipment List (SEL) to support acquisition of comparable equipment by DOJ for the first responder community. This equipment will conform to appropriate and applicable laws, regulations, and standards, such as those issued by the National Institute for Occupational Safety and Health and the National Fire Protection Association.

FEMA has developed and implemented the Rapid Response Information System (RRIS), which contains an inventory of Federal assets that could be made available to assist State and local response efforts, and a database on chemical and biological agents and protective measures. The inventory is being made available to Federal, State and local officials to assist them in assessing and obtaining the necessary equipment and resources for responding to terrorist incidents involving the use of nuclear, chemical or biological weapons.

Conclusion

Terrorism preparedness requires planning, training and exercising on a regular basis, and appropriate equipment, to ensure maximum readiness to respond to an actual incident. In responding to a terrorism incident, local responders will be the first to arrive at an incident site and may be forced to manage operations at the scene on their own for hours.

Statement of President Bush
Office of National Preparedness in FEMA
To Coordinate All Federal WMD Consequence
Management

THE WHITE HOUSE

Office of the Press Secretary

For Immediate Release   May 8, 2001

STATEMENT BY THE PRESIDENT

Domestic Preparedness Against Weapons of Mass Destruction

Protecting America's homeland and citizens from the threat of weapons of mass destruction is one of our Nation's important national security challenges. Today, more nations possess chemical, biological, or nuclear weapons than ever before. Still others seek to join them. Most troubling of all, the list of these countries includes some of the world's least-responsible states—states for whom terror and blackmail are a way of life. Some non-state terrorist groups have also demonstrated an interest in acquiring weapons of mass destruction.

Against this backdrop, it is clear that the threat of chemical, biological, or nuclear weapons being used against the United States—while not immediate—is very real. That is why our Nation actively seeks to deny chemical, biological, and nuclear weapons to those seeking to acquire them. That is why, together with our allies, we seek to deter anyone who would contemplate their use. And that is also why we must ensure that our Nation is prepared to defend against the harm they can inflict.

Should our efforts to reduce the threat to our country from weapons of mass destruction be less than fully successful, prudence dictates that the United States be fully prepared to deal effectively with the consequences of such a weapon being used here on our soil.

Today, numerous Federal departments and agencies have programs to deal with the consequences of a potential use of a chemical, biological, radiological, or nuclear weapon in the United States. Many of these Federal programs offer training, planning, and assistance to state and local governments. But to maximize their effectiveness, these efforts need to be seamlessly integrated, harmonious, and comprehensive.

Therefore, I have asked Vice President Cheney to oversee the development of a coordinated national effort so that we may do the very best possible job of protecting our people from catastrophic harm. I have also asked Joe Allbaugh, the Director of the Federal Emergency Management Agency, to create an Office of National Preparedness. This Office will be responsible for implementing the results of those parts of the national effort overseen by Vice President Cheney that deal with consequence management. Specifically it will coordinate all Federal programs dealing with weapons of mass destruction consequence management within the Departments of Defense, Health and Human Services, Justice, and Energy, the Environmental Protection Agency, and other federal agencies. The Office of National Preparedness will work closely with state and local governments to ensure their planning, training, and equipment needs are addressed. FEMA will also work closely with the Department of Justice, in its lead role for crisis management, to ensure that all facets of our response to the threat from weapons of mass destruction are coordinated and cohesive. I will periodically chair a meeting of the National Security Council to review these efforts.

No governmental responsibility is more fundamental than protecting the physical safety of our Nation and its citizens. In today's world, this obligation includes protection against the use of weapons of mass destruction. I look forward to working closely with Congress so that together we can meet this challenge.

Prepare to Prevent or Respond to Catastrophic Terrorist Attacks

Bremer Commission Report*

A terrorist attack in the United States using a biological agent, deadly chemicals, or nuclear or radiological material, even if only partially success-ful, would profoundly affect the entire nation, as would a series of conven-tional attacks or a single bombing that caused thousands of deaths. Given the trend toward more deadly terrorist attacks and indications that mass casual-ties are an objective of many of today's terrorists, it is essential that America be fully prepared to prevent and respond to this kind of catastrophic terror-ism.

The U.S. Government's plans for a catastrophic terrorist attack on the United States do not employ the full range of the Department of Defense's (DoD's) capabilities for managing large operations. Addition-ally, the interagency coordination and cooperation required to integrate the DoD properly into counterterrorism planning has not been accom-plished.

The Department of Defense's ability to command and control vast re-sources for dangerous, unstructured situations is unmatched by any other department or agency. According to current plans, DoD involvement is lim-ited to supporting the agencies that are currently designated as having the lead in a terrorism crisis, the FBI and the Federal Emergency Management Agency (FEMA). But, in extraordinary circumstances, when a catastrophe is beyond the capabilities of local, state, and other federal agencies, or is directly related to an armed conflict overseas, the President may want to designate DoD as a lead federal agency. This may become a critical operational consid-eration in planning for future conflicts. Current plans and exercises do not consider this possibility.

---

* From "Countering The Changing Threat Of International Terrorism," Re-port of the National Commission on Terrorism (pursuant to Public Law 277, 105th Congress), Amb. L. Paul Bremer III, Chairman, June 5, 2000. Commissioners: L. Paul Bremer III, Maurice Sonnenberg, Richard K. Betts, Wayne A. Downing, Jane Harman, Fred C. Iklé, Juliette N. Kayyem, John F. Lewis, Jr., R. James Woolsey.

An expanded role for the DoD in a catastrophic terrorist attack will have policy and legal implications. Other federal agencies, the states, and local communities will have major concerns. In preparing for such a contingency, there will also be internal DoD issues on resources and possible conflicts with traditional military contingency plans. These issues should be addressed beforehand.

Effective preparation also requires effective organization. The DoD is not optimally organized to respond to the wide range of missions that would likely arise from the threat of a catastrophic terrorist attack. For example, within DoD several offices, departments, Unified Commands, the Army, and the National Guard have overlapping responsibilities to plan and execute operations in case of a catastrophic terrorist attack. These operations will require an unprecedented degree of interagency coordination and communication in order to be successful.

There are neither plans for the DoD to assume a lead agency role nor exercises rehearsing this capability. Hence, these demanding tasks would have to be accomplished on an ad hoc basis by the military.

Recommendations:

o The President should direct the Assistant to the President for National Security Affairs, in coordination with the Secretary of Defense and the Attorney General, to develop and adopt detailed contingency plans that would transfer lead federal agency authority to the Department of Defense if necessary during a catastrophic terrorist attack or prior to an imminent attack.

o The Secretary of Defense should establish a unified command structure that would integrate all catastrophic terrorism capabilities and conduct detailed planning and exercises with relevant federal, state, and local authorities.

Given the urgency of near-term needs, long-term research and development (R&D) projects on technologies useful to fighting terrorism will be short-changed unless Congress and the President can agree on special procedures and institutional arrangements to work on research that is risky and has more distant payoffs.

Research and Development spending for new technologies to cope with catastrophic terrorism has significantly increased over the past three years. Most of the funds, however, are targeted on near-term improvements to meet immediate needs for better detectors, more vaccines, and requirements of first responders.

To prevent or cope with terrorist attacks in the future, in particular attacks using CBRN agents, the U.S. Government must make greater use of America's dominance in science and technology. No other country, much less any subnational organization, can match U.S. scientific and technological prowess in biotechnology and pharmaceutical production and quality control, electronics, computer science and other domains that could help overcome and defeat the technologies used by future terrorists. But this kind of R&D requires time—five to ten years or more—to develop new ideas, test hypotheses, craft preliminary applications, and test them. Developing mass production for successful applications further delays getting products into the hands of users.

The following list illustrates, but by no means exhusts, the type of projects that could constitute a long-term R&D program:
- New sensors to detect nuclear weapons in transit (e.g., gamma-ray imaging systems, including stimulation to elicit detectable emissions).
- High power ultraviolet beams to destroy BW agents and to clean up contaminated areas.
- New types of "tripwires" suitable for many different entry-points (e.g., explosive-sniffers, body scanner), and their proto-typing for mass-production.
- Advanced development of anti-virals for smallpox.

Recommendation:

o The President should establish a comprehensive and coordinated long-term Research and Development program to counter catastrophic terrorism.

Current controls on transfers of pathogens that could be used in biological terrorism are inadequate and controls on related equipment are nonexistent. In addition, current programs of the Department of Health and Human Services are not adequate to ensure physical security of pathogens or to monitor disease outbreaks overseas.

Terrorists, without serious risk of detection, could obtain pathogens from domestic natural sources, steal them, or import them into the United States. Most pathogens in the United States are tightly controlled, but regulation of laboratories as well as of dangerous agents during transport are designed to prevent accidents, not theft. Moreover, these controls are not as rigorous as controls over nuclear material.

Creating pathogens small and sturdy enough to disperse broadly over a target population for an effective period of time remains, fortunately, a complex process. Thus, regulating the sophisticated equipment required to turn pathogens into weapons could hamper terrorist efforts to acquire this capability.

However, no regulatory scheme is foolproof. Moreover, contagious diseases do not require sophisticated dispersion devices. Thus, it is important to have the ability to detect outbreaks of infectious diseases and to distinguish bioterrorist attacks from natural outbreaks. Some detection and analytical systems are in place domestically, but the international community's ability to distinguish natural disease from terrorism lags far behind even these modest U.S. efforts.

Recommendations:

o   The Secretary of Health and Human Services should strengthen physical security standards applicable to the storage, creation, and transport of pathogens in research laboratories and other certified facilities in order to protect against theft or diversion. These standards should be as rigorous as the physical protection and security measures applicable to critical nuclear materials.

o   The Congress should:

- Make possession of designated critical pathogens illegal for anyone who is not properly certified.
- Control domestic sale and transfer of equipment critical to the development or use of biological agents by certifying legitimate users of critical equipment and prohibiting sales of such equipment to non-certified entities.
- Require tagging of critical equipment to enable law enforcement to identify its location.
- The Secretary of Health and Human Services, working with the Department of State, should develop an international monitoring program to provide early warning of infectious disease outbreaks and possible terrorist experimentation with biological substances.

Toward A National Strategy For Combating Terrorism

Second Annual Gilmore Commission Report*

Executive Summary

We have been fortunate as a nation. The terrorist incidents in this country—however tragic—have occurred so rarely that the foundations of our society or our form of government have not been threatened. Nevertheless, the potential for terrorist attacks inside the borders of the United States is a serious emerging threat. There is no guarantee that our comparatively secure domestic sanctuary will always remain so. Because the stakes are so high, our nation's leaders must take seriously the possibility of an escalation of terrorist violence against the homeland.

The continuing challenge for the United States is first to deter and, failing that, to detect and interdict terrorists before they strike. Should an attack occur, local, State, and Federal authorities must be prepared to respond and mitigate the consequences of the attack.

To prepare to manage the consequences of such attacks effectively, the United States needs changes in the relationships among all levels of government. Our ability to respond cannot depend on a single level or agency of government. Rather we need a *national* approach, one that recognizes the unique individual skills that communities, States, and the Federal government possess and that, collectively, will give us the "total package" needed to

* Excerpt from *II. Toward A National Strategy For Combating Terrorism*, Second Annual Report to The President and The Congress of the Advisory Panel To Assess Domestic Response Capabilities For Terrorism Involving Weapons Of Mass Destruction, Gov. James S. Gilmore,III, chairman, December 15 2000. James Clapper, Jr. Vice Chairman, L. Paul Bremer, Raymond Downey, Richard Falkenrath, George Foresman, William Garrison, Ellen M. Gordon, James Greenleaf, William Jenaway, William Dallas Jones, Paul M. Maniscalco, John O. Marsh, Jr. Kathleen O'Brien, M. Patricia Quinlisk, Patrick Ralston, William Reno, Joseph Samuels, Jr., Kenneth Shine, Hubert Williams, Ellen Embrey.

address all aspects of terrorism.

While the Advisory Panel found much to commend, it also found problems at all levels of government and in virtually every functional discipline relevant to combating terrorism. The Panel believes these problems are particularly acute at high levels of the Federal Executive Branch. Hence, the present report highlights the related issues of national strategy and Federal organization, and recommends solutions for these and other problems.

Finding 1: The United States has no coherent, functional national strategy for combating terrorism.

The United States needs a functional, coherent national strategy for domestic preparedness against terrorism. The nation has a loosely coupled set of plans and specific programs that aim, individually, to achieve certain specific preparedness objectives. The Executive Branch portrays as its strategy a compilation of broad policy statements, and various plans and programs already under way. Many programs have resulted from specific Congressional earmarks in various appropriations bills and did not originate in Executive Branch budget requests; they are the initiatives of activist legislators. Although Federal agencies are administering programs assigned to them, the Executive Branch has not articulated a broad functional national strategy that would synchronize the existing programs and identify future program priorities needed to achieve national objectives for domestic preparedness for terrorism. Given the structure of our national government, only the Executive Branch can produce such a national strategy.

Recommendation 1: The next President should develop and present to the Congress a national strategy for combating terrorism within one year of assuming office.

The first step in developing a coherent national strategy is for the Executive Branch to define a meaningful, measurable expression of what it is trying to achieve in combating terrorism. To date, the Federal government's goals have been expressed primarily in terms of program execution. Rather, the national strategy must express goals in terms of the "end state" toward which the program strives. Since there exists no ready-made measure of a country's preparedness for terrorism (especially domestically), the Executive Branch must develop objective measurements for its program to combat terrorism, to track its progress, to determine priorities and appropriate funding levels, and to know when the desired "end state" has been achieved.

With meaningful objectives, logical priorities and appropriate policy prescriptions can be developed. That is the essence of any coherent strategy. Setting priorities is essential and can only be done after specific objectives have been clearly defined. For instance, should the nation seek a higher level of preparedness for its large urban centers than for its rural areas and, if so, how much higher? In the broad area of terrorism preparedness, what should be the relative importance of preparing for conventional terrorism, radiological incidents, chemical weapons, or biological weapons? With respect to biological weapons, which pathogens deserve priority? What priority and commensurate resources need to be devoted to defending against cyber attacks? A proper national strategy will provide a clear answer to these and many other questions. With these answers in hand it will be possible to design and manage an appropriate set of programs. The country is at a disadvantage, of course, in that a large number of programs have already been established and may have to be reconfigured—an inevitable consequence of their ad hoc origins.

Essential Characteristics of a Comprehensive Functional Strategy for Combating Terrorism

- *National* in scope, not just federal
- Appropriately resourced and based on measurable performance objectives
- Focused on the full range of deterrence, prevention, preparedness, and response across the spectrum of threats—domestic and international
- For domestic programs, built on requirements from and fully coordinated with relevant local, state, and federal authorities

Finding 2: The organization of the Federal government's programs for combating terrorism is fragmented, uncoordinated, and politically unaccountable.

Recommendation 2: The next President should establish a National Office for Combating Terrorism in the Executive Office of the President, and should seek a statutory basis for this office.

It should have at least five major sections, each headed by an Assistant Director:
1. Domestic Preparedness Programs
2. Intelligence
3. Health and Medical Programs

4. Research, Development, Test, and Evaluation (RDT&E), and National Standards
5. Management and Budget

The National Office for Combating Terrorism should exercise program and budget authority over Federal efforts to combat terrorism. It should have the authority to conduct a review of Federal agency programs and budgets to ensure compliance with the priorities established in the national strategy, as well as the elimination of conflicts and unnecessary duplication among agencies. The office should provide direction and priorities for research and development, and related test and evaluation (RDT&E) for combating terrorism, as well as for developing nationally recognized standards for equipment and laboratory protocols and techniques. It should coordinate programs designed to enhance the capabilities of and coordination among the various health and medical entities at all levels.

Finding 3: The Congress shares responsibility for the inadequate coordination of programs to combat terrorism.

Recommendation 3: The Congress should consolidate its authority over programs for combating terrorism into a Special Committee for Combating Terrorism—either a joint committee between the Houses or separate committees in each House—and Congressional leadership should instruct all other committees to respect the authority of this new committee and to conform strictly to authorizing legislation.

Finding 4: The Executive Branch and the Congress have not paid sufficient attention to State and local capabilities for combating terrorism and have not devoted sufficient resources to augment these capabilities to enhance the preparedness of the nation as a whole.

"Local" response personnel—community and State law enforcement officers, firefighters, emergency medical technicians, hospital emergency personnel, public health officials, and emergency managers—will be the "first responders" to virtually any terrorist attack anywhere in the nation. Federal resources may not arrive for many hours—if not days—after the attack. A disproportionately small amount of the total funds appropriated for combating terrorism is being allocated to provide direct or indirect assistance to State and local response efforts.

Recommendation 4: The Executive Branch should establish a strong institutional mechanism for ensuring the participation of high-level State

and local officials in the development and implementation of a national strategy for terrorism preparedness.
Finding 5: Federal programs for domestic preparedness to combat terrorism lack clear priorities and are deficient in numerous specific areas.

The Advisory Panel has reached consensus on a number of specific findings and recommendations, summarized below.

Specific Functional Recommendations

"Local" response entities—law enforcement, fire service, emergency medical technicians, hospital emergency personnel, public health officials, and emergency managers—will *always* be the "first response," and conceivably the only response. When entities at various levels of government are engaged, the responsibilities of all entities and lines of authority must be clear.

1. *Collecting Intelligence, Assessing Threats, and Sharing Information.* The National Office for Combating Terrorism should foster the development of a consolidated all-source analysis and assessment capability that would provide various response entities as well as policymakers with continuing analysis of potential threats and broad threat assessment input into the development of the annual national strategy.

2. *Operational Coordination.* The National Office for Combating Terrorism should encourage Governors to designate State emergency management entities as domestic preparedness focal points for coordination with the Federal government. The National Office should identify and promote the establishment of single-source, "all hazards" planning documents, standardized Incident Command and Unified Command Systems, and other model programs for use in the full range of emergency contingencies, including terrorism.

3. *Training, Equipping, and Exercising.* The National Office for Combating Terrorism should develop and manage a comprehensive national plan for Federal assistance to State and local agencies for training and equipment and the conduct of exercises, including the promulgation of standards in each area. The National Office should consult closely with State and local stakeholders in the development of this national plan.

4. *Health and Medical Considerations.* The National Office for Combating Terrorism should reevaluate the current U.S. approach to providing pub-

lic health and medical care in response to acts of terrorism, especially possible mass casualty incidents and most particularly bioterrorism.

5. *Research and Development, and National Standards.* The National Office for Combating Terrorism should establish a clear set of priorities for research and development for combating terrorism, including long-range programs.

6. *Providing Cyber Security Against Terrorism.* Cyber attacks inside the United States could have "mass disruptive," even if not "mass destructive" or "mass casualty" consequences.

Comparison of the 2000 Gilmore and Bremer Commission Reports

James Clapper, Jr.*

The charters and objectives of the Bremer Commission and the Gilmore Commission are, for the most part, very different. The Bremer Commission focused on international terrorism. The Gilmore Commission's clear mandate is on domestic preparedness—deterring, preventing, and responding to terrorist incidents inside the borders of the United States.

There are, nevertheless, several overlapping areas of interest between the two reports and the attendant findings and recommendations.

Both Panels agree on the increasing nature of the threat of international terrorism, including the potential for more attacks from international groups in side the borders of the United States.

Both panels specifically agree that certain measures must be taken to improve intelligence collection and dissemination on terrorists, including:

- Repealing the 1995 Director of Central Intelligence Guidelines as they apply to recruiting terrorist informants
- Reviewing and clarifying, as may be indicated, the Attorney General's Guidelines on Foreign Intelligence Collection and the Guidelines on General Crime, Racketeering Enterprise, and Domestic Security/ Terrorism Investigations
- Directing the Department of Justice Office of Intelligence Policy and Review not to require a process for initiating actions under the

---

* Lieutenant General, U.S. Air Force (Retired); Vice Chairman, Advisory Panel to Assess Domestic Response Capabilities for Terrorism Involving Weapons of Mass Destruction (Gilmore Commission). Excerpt from testimony before the Senate Committee on the Judiciary, Subcommittee on Technology, Terrorism, and Government Information, March 27, 2001.

Foreign Intelligence Surveillance Act that are more stringent than those required by statute.

Both Panels agree that significant improvements must be made in the ability of intelligence and law enforcement agencies to collect, analyze, disseminate and share intelligence and other information more effectively.

Both Panels agree that there must be a comprehensive strategy or plan for dealing with terrorism, including ways in which both the Executive Branch and the Congress develop and coordinate program and budget processes.

Both Panels agree in principal that Department of Defense (DoD) and U.S. Armed Forces may have a major role in preventing or responding to a terrorist attack, especially one involving a chemical, biological, radiological or nuclear device. We likewise strongly agree that insufficient planning, coordination, training, and exercises have been developed and implemented for the possibility of major DoD and military involvement. The one area in which we disagree has to do with "lead agency."

The Bremer Commission suggests that a response to a catastrophic attack may indicate the designation of DoD as Lead Agency. While we agree that DoD may have a major role, we firmly believe that the military must always be directly under civilian control. As a result, we recommend that the President always designate a Federal civilian agency other than the Department of Defense (DoD) as the Lead Federal Agency. Many Americans will not draw the technical distinction between the Department of Defense—the civilian entity—and the U.S. Armed Forces—the military entity. Although the Department of Defense and every major component of that department have civilian leaders, the perception will likely be that "the military" is in the lead.

This recommendation does not ignore the fact that the DoD, through all of its various agencies—not just the Armed Forces—has enormous and significant capabilities for command, control, communications, intelligence, logistics, engineer, and medical support and may play a major role in response to a terrorist attack, especially one with potentially catastrophic consequences. Those resources can still brought to bear but should, in our view, always be subordinated to another civilian agency.

V.
Loose Nukes and Bought Brains

A Report Card on DOE Nonproliferation Programs with Russia

Baker-Cutler Report*

Executive Summary

Introduction

Since the breakup of the Soviet Union, we have witnessed the dissolution of an empire having over 40,000 nuclear weapons, over a thousand metric tons of nuclear materials, vast quantities of chemical and biological weapons materials, and thousands of missiles. This Cold War arsenal is spread across 11 time zones and lacks the Cold War infrastructure that provided the control and financing necessary to assure that chains of command remain intact and nuclear weapons and materials remain securely beyond the reach of terrorists and weapons-proliferating states. This problem is compounded by the existence of thousands of weapons scientists who, not always having the resources necessary to adequately care for their families, may be tempted to sell their expertise to countries of proliferation concern.

The Task Force reached the following conclusions and recommendations:

1. The most urgent unmet national security threat to the United States today is the danger that weapons of mass destruction or weapons-usable material in Russia could be stolen and sold to terrorists or hostile nation states and used against American troops abroad or citizens at home.

2. Current nonproliferation programs in the Department of Energy, the Department of Defense, and related agencies have achieved impressive results

---

* From "DRAFT, A Report Card on the Department of Energy's Nonproliferation Programs with Russia," Sen. Howard Baker and Lloyd Cutler, Co-Chairs, Russia Task Force, The Secretary of Energy Advisory Board, United States Department of Energy, January 10, 2000.

thus far, but the Task Force concludes that the current budget levels are inadequate and the current management of the U.S. Government's response is too diffuse. The Task Force believes that the existing scope and management of the U.S. programs addressing this threat leave an unacceptable risk of failure and the potential for catastrophic consequences.

3. The new President and leaders of the 107th Congress face the urgent national security challenge of devising an enhanced response proportionate to the threat. The enhanced response should include: a net assessment of the threat; a clear achievable mission statement; the development of a strategy with specific goals and measurable objectives; a more centralized command of the financial and human resources required to do the job; and an identification of criteria for measuring the benefits for Russia, the United States, and the entire world.

The Task Force offers one major recommendation to the President and the Congress:

> **The President, in consultation with Congress and in cooperation with the Russian Federation, should quickly formulate a strategic plan to secure and/or neutralize in the next eight to ten years all nuclear weapons -usable material located in Russia and to prevent the outflow from Russia of scientific expertise that could be used for nuclear or other weapons of mass destruction.**

If this program is conceived in full cooperation with the Russian Federation, is adequately financed, and is implemented as part of a growing, open and transparent partnership, then the Task Force believes that Russia should be positioned to take over any work remaining at the end of the eight to ten year period.

Bearing this in mind, the Task Force report outlines an enhanced national security program. This program could be carried out for less than one percent of the U.S. defense budget, or up to a total of $30 billion over the next eight to ten years. The Russian Government would, of course, be expected to make a significant contribution commensurate with its own financial ability.

Background

As two former adversaries adapting to the end of the Cold War, the United States and Russia both have a responsibility to examine and address the dangers posed by the massive nuclear arsenal built up over the past five decades.

Important steps have already been taken with many ambitious milestones being met over the past decade. Former President Bush negotiated and President Clinton implemented what some have called the "contract of the century" with President Yeltsin. Under this agreement, the U.S. is purchasing 500 metric tons of HEU removed from former Soviet nuclear weapons, and this material is being converted to low enriched uranium fuel that is then used in civilian power reactors. To date, more than 110 metric tons of HEU, enough to build some 5,000 nuclear weapons, have been blended down and rendered impotent for nuclear weapons use. In its blended-down form, this material has been delivered to the international market to fuel civilian power reactors.

Since the Nunn-Lugar legislative initiative of 1991, the U.S. Government has established an array of threat reduction programs in both the Departments of Defense and Energy to assist in dismantling Russian nuclear and other weapons of mass destruction and to improve significantly the security of such weapons and materials. Additional work, under the aegis of the Department of State, has addressed the brain drain problem both in Russia and other countries of the former Soviet Union through programs such as the International Science and Technology Center (ISTC) Program. This program, together with DOE's Initiatives for Proliferation Prevention and its Nuclear Cities Initiative, has helped to redirect weapons scientists and engineers from defense work to civilian employment.

These U.S. programs have reduced the threat of diversion of nuclear weapons materials. To the best of our knowledge, no nuclear weapons or quantity of nuclear weapons-usable material have been successfully stolen and exported, while many efforts to steal weapons-usable material have been intercepted by Russian and international police operations.

Much more remains to be done, however. The Task Force observes that while we know a good deal about the size and state of the Russian weapons complex, there is still much that we do not know. More than 1,000 metric tons of HEU and at least 150 metric tons of weapons-grade plutonium exist in the Russian weapons complex.

Most of the cases involving the successful seizure and recovery of stolen nuclear weapons-usable material have occurred on the western border of Russia.

The southern border is less secure. Materials may be diverted through centuries old trade routes along Russia's mountainous border. In addition, many of the Russian nuclear sites remain vulnerable to insiders determined to steal enough existing material to make several nuclear weapons and to transport these materials to Iran, Iraq, or Afghanistan. At some sites, one well-placed insider would be enough. The Task Force was advised that buyers from Iraq, Iran and other countries have actively sought nuclear weapons-usable material from Russian sites.

In a worst-case scenario, a nuclear engineer graduate with a grapefruit-sized lump of HEU or an orange-sized lump of plutonium, together with material otherwise readily available in commercial markets, could fashion a nuclear device that would fit in a van like the one the terrorist Yosif parked in the World Trade Center in 1993. The explosive effects of such a device would destroy every building in the Wall Street financial area and would level lower Manhattan. In confronting this danger, the Russian Government has recognized that theft of nuclear weapons or nuclear weapons-usable material threatens Moscow or St. Petersburg as surely as it threatens Washington, DC or New York. Chechen terrorists have already threatened to spread radioactive material around Moscow; if they were armed with a nuclear device, the situation would be much worse. Success in countering this threat to both nations rests on a bedrock of shared vital interests.

The Threat Today

Russia today wrestles with a weakened ability to protect and secure its Cold War legacy. A number of factors have come together to present an immediate risk of theft of potential weapons of mass destruction: delays in payments to guards at nuclear facilities; breakdowns in command structures, including units that control weapons or guard weapons-usable material; and inadequate budgets for protection of stockpiles and laboratories housing thousands of potential nuclear weapons. Such threats are not hypothetical. Imagine if such material were successfully stolen and sold to a terrorist like Osama bin Laden, who reportedly masterminded the bombings of the U.S. embassies in Kenya and Tanzania and is the chief suspect in the recent attack on the U.S. destroyer *Cole*.

The Task Force Specifically Finds...

1. By and large, current DOE programs are having a significant and positive effect. Expansions of program scope and increases in funding, however, must take careful account of the pace at which funds can usefully be

expended in each individual program.

2. The strategic plan and the associated budgets should identify specific goals and measurable objectives for each program, as well as provide criteria for success and an exit strategy.

3. A major obstacle to further expansion and success of current programs is the continuation of differences between the U.S. and Russia over transparency and access. As a condition for a substantially expanded program, the U.S. and Russia should agree at a high level on the degree of transparency needed to assure that U.S.-funded activity has measurable impacts on program objectives and that U.S. taxpayer dollars are being spent as intended.

4. Given the gravity of the existing situation and the nature of the challenge before us, it is imperative that the President establish a high-level leadership position in the White House with responsibility for policy and budget coordination for threat reduction and nonproliferation programs across the U.S. Government.

5. The U.S. administration of these programs should seek to eliminate any unnecessary and overly restrictive controls that hamper swift and efficient action. To overcome potential impediments that often arise from "business as usual" practices within the Russian and U.S. bureaucracies, DOE and related agencies should take practical steps, including further enlargement of the DOE team working with the U.S. Ambassador in Moscow, to ensure the most efficient on-the-ground implementation of the programs in Russia.

6. It is imperative to mobilize the sustained interest and concern of the Congress. The Task Force urges the Congress to consider the creation of a joint committee on weapons of mass destruction, nuclear safety and nonproliferation, modeled after the former Joint Committee on Atomic Energy.

Nuclear Materials Protection, Control and Accounting (MPC&A) Program

Department of Energy Strategic Plan*

A. Need for Improved Nuclear Material Security

Problem and Its Magnitude

In the aftermath of the Cold War, the international community faces a common threat: the possibility that weapons-usable nuclear materials (plutonium [Pu] and highly enriched uranium [HEU]) could be stolen or diverted.

These materials are the essential ingredients of nuclear weapons. Loss of even small amounts of his dangerous material could enable additional states or a terrorist organization to build a nuclear weapon. The threat posed by this material is most urgent in Russia, the NIS, and the Baltic states, which inherited weapons-usable nuclear material when the Soviet Union collapsed in 1991. Experts believe that the former Soviet Union produced more than 1,200 tons of HEU and 150 tons of Pu.

More than half of this material resides in assembled nuclear weapons. Because they are strictly accounted for, difficult to transport, and heavily guarded within secure military installations, assembled nuclear weapons are considered to be much less vulnerable to theft or diversion than weapons-usable nuclear materials in other forms. Therefore, the greatest threat is presented by approximately 650 metric tons of weapons-usable nuclear material that exists in forms such as metals, oxides, solutions, and scrap.

This material, enough to produce more than 40,000 nuclear bombs, is spread among eight countries spanning eleven time zones. These materials are in use or stored at over 50 sites across Russia, the NIS, and the Baltics.

---

* Excerpts. U.S. Department of Energy, January 1998.

B. The Role of MPC&A in Nuclear Material Security

Modern, well-designed nuclear MPC&A systems provide a cost-effective and reliable way of securing nuclear material from both insider and outsider threats. Improving MPC&A systems at sites where nuclear material is inadequately protected is a critical component of U.S. national security strategy because such improvements prevent nuclear material from entering the smuggling pipeline, where it is difficult or impossible to retrieve. MPC&A improvements thus provide the first line of defense against nuclear smuggling which could lead to nuclear proliferation or nuclear terrorism.

Nearly all countries possessing nuclear materials have established MPC&A systems that are consistent with guide-lines developed by the International Atomic Energy Agency IAEA).

Over the years the United States has made major improvements to MPC&A systems at its nuclear facilities. In the 1960s, predictions of rapid growth in the commercial use of HEU and plutonium and high levels of material unaccounted for at some facilities prompted the U.S. Atomic Energy Commission to tighten regulations for nuclear material control and accounting. The United States began MPC&A upgrades in the 1970s, following the terrorist events surrounding the Munich Olympics. Such upgrades have continued at DOE facilities since that time, and have resulted in generally very substantial security systems for DOE facilities. Although recent reports indicated that even more resources and attention must be paid to DOE facility protection requirements, we are continually analyzing and taking steps to improve our nuclear MPC&A in response to changing hreats, while also seeking to responsibly manage associated costs, ensure public health and safety, and respect the environment. These upgrades are especially rele-vant to the current needs of nuclear facilities in the former Soviet Union to address changing threats and move toward more technology based MPC&A systems.

Major components of modern MPC&A systems are described below:

Physical protection systems are designed to detect and delay any unauthorized penetration of barriers and portals, and to respond with immediate investigation and use of force, if necessary. Physical protection measures are generally the most visible and pervasive components of a nuclear safeguards system. Guards, fences, multiple barriers to entry, limited access points, alarms, and motion detectors are all examples of elements of a physical protection system.

Material control systems are designed to limit access and use of nuclear material and to detect promptly the theft or diversion of the material should it occur. These systems may include portal monitors and other devices to control egress from storage sites. Material control is also achieved through the use of secure containers for nuclear material, seals, and identification codes that make it possible to verify easily the location and condition of nuclear material, as well as material use and storage rules and procedures.

Material accounting systems are designed to confirm the presence of nuclear material in inventory, to measure the loss of any material not accounted for, and to provide information for follow- up investigation. Material accounting systems include both traditional inventory systems and an array of equipment to measure the types and quantities of nuclear mate-rial in a given area.

Typically reinforcing the three major components of a MPC&A system is a program to ensure the reliability of the personnel who will be operating the system, including security screening, indoctrination, training, and personnel record keeping functions.

C. U.S. Initiatives to Improve Nuclear Material Security

The Cooperative Threat Reduction Program

Cooperative efforts to upgrade MPC&A in Russia, Ukraine, Belarus, and Kazakhstan were proposed in March, 1992, and were supported by funds made available by the "Soviet Nuclear Threat Reduction Act of 1991"—also known as the "Nunn-Lugar" act after its leading authors. This legislation and similar legislation during the period 1992-1995 provided funding for the Cooperative Threat Reduction (CTR) Program directed by the U.S. Department of Defense. Negotiations over these proposals progressed slowly, especially with Russia, and joint MPC&A projects at facilities containing weapons-usable nuclear material in these states did not begin until mid-1994. A significant milestone in initiating joint work on MPC&A was achieved by the CTR program in January, 1995, when an agreement between the U.S. Department of Defense and Russia's Ministry of Atomic Energy (Minatom) was amended to add $20 million for joint MPC&A upgrades. Similar agreements increasing available funds were signed with Ukraine, Belarus and Kazakhstan.

The Laboratory-to-Laboratory Initiative

In April, 1994, the DOE initiated a second approach to joint MPC&A cooperation with Russia that encouraged U.S. national laboratories to cooperate directly with the Russian Federation's nuclear institutes to improve MPC&A. This effort was designed to complement the original Government-to- Government approach and achieve more rapid joint progress on MPC&A. This initiative was known as the Laboratory-to-Laboratory program because it was based on the successful foundation of scientific collaborations established in 1992 between U.S. national laboratories and the Russian nuclear weapons institutes.

Presidential Involvement

In 1995, the MPC&A program was greatly strengthened by the direct involvement of the White House. In particular, the May 10, 1995, Clinton-Yeltsin Joint Statement on Nonproliferation reaffirmed the two states' commitment "to strengthen national and international regimes of control, accounting, and physical protection of nuclear materials and to prevent illegal traffic in nuclear materials."

More progress was achieved when Vice President Gore and Russian Prime Minister Chernomyrdin agreed to make MPC&A improvement a top priority for both governments. This agreement led to the June 1995 signing of a Joint Statement by for-mer U.S. Secretary of Energy Hazel O'Leary and Russian Atomic Energy Minister Viktor Mikhailov, initiating MPC&A upgrades at five key sites in Russia. At the same time, the DOE and Gosatomnadzor (GAN), the Russian nuclear regulatory agency, signed an agreement for cooperation that focused on creating a standardized national system for safeguarding nuclear material and providing MPC&A upgrades at six additional sites in Russia.

In September, 1995, when President Clinton issued a Presidential Decision Directive on "U.S. Policy on Improving Nuclear Material Security in Russia and the Other Newly Independent States" (PDD/NSC-41). This directive established cooperation with Russia, the NIS, and the Baltic states to improve the security of nuclear materials as one of the nation's top national security objectives. Under this directive the DOE was assigned formal responsibility within the U.S. government for directing the MPC&A program.

D. Program Guidelines

The original mission of the MPC&A program is to reduce the threat of nuclear proliferation and nuclear terrorism by rapidly improving the security of all weapons-usable nuclear aterial in forms other than nuclear weapons in Russia, the NIS, and the Baltics.

Goals and Strategies

1. Reach Agreement for MPC&A Cooperation with all Sites in Russia, the NIS, and the Baltics Containing Weapons-Usable Nuclear Material in Forms Other than Nuclear Weapons.
2. Implement Systematic and Rapid MPC&A Upgrades at all Sites
3. Ensure Long-Term Effectiveness of Improved MPC&A Systems
4. Achieve Technical Integrity and Openness

Frequently Used MPC&A Upgrades

1. Physical protection systems: locks, fences, barriers, gates, badging systems, and interior and exterior sensors, including video cameras and motion detectors.

2. Alarm systems and computers to process data from sensors, such as closed-circuit television and communication systems to improve response to alarms.

3. Nuclear material detectors installed at pedestrian and vehicle portals which detect attempts to remove nuclear material, including hand-held detectors for random guard-force checking.

4. Tamper-indicating devices to prevent unauthorized removal, computerized MPC&A systems, including barcode systems, to track nuclear material inventory.

5. Perimeter clearing and structural improvements to improve physical protection.

6. Computerized material accounting systems to maintain physical inventory and non-destructive assay measurements.

Moving Away from Doomsday and Other Dangers*

Sam Nunn

Supported by the generosity of Ted Turner, and guided by a distinguished board that Ted and I co-chair, the Nuclear Threat Initiative is a new foundation dedicated to reducing the global threat from nuclear, biological and chemical weapons. Our job is to increase public awareness, encourage dialogue, catalyze action, and promote new thinking about these dangers in this country and abroad. It is this last point—the need to think anew—that I want to emphasize today.

Ten years ago, just after President Gorbachev was released from house arrest following the failed coup, a U.S. Senator on an official visit to Moscow met with him in his Kremlin office, and asked him directly if he had retained command and control of the Soviet nuclear forces during the coup attempt. President Gorbachev did not answer, and that was answer enough. I was that Senator.

The Soviet empire was coming apart. I was optimistic that this break up would expand freedom and reduce the risk of global war, but I left Moscow in the early fall of 1991 convinced that it would also present a whole new set of dangers. Over the next two months, I formed a partnership with Senator Dick Lugar, Senator Pete Domenici, Senator Carl Levin, Senator John Warner, Senator Jeff Bingaman and others to address these new threats to our security. In the ten years since, much has been done, but the dangers persist and in some cases have increased. Let's take a look at a few events.

- In 1994 in Prague, authorities confiscated 2.7 kilograms of extremely potent nuclear bomb-making material.
- In 1995, Russian early warning systems initially misinterpreted a peaceful U.S. research rocket launch from Norway, which activated

---

* Excerpt from remarks of Sen. Sam Nunn before the National Press Club, Washington, D.C., March 29, 2001.

President Yeltsin's nuclear briefcase, and set in motion Russian procedures for a nuclear response.

- In the spring of 1995, members of the Japanese cult Aum Shinrikyo launched a sarin gas attack on the Tokyo subway. Before their organization was broken up, they were actively recruiting Russian scientists and also were working to develop biological weapons and to obtain the Ebola virus.
- In the spring of 1998, India and Pakistan, two countries that have fought three recent wars, exploded nuclear tests within days of each other. Both nations now have nuclear weapons; neither has sophisticated warning or safety systems, and there is a continuing insurgency along their shared border.
- In 1998, an employee at a Russian nuclear weapons laboratory was arrested trying to sell nuclear weapons designs to agents of Iraq and Afghanistan.
- Throughout the 1990s, thousands of Russian weapons scientists saw their jobs cut or wages slashed, and thousands responsible for the security of nuclear, chemical, and biological weapons and materials went months without pay.
- During this period, Iranian intelligence officers began making recruiting trips to Russia, offering biological weapons scientists many times their pay to move to Iran.
- In 1999, terrorist Usama Bin Laden, said: "To seek to possess the weapons that could counter those of the infidels is a religious duty."
- In our new century, this increased interest in acquiring nuclear weapons is matched by increased access to information. Today anyone with a computer and a modem can find rudimentary instructions for building a nuclear weapon on the internet.

These are known events. The larger danger lies in what we don't know.

As we enter the second decade of the post-Cold War world, let me repeat a statement often made, but too often not heard. The most significant, clear and present danger to the national security of the United States is the threat posed by nuclear and other weapons of mass destruction. Nothing else comes close. The public perception of the threat is low; the reality of the threat is high. There is a dangerous gap between the threat and our response. To close this gap, we must make a fundamental shift in the way we think about nuclear weapons, the spread of weapons of mass destruction, and our national security.

As President Reagan's former Undersecretary of Defense Fred Ikle has recently observed, a man from Mars comparing the U.S. nuclear posture today with that at the height of the Cold War would find them essentially indistinguishable.

The old threats we faced during the Cold War—a Soviet nuclear strike or an invasion of Europe—were threats made dangerous by Soviet strength. The new threats we face today—eroded early warning and increased reliance on early launch, and increased reliance on tactical nuclear weapons—are threats made dangerous by Russia's weakness. And these threats go far beyond deployed nuclear forces. Much of Russia's nuclear, biological, and chemical weapons and materials are poorly secured; its weapons scientists and security personnel poorly paid. This, too, is a consequence of Russia's economic weakness, and it multiplies the chance that weapons of mass destruction will come into the hands of rogue states or terrorists.

Not only are the threats today different; the means to meet them are different. We addressed the Cold War's threats by confrontation with Moscow, and over the long term, we cannot rule out a possible return to this confrontation. But most of today's greatest threats we can address only in cooperation with Russia. This is the overarching present day reality of our relationship.

This is not to say that we must embrace Russia as a friend or an ally. That will depend on Russia's behavior, and we will certainly continue to have frictions, frustrations, and disagreements. This is to acknowledge, however, that in spite of and because of its economic weakness, Russia will be a major factor, for better or for worse, across most of the spectrum of actual and potential threats we face.

We have a vital national security interest not only in assuring strategic stability between our two countries, we also have a vital national security interest in working with Russia to make sure that weapons of mass destruction do not end up in the hands of those who would not hesitate to use them against America and our allies or against Russia.

To some extent, this is something both countries have recognized. In the past ten years, we worked with Russia to persuade Ukraine, Kazakhstan, and Belarus to give up the nuclear weapons they inherited from the Soviet Union. We have also helped the Russians secure their nuclear weapons and materials to prevent theft and accidents; helped them convert nuclear weapons facilities to civilian purposes; and helped them employ their weapons scientists in peaceful purposes. There is a long way to go to complete this mission. We have just started to work with Russia to make improvements in joint early warning communications, to reduce the chance of catastrophic error. These are important steps, but we need giant strides.

I am puzzled by recent rumors which indicate that budgets for these essential threat reduction programs may be seriously reduced. If true, this would be heading backward. No one knows how long the present window of opportunity will remain open.

More than 1,000 tons of highly enriched uranium, and at least 150 tons of weapons-grade plutonium, exist in the Russian weapons complex, enough to build at least 60,000 nuclear weapons. Many storage sites are poorly secured. Thousands of weapons scientists are still without a steady paycheck, and terrorist groups and rogue states are trying to exploit the situation.

No investment pays a higher dollar-for-dollar dividend in national security than investment in threat reduction. None. I welcome The President's review of these programs, and I believe that they can be better coordinated and made more effective. The Bush Administration also is undertaking reviews of the U.S. nuclear posture, missile defenses, and conventional forces. As they take on this challenge, I urge them to be willing to think anew without any undue homage to inherited presumptions.

Our task is formidable, and our approach must be comprehensive. We must address the threats of nuclear, biological, and chemical weapons and multiple delivery systems, update our approach to deterrence, get an accounting of the numbers and deployments of tactical nuclear weapons, reduce the risk of an accidental launch, cut the risk of a terrorist attack, counter the threat of a rogue nation attack, and limit the spread of weapons of mass destruction. We will not be successful unless we are able to work with nations whose cooperation is essential for effective defenses against these multiple dangers.

Some will say we will never be at zero risk. I agree, but that should not affect our direction and our purpose. I believe that we must move in this direction, not at the expense of our security, but on behalf of it. Let me be clear, I am not talking about the total elimination of all nuclear weapons, a goal that generates much skepticism and disagreement. I am talking about risk management and risk reduction, an objective on which there can and should be broad common ground. To move in this direction, however, we have to face some difficult but fundamental questions that have been deferred far too long. Let me conclude my remarks by asking a few of them.

If our objective is to help move Russian and U.S. fingers further from the nuclear trigger, we must ask: Are there changes that the U.S. and Russia can make in how we operate our forces that would give each President more nuclear decision-making time, expanding minutes to hours, then perhaps hours to days? Can we get our best thinkers, including our military experts, together to discuss what can be done to ease the trigger pressure on both sides?

This discussion could lead to force structure changes, deployment changes, alert changes or reductions in the number of weapons, or all of these. Difficult—yes—but these steps in the long run may be more important in reducing the risk of a catastrophe than the absolute number of weapons.

If our objective is to ensure that nuclear weapons can't be launched by accident, then we must ask:

- Can we strengthen and build on the early warning system cooperation we have just started with Russia?
- Can we assure that the United States and Russia can quickly and accurately identify a nuclear attack from a third party, so that a rogue state or terrorist group could not trigger a nuclear exchange between Russia and the United States?

And while we are trying to prevent accidents, why not look seriously at the possibility of both the United States and Russia installing destruct packages on nuclear missiles, so that both of our countries can destroy our own missile launched by accident, before it can destroy a city or start a war. We have these destruct devices on test missiles; why not nuclear missiles?

If our objective is to ensure that nuclear, biological, and chemical weapons and materials don't fall into the hands of rogue nations and terrorists, we must ask: Is this a priority or an afterthought? If it's an afterthought—after what? What comes before it? If it is a priority, is that reflected in our effort and investment? Are our allies in Asia and Europe doing their share? If not, why not?

Securing Russia's Nuclear Weapons, Materials and Expertise

Rose Gottemoeller*

Introduction

It has been more than a decade since the Berlin Wall fell, opening a new era in history. While the Soviet threat is gone, dangers arising from the global spread of nuclear, chemical and biological weapons, and missiles for their delivery, remain with us. As a nation, we may face no greater challenge than to prevent these weapons from falling into the hands of those who would use them against us or our allies. To address this problem, the Clinton Administration has put in place the Expanded Threat Reduction Initiative (ETRI), a robust multi-agency and multi- imensional nonproliferation agenda.

A key to ETRI's success is the strong partnership of the Departments of Energy, Defense, and State and the complementary nature of the nonproliferation activities we are pursuing in cooperation with Russia. Department of Defense programs to enhance the safety, security, control and accounting of nuclear weapons fit perfectly with our work to secure fissile materials and nuclear weapons expertise. Our cooperation to promote nuclear material control and protection in the Russian Navy is an example of this partnership. Also, the Department of Energy's "brain drain" prevention programs build on the efforts of the State Department-supported International Science and Technology Center to transition former Soviet weapons scientists to peaceful work.

---

* Deputy Administrator for Defense Nuclear Nonproliferation (Acting) U.S. Department of Energy. Excerpt from statement before the Subcommittee on Emerging Threats and Capabilities, Committee on Armed Services, United States Senate, March 6, 2000.

Securing Nuclear Weapons Expertise

Our flagship brain drain prevention programs are the Nuclear Cities Initiative (NCI) and the Initiatives for Proliferation Prevention (IPP). Secretary Richardson and Minister for Atomic Energy Adamov established the NCI in late 1998 to cooperate with Russian efforts to create peaceful, commercial jobs for displaced nuclear weapons scientists and engineers in Russia's ten closed cities. NCI is a new type of brain drain prevention program in that it is focused on nuclear workers who are slated to leave the nuclear weapons complex as facilities, and their jobs, are eliminated. Our initial focus has been on three municipalities: Sarov (Arzamas-16), Snezhinsk (Chelyabinsk-70), and Zheleznogorsk (Krasnoyarsk-26).

This program is on track. Since April 1999, when my Office was first authorized to spend funds, we have commissioned an Open Computing Center in Sarov, an International Business Development Center in Zheleznogorsk (with similar centers to open soon in Snezhinsk and Sarov), upgraded telecommunications systems in all three cities, and signed an agreement at the end of December 1999 with the European Bank for Reconstruction and Development to open small business loan centers in the three cities, providing access to millions of dollars in potential financing.

We have also initiated high-level strategic planning efforts with the Ministry for Atomic Energy to establish goals, costs, and timelines for workforce reduction and facility closures in each of the three cities. The Sarov strategic plan identifies the reduction of as many as 6,000 employees of the Institute of Experimental Physics, a nuclear weapons design institute. Through the plan, we have also agreed to the accelerated shutdown of weapons assembly and disassembly at the Avangard plant: weapons assembly will halt by the end of 2000; weapons disassembly will halt by the end of 2003.

Like NCI, DOE's IPP program works to secure weapons of mass destruction expertise and know how. Since the program's inception in 1994, more than 6,000 weapons scientists in Russia and the Newly Independent States have been supported through 400 non-military projects. The program partners Russian and NIS scientists with specialists at the Department's national laboratories, and concentrates aggressively on the commercialization of projects that are cost- shared with U.S. industry. Major corporations—such as United Technologies, DuPont, and American Home Products—are participating in this program.

Securing Fissile Materials

Another core DOE activity is our Materials Protection, Control and Accounting (MPC&A) program, an essential bulwark against the nuclear weapons aspirations of terrorists and countries of proliferation concern. Through the MPC&A program, we have built a legacy of trust, solid working relationships and cooperation with Russian agencies, institutes and scientists, facilitating our efforts to improve the security for fissile materials at highest risk throughout the Russian nuclear complex.

By the end of this calendar year, we will have completed security upgrades at 36 sites and improved protection for 400 metric tons of highly enriched uranium and plutonium. We are also nearing completion of a separate implementing agreement with the Russian Ministry of Defense that will advance our MPC&A work at a number of very sensitive Russian Navy sites. Over the last year, working in cooperation with the Department of Defense, we completed security upgrades at a highly enriched uranium storage facility in Murmansk, the home base of the Russian Navy's Northern Fleet. Our sustainability program will ensure that Russia has the infrastructure to maintain and operate MPC&A systems over the long-term.

We are making solid progress on the MPC&A front. Nevertheless, economic turmoil, growing concern that insiders might sell nuclear material on the black market, and our recognition that the size and geographic scope of Russia's nuclear complex is larger than our original estimates in 1994, all suggest that our nonproliferation work in this area is not yet finished.

MPC&A is our first line of defense. Our "second line of defense" program is working to help Russia prevent unauthorized nuclear trade at nine key border crossing points and transportation centers—many of them possible transit points to Iran or North Korea. By the end of calendar year 2000, we plan to place radiation detection equipment at all nine points. We are also developing a detection equipment training manual, which will guide the work of more than 30,000 front-line Russian customs officials. We have additional nuclear material security programs focused on MPC&A improvements in former Soviet states outside of Russia.

Fissile Materials Disposition

On the international front, we are continuing our efforts in partnership with Russia to demonstrate a number of plutonium disposition technologies, demonstrations that will accelerate Russia's ability to build the facilities needed to dispose of its own surplus plutonium.

Heu Transparency And Implementation

Our work with Russia to convert surplus highly enriched uranium from the Russian military stockpile into a non-weapon-usable form is also progressing well. The 1993 U.S.-Russia HEU Purchase Agreement—also known by the title "Megatons to Megawatts"—remains one of the more impressive nonproliferation achievements of the last decade. Through the end of calendar year 1999, more than 80 metric tons of weapons grade uranium—enough material for 3,200 weapons—had been removed from the Russian military program under this Agreement and converted to low enriched uranium for commercial sale. Already, Russia has received close to $1.5 billion as compensation for converted HEU.

Building For Future Success

The President's FY 2001 budget request for the Expanded Threat Reduction Initiative included a proposed $100 million for a Department of Energy nonproliferation program with Russia. Activities included in this new program will supplement existing efforts to reduce proliferation dangers in the Russian military nuclear complex, while focusing attention on an area that heretofore has not been addressed, that is, separated plutonium produced in Russia's civil nuclear sector. This effort should be viewed in the context of our broader efforts with Russia to end the production of fissile materials and reduce existing stockpiles, an effort that includes, among others, the Plutonium Disposition program, the HEU Purchase Agreement, and the Plutonium Production Reactor Agreement.

VI.
Intelligence and Technology

Good Intelligence Is The Best Weapon Against International Terrorism

Bremer Commission Report*

Obtaining information about the identity, goals, plans, and vulnerabilities of terrorists is extremely difficult. Yet, no other single policy effort is more important for preventing, preempting, and responding to attacks.

Eliminate Barriers to Aggressive Collection of Information on Terrorists

Complex bureaucratic procedures now in place send an unmistakable message to Central Intelligence Agency (CIA) officers in the field that recruiting clandestine sources of terrorist information is encouraged in theory but discouraged in practice.

CIA has always had a process for assessing a potential informant's reliability, access, and value. However, the CIA issued new guidelines in1995 in response to concern about alleged serious acts of violence by Agency sources. The guidelines set up complex procedures for seeking approval to recruit informants who may have been involved in human rights violations. In practice, these procedures have deterred and delayed vigorous efforts to recruit potentially useful informants. The CIA has created a climate that is overly risk averse. This has inhibited the recruitment of essential, if sometimes unsavory, terrorist informants and forced the United States to rely too heavily on foreign intelligence services. The adoption of the guidelines contributed to a marked decline in Agency morale unparalleled since the 1970s, and a significant number of case officers retired early or resigned.

Recommendations:

   o The Director of Central Intelligence should make it clear to the Central Intelligence Agency that the aggressive recruitment of human

---

* From "Countering The Changing Threat Of International Terrorism," Report of the National Commission on Terrorism (pursuant to Public Law 277, 105th Congress), Amb. L. Paul Bremer III, Chairman, June 5, 2000. Commissioners: L. Paul Bremer III, Maurice Sonnenberg, Richard K. Betts, Wayne A. Downing, Jane Harman, Fred C. Iklé, Juliette N. Kayyem, John F. Lewis, Jr., R. James Woolsey.

intelligence sources on terrorism is one of the intelligence community's highest priorities.

o The Director of Central Intelligence should issue a directive that the 1995 guidelines will no longer apply to recruiting terrorist informants. That directive should notify officers in the field that the pre-existing process of assessing such informants will apply.

The Federal Bureau of Investigation (FBI), which is responsible for investigating terrorism in the United States, also suffers from bureaucratic and cultural obstacles to obtaining terrorism information.

The World Trade Center bombers and the foreign nationals arrested before the millennium sought to inflict mass casualties on the American people. These incidents highlight the importance of ensuring that the FBI's investigations of international terrorism are as vigorous as the Constitution allows.

The FBI's terrorism investigations are governed by two sets of Attorney General guidelines. The guidelines for Foreign Intelligence Collection and Foreign Counterintelligence Investigations (FI guidelines), which are classified, cover the FBI's investigations of international terrorism, defined as terrorism occurring outside the United States or transcending national boundaries. Domestic terrorism is governed by the Attorney General guidelines on General Crimes, Racketeering Enterprise and Domestic Security/Terrorism Investigations (domestic guidelines). The domestic guidelines would apply, for example, to an investigation of a foreign terrorist group's activities in the United States if the FBI does not yet have information to make the international connection required for the Fl guidelines.

Recommendation:
o The Attorney General and the Director of the Federal Bureau of Investigation should develop guidance to clarify the application of both sets of guidelines. This guidance should specify what facts and circumstances merit the opening of a preliminary inquiry or full investigation and should direct agents in the field to investigate terrorist activity vigorously, using the full extent of their authority.

The Department of Justice applies the statute governing electronic surveillance and physical searches of international terrorists in a cumbersome and overly cautious manner. [Commissioner Kayyem did not concur with the content of this section.]

Pursuant to the Foreign Intelligence Surveillance Act (FISA), the FBI can obtain a court order for electronic surveillance and physical searches of foreign powers, including groups engaged in international terrorism, and agents of foreign powers.

Applications from the FBI for FISA orders are first approved by the Office of Intelligence Policy and Review (OIPR) in the Department of Justice before being presented to a judge of the FISA Court for approval. OIPR has not traditionally viewed its role as assisting the FBI to meet the standards for FISA applications in the same way that the Criminal Division of DoJ assists the FBI investigators to meet the standards for a wiretap. Also, OIPR does not generally consider the past activities of the surveillance target relevant in determining whether the FISA probable cause test is met.

During the period leading up to the millennium, the FISA application process was streamlined. Without lowering the FISA standards, applications were submitted to the FISA Court by DoJ promptly and with enough information to establish probable cause.

Recommendations:
o   The Attorney General should direct that the Office of Intelligence Policy and Review not require information in excess of that actually mandated by the probable cause standard in the Foreign Intelligence Surveillance Act statute.
o   To ensure timely review of the Foreign Intelligence Surveillance Act applications, the Attorney General should substantially expand the Office of Intelligence Policy and Review staff and direct it to cooperate with the Federal Bureau of Investigation.

Promote the Flow of Terrorism Information From Law Enforcement to Policymakers and Analysts

The law enforcement community is neither fully exploiting the growing amount of information it collects during the course of terrorism investigations nor distributing that information effectively to analysts and policymakers.

Recommendations:
o   The Director of the Federal Bureau of Investigation should establish and equip a dedicated staff of reports officers to develop terrorism and foreign intelligence information obtained at field offices and head-

quarters for prompt dissemination to other agencies, especially those within the intelligence community, while protecting privacy and pending criminal cases.

Intelligence and the Changing Face of Terrorism

Anthony H. Cordesman*

"Terrorism" is a topic that arouses so much fear and revulsion that there is a natural tendency to "cry wolf," and to confuse the potential threat with one that is actually occurring. Similarly, any discussion of the new threats posed by weapons of mass destruction and information warfare involves threats that are so serious that there is an equal tendency to respond like Chicken Little and worry that the sky is falling.

The Changing Face of Terrorism and Technology

In saying this, I am all too well aware that no victim of terrorism, or their loved ones, are going to be consoled by the fact that they are a relatively small statistic. The political symbolism of successful terrorist attacks is also often far greater than the casualties, and even an empty threat can help to undermine the fabric of social trust upon which our democracy is based.

Equally important, the fact we have not yet encountered an attack in the US as serious as the strikes on our Embassies in Kenya and Tanzania, or as potentially threatening as Aum Shinrikyo, is in no way a guarantee for the future. Rather than exaggerate current threats, we need to be very conscious of the fact that the nature and seriousness of the threat can change suddenly and with little warning.

We need to bridge the gap between the way in which the US government prepares for asymmetric warfare and to deal with the threat of terrorism—not only in terms of intelligence analysis, but our defense and response

---

* Arleigh A. Burke Chair in Strategy, Center for Strategic and International Studies, Washington, D.C. Excerpt from "The Changing Face of Terrorism and Technology, and the Challenge of Asymmetric Warfare," testimony before the Senate Judiciary Subcommittee on Technology, Terrorism, and Government Information, March 27, 2001.

planning for Homeland Defense. We also must include intelligence analysis of capabilities and not just intentions. History shows us that the fact that foreign countries and leaders are deterred, or show restraint today, is no guarantee they will behave the same way under crisis conditions.

We need to ensure the effective fusion of intelligence community efforts, military planning, and civil defense and response planning. We should not leave any gap where the Department of Defense seriously plans for large-scale nuclear and biological attacks and civil Departments and Agencies focus on relatively low-level conventional explosives and limited chemical attacks.

We need to be equally careful not to compartment our analysis of information warfare so that the Department worries about true information warfare while civil departments and agencies worry about hacking and cracking at much lower levels of threat.

Finally, we need to consider the full implications of our call for missile defense, and of our counterproliferation activities. The more we succeed in blocking overt threats, the more we will drive states towards finding alternative means of attack. It makes little sense to close the barn door and leave the windows open.

We need to reexamine the problem of vulnerability. We cannot hope to accurate predict our attacker or their means of attack, but we can do much to improve our analysis of vulnerability and shape our intelligence and planning effort around the need to detect threats to our greatest vulnerabilities. To be specific, there are several areas of vulnerability that need special attention:

o   *We need to conduct and systematically update our analysis of the vulnerability of our critical infrastructure*, including financial systems, information systems, communications systems, utilities, and transportation nets and make sure our intelligence can focus on potential threats.

o   *We need to reexamine our vulnerability to the chemical threat* in the light of fourth generation weapons, and the growing ease with which states, extremists, and terrorists can obtain them.

o   *We need to rethink the risk of biological attack:* We need to look beyond the risk of the limited use of crude, long-known weapons and toxins, and assess the extent to which genetic weapons are increasing our vulnerabilities. We also need to look beyond single agent non-infectious attacks on human beings, and consider multiple agent attacks, infectious attacks, and/or attacks on our agriculture.

o *We need to reconsider the cumulative risk of covert or terrorist nuclear attack:* It still seems unlikely that any state or terrorist movement could both acquire a nuclear device in the near future, and be willing to take the risk of using it. The cumulative risk over time, however, is sufficiently great to justify more analysis of our key vulnerabilities.

It is important to note that the US intelligence community and Department of Defense is already addressing many of these issues, as is the National Security Council and a broader federal Homeland defense effort. At the same time, these are all areas where Congressional oversight can play a major role in assessing the quality of the intelligence effort and the broader effort within the Executive Branch.

Other Problems in Intelligence

Let me make several comments focused on the problem of intelligence coverage of terrorism and asymmetric warfare. There are some things that never seem to change:

- **It is far easier to call for strategic warning than to get it, or get policymakers to act on it of they do receive it.** We can always improve our analysis of warning indicators. In fact, the intelligence community does this all the time. We cannot, however, count on any method of analysis sorting through the constant "noise level" in these indicators and providing reliable probability analysis or warning. Furthermore, we cannot count on policymakers reacting.

  We should improve our analysis, but no system of warning, defense, and response can *rely* on strategic warning. Moreover, it is my impression that even when the intelligence community does make improvements, decision-makers choose to ignore unpopular or expensive warning or demand that the community free them from the burden of ambiguity and uncertainty.

  It is always easy for decision-makers to demand prophecy and attack intelligence analysis when they don't get it. This may explain why there are so many calls for improved strategic warning and so few calls for improved decision-maker response.

- **It is far easier to call for better HUMINT than it is to get it.** I have listened to three decades of calls for improved human intelligence. In practice, however, it remains as underfunded as ever, and partly because it is so difficult to make cost-effective investments and to be sure they pay off. Far too often, successes are matters of chance and not of the scale of effort.

Yes, we should improve HUMINT—where we can show there is a feasible plan and a cost-effective path for success. However, calling for improved HUMINT all too often is both a confession of the severe limits of National Technical Means and a substitute for serious planning and effort.

- **New intelligence toys are not new systems, and systems always have limitations.** The other side of this coin is that we probably face growing limitations in our imagery and signals intelligence capabilities in many of the areas that affect our vulnerability to asymmetric warfare and terrorism. These are not a problem that should be addressed in open testimony, nor can I claim that my background in these issues is up-to-date. However, it is far from clear that some of the extremely expensive improvements we plan in National Technical Means will really pay off in the areas we are discussing today, or that some of the new tactical detectors and sensors being developed are integrated into effective systems. There may well be a need for independent net intelligence assessment of our probable future capabilities in these areas.

- **We need more focus on weaponization, weapons effects, and different kinds of vulnerability.** Proliferation and changes in information warfare are creating major new challenges in how the community should assess the weapons available to state and extremist actors. This is particularly true of biotechnology and information warfare, but it also involves the risk of "dirty," unsafe, and unpredictable nuclear weapons. Most weapons effects analysis is badly dated, and related to use against military targets. Weaponization analysis often does not address the acute uncertainty that may occur in weapons effects, and most vulnerability analysis is now dated. The technical issues of what attackers can really do, the problem intelligence may face in characterizing their resources, and the risk of combinations of new methods of attack—combining information systems and CBRN attacks, cocktails of biological weapons, etc. needs more attention.

- **We need an effective bridge between foreign intelligence and law enforcement that responds to the scale of the emergency.** We now have a wide range of barriers between foreign intelligence collection, surveillance of US citizens and activities within the US, military operations, and law enforcement activities. In general, these involve useful and necessary protections of American civil liberties. If, however, the threat rises to the level of a tangible risk an attack may use effective biological weapons, use nuclear weapons, or cripple our critical infrastructure, we need some way to react to a true national emergency that eliminates as many of these barriers as possible, and which does so at the state and local level and not just the federal one. We have long talked about the need for the "fusion" of intelligence and operations in warfighting. We may well face a similar need in Homeland defense, and the "fusion" of foreign intelligence and law enforcement activity will be critical.

Whenever new threats emerge, there is a natural tendency to call for new organizations, czars, and interagency structures. It is far easier to say that a new organization is needed than to get into the nitty gritty of actually having to improve existing capabilities or develop new ones. A set of problems involving this many uncertainties and new skills may or may not require new federal organizations, and new organizations within the intelligence community.

Combating Terrorism: Coordination of Non-Medical R&D Programs

Page Stoutland*

The Energy Department's Chemical and Biological Nonproliferation Program (CBNP) was initiated in FY 1997 in response to the Defense Against Weapons of Mass Destruction Act ("Nunn-Lugar-Domenici"). The mission of the CBNP is to develop, demonstrate, and deliver systems and the supporting technologies that will lead to major improvements in the U.S. capability to prepare for and respond to chemical or biological attacks. The program builds upon existing DOE capabilities and is focused on developing detection and response systems to improve our domestic preparedness. In selected areas we also support the needs of the Defense and Intelligence Communities. Our FY 2000 budget is $40.0 million; a $21.5 million increase over the FY 1999 budget. Our request for FY 2001 is $42 million.

DOE's and the national laboratories' involvement in this area builds upon a long history of supporting nonproliferation and national security policy. As part of its primary nuclear science and technology mission, DOE has developed substantial capabilities in areas that are directly related to countering the chemical and biological threat. These capabilities, in areas such as genomic sequencing, development of new DNA-based diagnostics, and advanced modeling and simulation, and the linking of these capabilities with our expertise in nonproliferation and national security, form the basis for DOE's role in combating chemical and biological threats. In addition to DOE-supported efforts, our national laboratories conduct over $50 million per year in chemical and biological defense R&D for other government agencies in direct support of their missions.

* Dr. Stoutland is Director, Chemical and Biological Nonproliferation Program Office of Defense Nuclear Nonproliferation, National Nuclear Security Administration (NNSA), U.S. Department of Energy. Excerpt from statement before House Committee on Government Reform, Subcommittee on National Security, Veterans Affairs, and International Relations, March 22, 2000.

Technology plays a critical role in defending the U.S. population against attacks with chemical and biological weapons. These emerging threats, whether of domestic or foreign origin, are rooted in science and technology and any effective response must draw on similar expertise. Technology, however, is only one dimension of the complex system of people, organizations and policies, operational procedures, physical resources, and information flow that comprises a preparedness and response capability. In this context, it is important to recognize the complex issues associated with protecting civilians from chemical or biological attacks that are distinct from the issues the military faces on the battlefield. Technology must be developed with these factors in mind to effectively anticipate and meet operational needs..

Requirements

In a general sense, the CBNP R&D investments are guided by a process that considers the threat and the related vulnerabilities, and the benefit that a particular technology or system would have were it to be developed. We have undertaken a number of specific activities to identify the highest impact areas for R&D that build upon threat characterization and recommendations regarding specific equipment requirements.

Characterizing the threat environment is important for guiding our R&D activities. DOE does not conduct threat assessments in the chemical and biological areas. Instead, we rely on the FBI, the Defense and Intelligence Communities and public health assessments as appropriate. These assessments, which for example, consider the agents most likely to be used, are then used to guide our R&D activities. Implicit in this process is the recognition of the uncertainties inherent in estimating the nature and magnitude of the threat, and that these uncertainties must be factored into our planning.

Threat assessments as well as other factors are necessary for the formation of equipment and operational needs. These needs will ultimately be the result of a complex process that involves policy makers, technologists, first responders, the medical community, and others. There are no formal requirements for countering the domestic chemical and biological threat. This is not because we or others have not considered the issue, but rather is representative of the challenges implicit in arriving at a set of needs or requirements that would serve a diverse set of users and act as meaningful targets for R&D programs. Lists of needs must be translated into the highest priority areas for R&D if they are to usefully guide our research activities.

It is useful to contrast this situation with that of the military's requirements process. The military is a vertically integrated organization, with researchers directly supporting users all of whom ultimately report to the Secretary of Defense. The civilian situation is much more complex as there are many users in many different organizations with very different needs. In addition, the science and technology infrastructures and expertise often reside in organizations different from those with the operational responsibilities.

Our analytical studies program component directly contributes to the development of an overall U.S. strategy to counter the CB threat. Presently, within this program element we are conducting a high-level study we call the Defense of Cities Study that aims to develop an analytical framework by which to compare the various chemical and biological defense options available to policy makers.

Recent Highlights

A central part of the CBNP is the development of detection systems. Improved detection capabilities are critical—domestically, even small quantities of chemical or biological agents can have severe effects, and false alarms can not be tolerated. The DOE program is developing a suite of detection systems. One, a chemical and biological toxin detector will be a hand-held unit able to rapidly detect many different toxic agents with a false alarm rate of less than 1 in 10,000 measurements. This detector is possible because of recent advances in micro-machining technologies and in the fabrication of miniature lasers and optical components. This year we will demonstrate a hand-held prototype in the laboratory—in two years it will be demonstrated in a rugged field version.

We are building other detectors for the very different application of detecting biological pathogens such as anthrax. This year one of our laboratories is building half a dozen hand-held biodetectors which will be given to first responders and others for "beta testing" in the field. If successful, we, in conjunction with commercial partners, will build many more.

Domestic Demonstration and Application Programs (DDAPs)

The most important component of the CBNP for understanding user needs is the demonstration programs, or DDAPs, which are designed to field and demonstrate complete prototype systems that use technology developed within the CBNP or elsewhere. We work closely with users who host the demonstration, and in an iterative way determine their needs. It is important to emphasize here the important difference between a stated need for a particular piece of hardware, and the requirement for a system with particular performance specifications.

Two programs are currently underway: PROTECT: Program for Response Options and Technology Enhancements for Chemical/Biological Terrorism and BASIS: Biological Aerosol Sentry and Information System. Both focus on the demonstration of early detection, identification, and warning (DI&W) systems. In PROTECT we are working closely with the Department of Transportation and a number of major U.S. subway systems to examine systematically and rigorously the vulnerability of subway systems to chemical or biological attack. Using computer models we can estimate not only what the effects of an attack might be, but how to most effectively respond to them by, for example, changing the air flow in the subway system. Our scientists have estimated that, if one can respond within minutes with appropriate actions (using existing equipment), over 1800 lives would be saved in a small-scale sarin nerve gas attack, when compared to how we are able to respond today. The reduction in potential casualties could be 10 to 100 times greater in the case of a deadlier biological agent such as anthrax.

Mitigating actions depend critically upon prompt detection of the attack. We are now aggressively moving forward both in testing chemical detectors, and in improving the computer models and related information systems that are essential to enable the rapid decisions necessary to realize these goals. Next year a demonstration of a complete system will take place involving one subway station, and the following year a network of five stations will be demonstrated.

Coordination

The CBNP is designed to complement other U.S. Government programs, while relying on the unique capabilities of the DOE laboratories. As part of the coordination process, we either participate directly or follow the status of the Technical Support Working Group (TSWG), the National Defense Preparedness Office (NDPO), and the NSC-led Weapons of Mass Destruction Preparedness Group (WMDP) efforts. Within the WMDP exists an R&D subgroup chaired by the White House Office of Science and Technology Policy, which coordinates R&D that addresses the domestic chemical and biological threat, and facilitates the identification of needs. In addition to these groups we participate in a number of formal coordination mechanisms with the Defense and Intelligence Communities such as the Counterproliferation Program Review Committee (CPRC). Importantly, within the last year the CPRC has formed a Chemical and Biological Defense Focus Group to specifically help coordination in the chemical and biological area. Informal coordination occurs routinely via information exchanges between the CBNP and the DoD, HHS, DOJ, and other agencies. We also sponsor an annual meeting to review the status of the DOE program.

Detection and warning systems enable prompt responses that can limit exposures to lethal agents and provide timely information to the medical community, ultimately saving lives and dollars.

Our program builds upon existing capabilities of the DOE national laboratories, and has begun to reach out to the industrial and academic communities. The program emphasizes the near-term fielding of detection and warning systems to protect key events and facilities, while developing more robust capabilities for the longer term.

Forensic Science Center*
Lawrence Livermore National Laboratory

The Forensic Science Center at Lawrence Livermore National Laboratory delivers a full range of forensic science capabilities to detect terrorism and illegal activities. The Center houses a variety of state-of-the-art analytical tools ranging from gas chromatograph–mass spectrometers (GC–MS) to ultratrace chemical and DNA techniques. The Center's multidisciplinary staff provides expertise in organic and inorganic analytical chemistry, nuclear science, biochemistry, and genetics useful for supporting law enforcement and for verifying compliance with international treaties and agreements.

Identifying chemical samples

Unknown samples arrive at the Center in many different forms and states of stabilization. Some are water, vegetation, or soil samples; others are "wipes" of substances that may be related to clandestine weapons-production activities. The following new technologies are helping us precisely analyze and interpret such samples accurately.

• A portable chemistry analyzer known as an ion cyclotron resonance mass spectrometer (ICR-MS) can be configured to detect specific chemicals at very low levels of concentration. The low power requirements of the ICR-MS and its simple electronic circuitry, together with the compactness of the spectrometer, the vacuum system, and the computer, permit a small package no larger than a 3-lb coffee can. We are also developing a version that can be left unattended in the field to perform diagnostic chemical analyses.

• A miniature GC–MS, completely self-contained in a 28-kg (~61-lb) suitcase-sized package, can detect ultratrace (microgram or less) quantities of narcotics and compounds related to chemical-warfare agents, including their precursors and decomposition products. This instrumentation is ideally suited to support most nonproliferation and law enforcement efforts and investigations related to chemical pollutants released into the environment. The miniature GC–MS is now carried inside a suitcase, and we are working to reduce its size further so that it can fit into a briefcase.

---

* Source: Lawrence Livermore National Laboratory fact sheets.

- A new ion storage-time-of-flight (IS/TOF) mass allows extremely low levels (a few parts per trillion) of chemicals in air to be collected and detected very rapidly. This new instrument is unique in that it can acquire data on the order of thousands of spectra per second, making it suitable for high-speed aircraft sampling of air samples. Potential applications include identifying hazardous and chemical spills, monitoring industrial stacks and materials for volatile compounds, detecting concealed contraband, and surveying the environment. This instrument is particularly useful for sampling a released plume of smoke or airborne chemical that is only available for an instant of time.

- An imaging laser-ablation mass spectrometer, combining three technologies—an ion trap mass spectrometer for analysis, a high-powered microscope for viewing, and a laser for ionizing samples—into a single system entirely new for forensic analysis.

Sampling material is placed on the tip of a probe that is inserted into the source region of an ion trap mass spectrometer. With a microscope outside the vacuum chamber, the sampling material is viewed from above at 250x magnification. A laser beam is then directed at precisely the 10- to 50-micrometer spot on the probe tip from which the sample's mass spectral data is desired. The intensity of the laser beam can be adjusted to instantaneously vaporize more or less sampling material, depending on the size of the sample. The laser ionizes the material, and the mass spectrometer sorts these fragments according to their molecular weights. Once sorted, each chemical component produces a characteristic mass spectral fragmentation pattern that is used by the operator to identify the entire sample.

Chemical and Toxin Detection

John Vitko*

The problem with the terrorist threat in the chemical area is that it it's very broad. I have a little concern about the focus on anthrax and plague and smallpox. We may do ourselves, the community, and the nation a disservice in thinking of terrorist threats only in terms of those instead of the broad range of materials that a terrorist might choose because of factors like availability, familiarity, known effects, etc. I think we need a system that covers a broad range of chemical threats, running from toxic industrial materials through chemical agents, through biotoxins, to pathogens.

There are several parameters that affect how you think about these in terms of detection systems. One is their relative toxicity. If you normalize to sarin as one, most toxic industrial materials are one tenth to one hundred times as potent, i.e. they are significantly weaker. Biotoxins though are getting the name of super poisons and are tens to thousands of times more potent with botulinum being the most toxic poison known to man. Lethality is one key parameter, the other key parameter is the time to effect. With a chemical agent attack, people are going to be affected promptly. When the first responders arrive at the scene, people will already be ill and the diagnosis of the agent will be based less on any detector reading, and more on the exhibited symptoms of the individual. But that's not the case if you're dealing with toxins, where time to effect can be hours to days. Thus toxins fall in between the case of chemical agents where you have immediate knowledge and pathogens where you might not be aware of an 'attack' until several days after the event. So we need to look at the range of these.

Appropriately, we focus on one of three key scenarios that the National Research Council (NRC) considered in their study on bioterrorism and the medical response, covert biological attack. We don't know it occurred, and

---

* Dr. Vitko is at the Sandia National Laboratory. Excerpt from presentation to RAND Symposium, "Bioterrorism: Homeland Defense: The Next Steps," February 8-10 2000, Santa Monica, CA.

we can only tell when it has happened by the symptoms the people are reporting. Importantly, there are two other scenarios we should consider. The first is a high value situation—e.g., a subway or a government building—where we continuously want to monitor. The requirement for continuous operations and extremely low false positives puts some very different and demanding requirements on the detection system.

The second scenario is the typical HAZMAT scenario. Here if it's chemical attack we'll likely be able to tell what the agent is by the medical symptoms. The detection system impact will be mainly in assessing secondary contamination to both the first responder and the medical community. It turns out that without accurate knowledge of the agent and its concentration, first responders must wear self-contained breathing apparatus, which slows and limits their access to the scene and to the treatment of injured parties. If first responders had sensors that were timely and sensitive they might in fact be freed from that burden and be able to do a lot more than is currently possible. Different scenarios that have different detection requirements.

In terms of false alarms, you are not so concerned about a false positive. What you are concerned about is a false negative, where the environment is unsafe for the responder to unsuit, unmask, do whatever, and then act. As to detection sensitivities, a simple calculation gives some of the numbers involved. The "LCt 50" for sarin is 100 milligrams per meter cubed in a minute (the product of the aerosol concentration and exposure time that is lethal to 50 percent of a group at an assumed breathing rate). For a release of one kilogram of sarin in a large building, 100 meters by 100 meters by 10 meters, at 100% efficienct uniform dispersal, the average concentration is 10 milligrams per cubic meter, so one can get a LCt 50 exposure in ten minutes.

But the level that of real concern to the HAZMAT responder is the permissible exposure level for workers on an 8-hour basis. These are what OSHA and are several orders of magnitude more stringent. When multiplied by the "protective factor" on the protective gear, this tells you whether you need to have a self contained breathing apparatus in responding . So it's in this domain where the sensitivity starts getting interesting. You see quantitatively what a kilogram of sarin can do, and then by scaling you can determine what super toxins that tend to be 1000 times more potent.

So what are the tools we currently have for chemical agent and bio toxin detection? In smaller towns, there is still typical HAZMAT equipment where you're dealing with pH papers and with combustible gas meters that don't help you a lot in chem-bio scenarios. For larger cities, like Los Angeles, the equipment is largely borrowed from the DoD. Representative examples include the chemical agent monitor or CAM, which is an ion mobility spectrometer that measures the mass and the charge of the agent you are detecting. The CAM provides a qualitative indication of whether you have a nerve or other chemical agent present. It is used to check whether contamination is present on equipment and people. If you want to unmask, you need a more sensitive detector such as the M256A1 kit. This uses wet chemistry tests, exposing a filter paper that is coated with an enzyme for ten minutes. It will tell you whether you have an agent present or not with much greater sensitivity than the CAM. This is a slow process. It's a 15-minute test. And yet, these sensitivities are about 500 times above the permissible exposure level and about 10 times above what we can allow with the kind of protective factors we now have on personal protective equipment.

Most of the DoD's existing detection equipment is for chemical agent detection. When it comes to detecting biotoxins, the primary existing field method is based on immunoassays, in which antibodies bind to the toxin and induce an observable color change.

Having briefly reviewed the existing DoD chem-bio detection equipment that might be suitable for a first responder, let's now look at some of the systems currently under development or in R & D. The joint services (Army, Air Force, Navy, Marines) are developing the joint chemical agent detector or JCAD. JCAD is the first DoD chemical agent detector to use surface acoustic wave (SAW) detectors. SAWs are tiny vibrating crystals, whose frequency shifts when a small amount of chemical agent absorbs to their surface. It's designed in a way that it should have fewer false alarms, than an ion mobility spectrometer which can be subject to interferants such as perfume, exhaust, paint, and after-shave lotion, interferants you might encounter in a normal enclosed space that you wouldn't necessarily encounter on a battlefield. JCAD is scheduled to be available in the next 3-4 years and will be mass-produced for the military so it should come out as a relatively low cost unit that's deployable.

Shifting our attention to biotoxins, there are several advanced antibody-based technologies under development. I will highlight the work from the Naval Research Laboratory. The current emphasis in antibody based detection is to move from single assays which detect a single agent to multiplexed assays which can detect a range of agents. A coverplate contains fluid transport channels which run at right angles to the antibody stripes. You place a drop of the sample on the microscope slide. It migrates down the channels and where it crosses an antibody to the toxin it contains, you get a hit—e.g., ricin, SEB, botulinum.

Sandia National Laboratories and Oakridge National Laboratory are developing a hand held unit that detects both chemical agents and bio toxins, and has the potential for extensibility to viruses and bacteria. Basically what

204 • Super Terrorism

it does is take advantage of a lot of new small detector, small separation technologies. It separates a complex mixture, either gas phase or liquid phase, into the separate chemical compounds that make up that mixture. Then in the case of gas phase samples, it uses surface acoustic wave devices to detect and weigh the individual compounds. In the case of liquid phase samples, it uses a tiny laser diode to excite a fluorescent 'tag' on the compound, thereby providing ultra sensitive detection. You don't have to know in advance what it is that you're detecting. It sorts them out from each other and it sorts them out from the interferents you have. So if you have smokes, perfumes, dyes, aftershave lotions, paint exhaust, subway goop, whatever it is, it sorts it out. Advances in miniaturization will soon allow you to do multiple independent separations in a small hand-held unit in under 5 minutes.

Current chemical and biotoxin detectors are largely derived from military applications and have a number of significant limitations when applied to first responder situations. Fortunately, there are technologies now under development that address a number of these limitations in that they deal with a much broader range of agents, they have improved sensitivity, and they have the kinds of low false alarm rates that you need for facility monitoring. Importantly, they may also provide the sensitivity to know when you need personal protection equipment.

Advanced Bio Countermeasures at DARPA

Larry Dubois*

The program at DARPA in the development of technologies to counter the threat of biological warfare spends about a $100 million annually. I would like to a couple of examples of the technologies that we are developing and getting out into the field.

If you look at the spectrum of biological warfare and what needs to be done to defend against it, you see a time line. Before a viral event, we have to worry about trying to prevent it and the proliferation of biological agents. Then after the event, we need some sort of a sensor to detect the form, we need to protect towns, deal with consequence management issues, and finally be able to diagnose the exposure and treat it and ultimately to decontaminate the area. This is a very broad spectrum, and each item points to a technological solution or technological development that can enhance our ability to respond.

DARPA, within the Department of Defense, is geared towards looking into the future and taking potentially high risk solutions to problems. We've put together a fairly extensive program really to thwart the use of biological warfare agents. This is for both military and terrorist components.

We define biological warfare agents broadly. We have the traditional bacterial and viral threats, but they also include bioengineered threats, which is a real problem we're going to have to deal with in the future; as well as toxins. There are four major thrusts within our program.

The first is pathogen countermeasures, primarily developing therapeutics to deal with the problem and advanced diagnostics, to tell us whether people have been exposed to biological warfare agents or whether they hap-

---

*Dr. Dubois is Director of the Defense Sciences Office in the Defense Advanced Research Project Agency (DARPA). Excerpt from presentation to seminar on "Emerging Threats Of Biological Terrorism: Recent Developments," Potomac Institute for Policy Studies, Arlington, VA, June, 16, 1998.

pen to have the flu. We have a fairly extensive program in sensors, and finally one in consequence management. And the two that I will focus on are the areas of pathogen countermeasures and sensor development.

Our medical countermeasure program has several different aspects to it from immunization to antibacterials, antivirals, and antitoxins. It's a three-pronged attack on the problem. The first is really to defeat the pathogen's ability to enter the body and reach target tissues.

We're also still looking at targeting common methods of pathogenesis. The reason for that is the following: There are dozens, some people would say hundreds, of different potential agents. If you throw in all of the bioengineered threats, there are literally an innumerable amount of potential agent threats we have to deal with. If you have to deal with an individual therapeutic or individual vaccine for every single one of those threats, it would be an impractical amount of work. So we're trying to look at common tableaus. Are there ways of developing therapeutics that attack all classes of pathogens?

Finally, we're interested in modulating humans' own biological response to the presence of pathogens. In many cases, what happens is our human body kills our own cells while responding to the presence of a pathogen, as opposed to the pathogen itself actually killing us. Let me give you a couple of examples of the kind of far-reaching technological advances we're looking at. First is the development of modified red blood cells, and the idea is the following: We have lots of red blood cells circulating through our system constantly and clearly performing very, very useful functions, but most of the surface of the red blood cell isn't being used for much. So one of the projects that we have going with the University of Virginia is to modify the surface of a relatively small number of these red blood cells by attaching a heteropolymer.

This heteropolymer has two different linker groups on either end of it. One is a linker that bonds specifically to the red blood cell, and the other linker group is one that bonds to a specific target pathogen. What happens is you can inject this heteropolymer into the bloodstream. A simple shot will do, either pre-exposure or post-exposure.

The antibody on the surface of this heteropolymer can bind very tightly to the pathogen, and as the red blood cells circulate throughout the body, the target pathogen is destroyed in the liver and the spleen. What's been demonstrated is a million-fold reduction in the amount of virus in the bloodstream in an hour. These heteropolymers that are bound to the red blood cells are stable for over seven days, and as I said , you can either give them pre-exposure or post-exposure.

The studies to date have worked on inactivated species, things like Ebola, Marburg, dengue, viruses. We've started the work now, and there are a lot of agents being pursued in collaboration with the drugs at USAMRIID, and the work that's discussed here has been done in nonhuman primates. So we're very, very close to taking this technology and transitioning it out and starting to look at real species and then ultimately in human clinical trials. So that's one example of the kinds of things that we're doing that's really far-reaching, actually to use your blood cells to scrub out infection.

Another area we're working on could be used against agents that are within the human body. It's actually like liposomes, like a soap, if you will, that does a superb job of actually killing a wide variety of agents. It's harmless to plants and animals and humans, but it does a great job on pathogens. A very dilute solution of this particular liposome or soap solution will kill 99 plus percent of various spores in just a few hours. As I said, it can be used internally or externally.

But ideally what we'd like to know is whether we've been exposed in the first place. We have a fairly extensive bio-sensor program with the goal of making things smaller, lighter, cheaper, with very high sensitivity, a low false alarm rate, and of course, to be very automated and very fast.

A number of detection schemes today use DNA as a basis of determining what the pathogen is. The problem is there's only one copy of DNA in an individual pathogen cell. So we've taken a different attack, and that's to look at the RNA. In this case, there are maybe 60,000 copies of the RNA in an individual cell. So you don't have to go through the somewhat time-consuming process of amplifying or increasing the number of DNA molecules. We've developed very relatively small integrated chips, integrated circuits, that have a variety of different antibodies on the surface, and with florescent markers it can be used to determine what kind of a pathogen we have.

It actually determines things like the genus of the species. It can determine if something's pathogenic or not pathogenic. It's also relatively rapid and small, and ultimately when it gets developed, it will be a relatively low-cost way of determining whether one has been exposed to pathogens.

Ultimately, humans are the final sort of detector, if you will, of pathogens, much the way that back in the old days when miners went down into the mines and had this idea of taking a canary with them because they're very, very sensitive to the lack of oxygen and the presence of CO and things like that.

We have the a similar concept now that we're working on for detectors for biological warfare agents, and that is can we use individual cells or tissues as sensors for biological or chemical agents, not actually carrying little canaries around, but in this case, carrying around individual cells and using them with the idea that if something is harmful to these cells, then it will be harmful to us as humans. And ultimately, the detectors should be small and compact and robust since they are cell size.

And the interesting thing about cells—and this is an example of some of the work that's gone on in nerve cells—is they can be sensitive to a wide variety of different species. Each species changes the pathway of how the cell operates in a slightly different way. This happens to be nerve cells that are living on small microelectronic circuits. They can live there for a couple of weeks. Clearly, we need to make them live longer and improve a number of robustness or viability issues, but the concept, I think, is sound.

There are cells that can react to a wide variety of different species and actually can be used for detection of signals. This is just a real brief overview of the kinds of things that we're working on. For the most part, the DARPA charter is to do long-range far-thinking research.

VII.
Laws and Directives

Presidential Decision Directives

PDD-39: U.S. Policy On Combating Terrorism*

Federal Agencies' Efforts to
Implement National Policy and Strategy

This unclassified abstract of Presidential Decision Directive 39 (PDD 39) is reproduced verbatim. The National Security Council (NSC) reviewed and approved it for distribution to federal, state, and local emergency response and consequence management personnel.

1. General. Terrorism is both a threat to our national security as well as a criminal act. The Administration has stated that it is the policy of the United States to use all appropriate means to deter, defeat and respond to all terrorist attacks on our territory and resources, both people and facilities, wherever they occur. In support of these efforts, the United States will:

- Employ efforts to deter, preempt, apprehend and prosecute terrorists.
- Work closely with other governments to carry our counterterrorism policy and combat terrorist threats against them.
- Identify sponsors of terrorists, isolate them, and ensure they pay for their actions.
- Make no concessions to terrorists.

2. Measures to Combat Terrorism. To ensure that the United States is prepared to combat terrorism in all its forms, a number of measures have been directed. These include reducing vulnerabilities to terrorism, deterring and responding to terrorist acts, and having capabilities to prevent and manage the consequences of terrorist use of nuclear, biological, and chemical (NBC) weapons, including those of mass destruction.

    a. Reduce Vulnerabilities. In order to reduce our vulnerabilities to terrorism, both at home and abroad, all department/agency heads have been directed to ensure that their personnel and facilities are fully protected against terrorism. Specific efforts that will be conducted to en-

* Excerpt from Report GAO/NSIAD-97-254, Appendix I, General Accounting Office, September 9, 1997.

sure our security against terrorist acts include the following:

- Review the vulnerability of government facilities and critical national infrastructure.
- Expand the program of counterterrorism.
- Reduce vulnerabilities affecting civilian personnel/facilities abroad and military personnel/facilities.
- Reduce vulnerabilities affecting U.S. airports, aircraft/passengers and shipping, and provide appropriate security measures for other modes of transportation.
- Exclude/deport persons who pose a terrorist threat.
- Prevent unlawful traffic in firearms and explosives, and protect the President and other officials against terrorist attack.
- Reduce U.S. vulnerabilities to international terrorism through intelligence collection/analysis, counterintelligence, and covert action.

b. **Deter.** To deter terrorism, it is necessary to provide a clear public position that our policies will not be affected by terrorist acts and we will vigorously deal with terrorist/sponsors to reduce terrorist capabilities and support. In this regard, we must make it clear that we will not allow terrorism to succeed and that the pursuit, arrest, and prosecution of terrorists is of the highest priority. Our goals include the disruption of terrorist-sponsored activity including termination of financial support, arrest and punishment of terrorists as criminals, application of U.S. laws and new legislation to prevent terrorist groups from operating in the United States, and application of extraterritorial statutes to counter acts of terrorism and apprehend terrorists outside of the United States. Return of terrorists overseas, who are wanted for violation of U.S. law, is of the highest priority and a central issue in bilateral relations with any state that harbors or assists them.

c. **Respond.** To respond to terrorism, we must have a rapid and decisive capability to protect Americans, defeat or arrest terrorists, respond against terrorist sponsors, and provide relief to the victims of terrorists. The goal during the immediate response phase of an incident is to terminate terrorist attacks so that the terrorists do not accomplish their objectives or maintain their freedom, while seeking to minimize damage and loss of life and provide emergency assistance. After an incident has occurred, a rapidly deployable interagency Emergency Support Team (EST) will provide required capabilities on scene: a Foreign Emergency Support Team (FEST) for foreign incidents and a Domestic Emergency Support Team (DEST) for domestic incidents. DEST membership will be limited to those agencies required to respond to the specific incident. Both teams will include elements for specific types of incidents such as nuclear, biological or chemical threats.

The Director, Federal Emergency Management Agency (FEMA), will ensure that the Federal Response Plan is adequate for consequence management activities in response to terrorist attacks against large U.S. populations, including those where weapons of mass destruction are involved. FEMA will also ensure that State response plans and capabilities are adequate and tested. FEMA, supported by all Federal Response Plan signatories, will assume the Lead Agency role for consequence management in Washington, D.C., and on scene. If large scale casualties and infrastructure damage occur, the President may appoint a Personal Representative for consequence management as the on scene Federal authority during recovery. A roster of senior and former government officials willing to perform these functions will be created and the rostered individuals will be provided training and information necessary to allow them to be called upon on short notice.

Agencies will bear the costs of their participation in terrorist incidents and counterterrorist operations, unless otherwise directed.

d. **NBC Consequence Management.** The development of effective capabilities for preventing and managing the consequences of terrorist use of nuclear, biological or chemical (BC) materials or weapons is of the highest priority. Terrorist acquisition of weapons of mass destruction is not acceptable and there is no higher priority than preventing the acquisition of such materials/weapons or removing this capability from terrorist groups. FEMA will review the Federal Response plan on an urgent basis, in coordination with supporting agencies, to determine its adequacy in responding to an NBC-related terrorist incident; identify and remedy any shortfalls in stockpiles, capabilities or training; and report on the status of these efforts in 180 days.

PDD-41: Further Reducing The Nuclear Threat*

In April 1994, a new program of cooperation on nuclear materials protection, control, and accounting (MPC&A) was initiated between (1) the US Depart-

---

* Excerpt from White House Statement, September 28, 1995.

ment of Energy and its laboratories and (2) nuclear institutes and enterprises of the Russian Federation. One purpose of the program is to accelerate progress toward a goal that is vital to the national security interests of both countries: reducing the risk of nuclear weapons proliferation by strengthening MPC&A systems. The program has made significant progress and has expanded to include many additional Russian participants. It has also fostered a spirit of mutual understanding, partnership, and respect between US and Russian nuclear specialists, which has paved the way for advances in other MPC&A and nuclear security cooperative efforts.

The US Department of Energy (DOE) is cooperating with Russia, the Newly Independent States (NIS), the Baltics, and and the Ukrainian Government to help prevent the proliferation of nuclear weapons through the improvement of national systems of nuclear material protection, control, and accounting (MPC&A). US cooperation with Russia is carried out under the DOE MPC&A Program and the Ninn-Lugar funded Cooperative Threat Reduction program for Russia. Presidential Decision Directive (PDD)-41 designated DOE as the government agency with primary responsibility for MPC&A efforts in Russia, the NM, and Baltics. Cooperation is conducted in coordination with the Nuclear Regulatory Commission (NRC) for the development of a strong, independent national regulatory agency in Russia. DOE also coordinates these efforts with the European Community and other countries.

Clinton Directive Aims To Further Reduce Nuclear Threat:

Today, the United States is taking another step to reduce the nuclear threat. The president has directed his administration to launch an accelerated plan to improve the security of nuclear materials. Working with Russia and the other states of the former Soviet Union, we will deepen out cooperation to reduce the risk of illicit transfers of nuclear weapons, fissile materials, and other dangerous nuclear and radioactive substances to states or terrorists.

Even as the threat of nuclear war recedes, we must confront the urgent challenge of ensuring that nuclear weapons and materials do not fall into the wrong hands. For that reason, President Clinton has made the security of nuclear materials a matter of the highest priority. Already we have achieved an unprecedented level of direct cooperation among our governments. U.S. nuclear material security experts are now working closely with their counterparts at more than two dozen sites across the former Soviet Union to identify and remedy potential weaknesses in systems designed to protect nuclear materials. These efforts complement other initiatives to increase nuclear material security—such as the shipment of highly-enriched uranium out of Kazakhstan for safekeeping under Operation Sapphire; the transfer of nuclear weapons from Ukraine to Russia for dismantlement; and the agreement with Russia under which 500 metric tons of highly-enriched uranium from nuclear warheads are already being converted to much safer low-enriched uranium fuel for electricity production in civilian nuclear reactors.

The directive we are issuing today calls for concrete steps to deepen and accelerate our cooperation with the FSU to protect, control and account for nuclear materials; to continue our joint efforts to assure the security of nuclear weapons themselves; and to increase the integration of our diplomatic, law enforcement and intelligence efforts.

Working together, we are reducing the nuclear danger we all face and making the lives of the American people, and people around the world, safer.

PDD-62: Combating Terrorism*

Since he took office, President Clinton has made the fight against terrorism a top national security objective. The President has worked to deepen our operation with our friends and allies abroad, strengthened law enforcement's counterterrorism tools and improved security on airplanes and at airports. These efforts have paid off as major terrorist attacks have been foiled and more terrorists have been apprehended, tried and given severe prison terms.

Yet America's unrivaled military superiority means that potential enemies—whether nations or terrorist groups—that choose to attack us will be more likely to resort to terror instead of conventional military assault. Moreover, easier access to sophisticated technology means that the destructive power available to terrorists is greater than ever. Adversaries may thus be tempted to use unconventional tools, such as weapons of mass destruction, to target our cities and disrupt the operations of our government. They may try to attack our economy and critical infrastructure using advanced computer technology.

President Clinton is determined that in the coming century, we will be capable of deterring and preventing such terrorist attacks. The President is

---

* Excerpt from Fact Sheet, the White House, Office of the Press Secretary (Annapolis, Maryland), May 22, 1998.

convinced that we must also have the ability to limit the damage and manage the consequences should such an attack occur.

To meet these challenges, President Clinton signed Presidential Decision Directive 62. This Directive creates a new and more systematic approach to fighting the terrorist threat of the next century. It reinforces the mission of the many U.S. agencies charged with roles in defeating terrorism; it also codifies and clarifies their activities in the wide range of U.S. counter-terrorism programs, from apprehension and prosecution of terrorists to increasing transportation security, enhancing response capabilities and protecting the computer-based systems that lie at the heart of America's economy. The Directive will help achieve the President's goal of ensuring that we meet the threat of terrorism in the 21st century with the same rigor that we have met military threats in this century.

The National Coordinator

To achieve this new level of integration in the fight against terror, PDD-62 establishes the Office of the National Coordinator for Security, Infrastructure Protection and Counter-Terrorism. The National Coordinator will oversee the broad variety of relevant polices and programs including such areas as counter-terrorism, protection of critical infrastructure, preparedness and consequence management for weapons of mass destruction. The National Coordinator will work within the National Security Council, report to the President through the Assistant to the President for National Security Affairs and produce for him an annual Security Preparedness Report. The National Coordinator will also provide advice regarding budgets for counter-terror programs and lead in the development of guidelines that might be needed for crisis management.

Antiterrorism and Effective Death Penalty Act of 1996:
A Summary

Charles Doyle*

The Antiterrorism and Effective Death Penalty Act of 1996 is the product of legislative efforts stretching back well over a decade and stimulated to passage in part by the tragedies in Oklahoma City and the World Trade Center.

Title I of the Act substantially amends federal habeas corpus law as it applies to both state and federal prisoners whether on death row or imprisoned for a term of years by providing: a bar on federal habeas reconsideration of legal and factual issues ruled upon by state courts in most instances; creation of a general 1 year statute of limitations ; creation of a 6 month statute of limitation in death penalty cases; encouragement for states to appoint counsel for indigent state death row inmates during state habeas or unitary appellate proceedings; and a requirement of appellate court approval for repetitious habeas petitions.

Title II recasts federal law concerning restitution, expands the circumstances under which foreign governments that support terrorism may be sued for resulting injuries, and increases the assistance and compensation available to the victims of terrorism.

TITLE III—INTERNATIONAL TERRORISM PROHIBITIONS

Title III is designed to help sever international terrorists from their sources of financial and material support. It enlarges the proscriptions against assisting in the commission of various terrorist crimes. It authorizes the regulation of fundraising by foreign organizations associated with terrorist activities. It adjusts the Foreign Assistance Act to help isolate countries who support terrorists and to bolster counterterrorism efforts of other countries.

---

* Senior Specialist, American Law Division, Congressional Research Service. Excerpt from CRS Report, June 3, 1996.

Subtitle A—Prohibition on International Terrorist Fundraising

Subtitle A does three things. It establishes the procedure under which a foreign organization may be designated as a terrorist organization. It proscribes providing such an organization with "material support." And it establishes a system of civil penalties for banks and other financial institutions that fail to freeze and report the assets of such organizations.

Subtitle B—Prohibition on Assistance to Terrorist States

Subtitle B seeks to isolate countries that support terrorism by
— outlawing financial transactions with countries that support terrorism;
— prohibiting material support for commission of a wider range of terrorist offenses; and
— using the Foreign Assistance Act to quarantine countries that sponsor terrorism and bolster counterterrorism efforts of countries that resist it.

TITLE V—NUCLEAR, BIOLOGICAL AND CHEMICAL WEAPONS RESTRICTIONS

Title V adjusts the restrictions on possession and use of materials capable of producing catastrophic damage in the hands of terrorists.

Subtitle A—Nuclear Materials

Sec. 501 states findings and purpose concerning illicit nuclear proliferation.

Sec. 502 expands existing proscriptions concerning the misuse of nuclear materials to include nuclear byproducts; adds environmental harm to the damage that can trigger criminal penalties; and supplements the jurisdictional conditions under which the U.S. may prosecute to include instances where the federal government is the target of threats or extortion based on crimes involving nuclear materials or their byproducts, 18 U.S.C. 831.

Sec. 503 directs the Attorney General and Secretary of Defense to report to Congress within 6 months on the extent of the theft of firearms, explosives and other terrorist useful materials from military arsenals.

Subtitle B—Biological Weapons Restrictions

Sec. 511 makes it a federal crime to threaten to use a weapon of mass destruction (it was previously a crime to use, attempt to use or conspire to use such a weapon, 18 U.S.C. 2332a) or to threaten, attempt or conspire to use a biological weapon (18 U.S.C. 175).

It enlarges the definitions of 18 U.S.C. 178 (used to outlaw misuse of biological weapons) to include components of (a) infectious substances, (b) toxic materials including those to which the definition was previously limited, and (c) recombinant molecules.[53]

It adds these new defined biological weapons to the definition of weapons of mass destruction for purposes of the prohibition against misconduct associated with those weapons (the prior definition used "disease organism" instead), 18 U.S.C. 2332a(a).

It directs the Secretary of Health and Human Services to promulgate regulations identifying biological agents that pose a potential threat to public health and safety and governing their intentional or inadvertent transfer, 42 U.S.C. 262 note.

Subtitle C—Chemical Weapons Restrictions

Sec. 521 makes it a federal crime to unlawfully use chemical weapons within the U.S. or against federal property or against an American overseas, 18 U.S.C. 2332c (it was already a federal crime to unlawfully use poison gas under the same jurisdictional circumstances, 18 U.S.C. 2332a); the section also calls for an interagency task force to study the feasibility of establishing a research facility to study chemical and biological weapons.

Title VI provides implementing legislation for the Convention on the Marking of Plastic Explosives for the Purpose of Detection negotiated in Montreal on March 1, 1991.

TITLE VII—CRIMINAL LAW MODIFICATIONS TO COUNTER TERRORISM

Title VII makes a number of changes in existing federal criminal law and procedure, primarily expanding the reach of federal law and increasing penalties to more effectively combat terrorism. It makes it a federal crime to kill, kidnap or assault any federal officer or employee, to conspire in the United States to commit crimes of violence overseas, or to commit a crime of violence within the United States with related conduct such as a conspiracy occurring overseas. It also increases the penalties for misconduct involving explosives and for conspiracy to commit several of the federal crimes associated with international terrorists.

TITLE VIII—ASSISTANCE TO LAW ENFORCEMENT

Title VIII authorizes the appropriation of an additional $1 billion to fund anti-terrorism law enforcement efforts, authorizes overseas law enforcement placement and training as well as parking bans around federal buildings in D.C., and calls for various studies involving counterfeiting, computer crime, the focus of federal law enforcement, wiretapping, violence against federal

Sec. 819 authorizes appropriations of $5 million for FY1997 to enable the Attorney General to make grants to be used for training and equipment to enhance the capability of city fire and emergency agencies to respond to terrorist attacks.

Sec. 820 authorizes appropriations of $20 million for FY1997 and $10 million for FY1998 to enable the Department of Justice to assist foreign countries in the area of counterterrorism technology.

Defense Against Weapons of Mass Destruction Act of 1996*

The Nunn-Lugar-Domenici
Domestic Preparedness Initiative

Public Law: 104-201 (09/23/96)
TITLE XIV—DEFENSE AGAINST WEAPONS OF MASS DESTRUCTION

Subtitle A—Domestic Preparedness

SEC. 1411. RESPONSE TO THREATS OF TERRORIST USE OF WEAPONS OF MASS DESTRUCTION.

(a) ENHANCED RESPONSE CAPABILITY—In light of the potential for terrorist use of weapons of mass destruction against the United States, the President shall take immediate action—

(1) to enhance the capability of the Federal Government to prevent and respond to terrorist incidents involving weapons of mass destruction; and

(2) to provide enhanced support to improve the capabilities of State and local emergency response agencies to prevent and respond to such incidents at both the national and the local level.

SEC. 1412. EMERGENCY RESPONSE ASSISTANCE PROGRAM.

(a) PROGRAM REQUIRED—

(1) The Secretary of Defense shall carry out a program to provide civilian personnel of Federal, State, and local agencies with training and expert advice regarding emergency responses to a use or threatened use of a weapon of mass destruction or related materials.

(2) The President may designate the head of an agency other than the Department of Defense to assume the responsibility for carrying out the program on or after October 1, 1999, and relieve the Secretary of Defense of that responsibility upon the assumption of the responsibility by the designated official.

---

* Excerpt from Defense Against Weapons of Mass Destruction Act of 1996.

(3) In this section, the official responsible for carrying out the program is referred to as the 'lead official'.

(b) COORDINATION—In carrying out the program, the lead official shall coordinate with each of the following officials who is not serving as the lead official:

(1) The Director of the Federal Emergency Management Agency.

(2) The Secretary of Energy.

(3) The Secretary of Defense.

(4) The heads of any other Federal, State, and local government agencies that have an expertise or responsibilities relevant to emergency responses described in subsection (a)(1).

(c) ELIGIBLE PARTICIPANTS—The civilian personnel eligible to receive assistance under the program are civilian personnel of Federal, State, and local agencies who have emergency preparedness responsibilities.

(e) AVAILABLE ASSISTANCE—Assistance available under this program shall include the following:

(1) Training in the use, operation, and maintenance of equipment for—

(A) detecting a chemical or biological agent or nuclear radiation;

(B) monitoring the presence of such an agent or radiation;

(C) protecting emergency personnel and the public; and

(D) decontamination.

(2) Establishment of a designated telephonic link (commonly referred to as a 'hot line') to a designated source of relevant data and expert advice for the use of State or local officials responding to emergencies involving a weapon of mass destruction or related materials.

(3) Use of the National Guard and other reserve components for purposes authorized under this section that are specified by the lead official (with the concurrence of the Secretary of Defense if the Secretary is not the lead official).

(4) Loan of appropriate equipment.

(f) LIMITATIONS ON DEPARTMENT OF DEFENSE ASSISTANCE TO LAW ENFORCEMENT AGENCIES—Assistance provided by the Department of Defense to law enforcement agencies under this section shall be provided under the authority of, and subject to the restrictions provided in, chapter 18 of title 10, United States Code.

(g) ADMINISTRATION OF DEPARTMENT OF DEFENSE ASSISTANCE—The Secretary of Defense shall designate an official within the Department of Defense to serve as the executive agent of the Secretary for the coordination of the provision of Department of Defense assistance under this section.

(h) FUNDING—
(1) Of the total amount authorized to be appropriated under section 301, $35,000,000 is available for the program required under this section.
(2) Of the amount available for the program pursuant to paragraph (1), $10,500,000 is available for use by the Secretary of Defense to assist the Secretary of Health and Human Services in the establishment of metropolitan emergency medical response teams (commonly referred to as 'Metropolitan Medical Strike Force Teams') to provide medical services that are necessary or potentially necessary by reason of a use or threatened use of a weapon of mass destruction.
(3) The amount available for the program under paragraph (1) is in addition to any other amounts authorized to be appropriated for the program under section 301.

SEC. 1413. NUCLEAR, CHEMICAL, AND BIOLOGICAL EMERGENCY RESPONSE.
(a) DEPARTMENT OF DEFENSE—The Secretary of Defense shall designate an official within the Department of Defense as the executive agent for—
(1) the coordination of Department of Defense assistance to Federal, State, and local officials in responding to threats involving biological or chemical weapons or related materials or technologies, including assistance in identifying, neutralizing, dismantling, and disposing of biological and chemical weapons and related materials and technologies; and
(2) the coordination of Department of Defense assistance to the Department of Energy in carrying out that department's responsibilities under subsection (b).
(b) DEPARTMENT OF ENERGY—The Secretary of Energy shall designate an official within the Department of Energy as the executive agent for
(1) the coordination of Department of Energy assistance to Federal, State, and local officials in responding to threats involving nuclear, chemical, and biological weapons or related materials or technologies, including assistance in identifying, neutralizing, dismantling, and disposing of nuclear weapons and related materials and technologies; and
(2) the coordination of Department of Energy assistance to the Department of Defense in carrying out that department's responsibilities under subsection (a).
(c) FUNDING—Of the total amount authorized to be appropriated un-

der section 301, $15,000,000 is available for providing assistance described in subsection (a).

SEC. 1414. CHEMICAL-BIOLOGICAL EMERGENCY RESPONSE TEAM.

(a) DEPARTMENT OF DEFENSE RAPID RESPONSE TEAM—The Secretary of Defense shall develop and maintain at least one domestic terrorism rapid response team composed of members of the Armed Forces and employees of the Department of Defense who are capable of aiding Federal, State, and local officials in the detection, neutralization, containment, dismantlement, and disposal of weapons of mass destruction containing chemical, biological, or related materials.

SEC. 1415. TESTING OF PREPAREDNESS FOR EMERGENCIES INVOLVING NUCLEAR, RADIOLOGICAL, CHEMICAL, AND BIOLOGICAL WEAPONS.

(a) EMERGENCIES INVOLVING CHEMICAL OR BIOLOGICAL WEAPONS—

(1) The Secretary of Defense shall develop and carry out a program for testing and improving the responses of Federal, State, and local agencies to emergencies involving biological weapons and related materials and emergencies involving chemical weapons and related materials.

(2) The program shall include exercises to be carried out during each of five successive fiscal years beginning with fiscal year 1997.

(3) In developing and carrying out the program, the Secretary shall coordinate with the Director of the Federal Bureau of Investigation, the Director of the Federal Emergency Management Agency, the Secretary of Energy, and the heads of any other Federal, State, and local government agencies that have an expertise or responsibilities relevant to emergencies described in paragraph (1).

(b) EMERGENCIES INVOLVING NUCLEAR AND RADIOLOGICAL WEAPONS—

(1) The Secretary of Energy shall develop and carry out a program for testing and improving the responses of Federal, State, and local agencies to emergencies involving nuclear and radiological weapons and related materials.

(2) The program shall include exercises to be carried out during each of five successive fiscal years beginning with fiscal year 1997.

(3) In developing and carrying out the program, the Secretary shall coordinate with the Director of the Federal Bureau of Investigation, the

Director of the Federal Emergency Management Agency, the Secretary of Defense, and the heads of any other Federal, State, and local government agencies that have an expertise or responsibilities relevant to emergencies described in paragraph (1).

(c) ANNUAL REVISIONS OF PROGRAMS—The official responsible for carrying out a program developed under subsection (a) or (b) shall revise the program not later than June 1 in each fiscal year covered by the program. The revisions shall include adjustments that the official determines necessary or appropriate on the basis of the lessons learned from the exercise or exercises carried out under the program in the fiscal year, including lessons learned regarding coordination problems and equipment deficiencies.

(d) OPTION TO TRANSFER RESPONSIBILITY—

(1) The President may designate the head of an agency outside the Department of Defense to assume the responsibility for carrying out the program developed under subsection (a) beginning on or after October 1, 1999, and relieve the Secretary of Defense of that responsibility upon the assumption of the responsibility by the designated official.

(2) The President may designate the head of an agency outside the Department of Energy to assume the responsibility for carrying out the program developed under subsection (b) beginning on or after October 1, 1999, and relieve the Secretary of Energy of that responsibility upon the assumption of the responsibility by the designated official.

(e) FUNDING—Of the total amount authorized to be appropriated under section 301, $15,000,000 is available for the development and execution of the programs required by this section, including the participation of State and local agencies in exercises carried out under the programs.

Subtitle B—Interdiction of Weapons of Mass Destruction and Related Materials

SEC. 1421. PROCUREMENT OF DETECTION EQUIPMENT UNITED STATES BORDER SECURITY.

Of the amount authorized to be appropriated by section 301, $15,000,000 is available for the procurement of—

(1) equipment capable of detecting the movement of weapons of mass destruction and related materials into the United States;

(2) equipment capable of interdicting the movement of weapons of mass destruction and related materials into the United States; and

(3) materials and technologies related to use of equipment described in paragraph (1) or (2).

SEC. 1424. INTERNATIONAL BORDER SECURITY.

(a) SECRETARY OF DEFENSE RESPONSIBILITY—The Secretary of Defense, in consultation and cooperation with the Commissioner of Customs, shall carry out programs for assisting customs officials and border guard officials in the independent states of the former Soviet Union, the Baltic states, and other countries of Eastern Europe in preventing unauthorized transfer and transportation of nuclear, biological, and chemical weapons and related materials. Training, expert advice, maintenance of equipment, loan of equipment, and audits may be provided under or in connection with the programs.

(b) FUNDING—Of the total amount authorized to be appropriated by section 301, $15,000,000 is available for carrying out the programs referred to in subsection (a).

(c) ASSISTANCE TO STATES OF THE FORMER SOVIET UNION— Assistance under programs referred to in subsection (a) may (notwithstanding any provision of law prohibiting the extension of foreign assistance to any of the newly independent states of the former Soviet Union) be extended to include an independent state of the former Soviet Union if the President certifies to Congress that it is in the national interest of the United States to extend assistance under this section to that state.